Democracy and Rule of Law in the European Union

Flora A.N.J. Goudappel · Ernst M.H. Hirsch Ballin
Editors

Democracy and Rule of Law in the European Union

Essays in Honour of Jaap W. de Zwaan

ASSER PRESS

Springer

Editors
Flora A.N.J. Goudappel
Rotterdam
The Netherlands

Ernst M.H. Hirsch Ballin
Tilburg - The Hague
The Netherlands

ISBN 978-94-6265-065-7 ISBN 978-94-6265-066-4 (eBook)
DOI 10.1007/978-94-6265-066-4

Library of Congress Control Number: 2015953808

Published by T.M.C. ASSER PRESS, The Hague, The Netherlands www.asserpress.nl
Produced and distributed for T.M.C. ASSER PRESS by Springer-Verlag Berlin Heidelberg

Printed on acid-free paper

Springer Science+Business Media B.V. Dordrecht is part of Springer Science+Business Media
(www.springer.com)

Foreword

Professor Jaap de Zwaan retired from Erasmus School of Law of the Erasmus University Rotterdam in March 2014. He had been a highly valued colleague for over 16 years. Following a career in the legal profession and almost 20 years at the Dutch Ministry of Foreign Affairs, Professor De Zwaan opted for the academic world in 1998. From his appointment on 1 January 1998 until becoming a professor emeritus on 14 March 2014, he was Professor of European Law at Erasmus University Rotterdam. As holder of this chair, he made major contributions to the education and research of the law school. Professor De Zwaan, a highly regarded lecturer, ensured that European law was given the prominent place in the curriculum that it continues to have today. As a researcher, he published many works on European integration and supervised many doctoral candidates. Reflecting his passion for European integration, from 1998 to 2014, Professor De Zwaan also held the Jean Monnet Chair in Future Developments of the European Union.

In addition to his academic achievements, Professor De Zwaan was a very accomplished administrator. He was the Faculty of Law's dean of internationalization from 1999 to 2001 and, from 2001 to 2004, head of the faculty as dean. In this capacity, he was responsible for overseeing two major and complex structural reforms that were taking place in the Dutch academic world at the time, namely the administrative reorganization under the University Government (Modernisation) Act and the shift to the bachelor–master structure. With a diplomatic management style aimed at fostering cohesion and cooperation, Professor De Zwaan ensured that Erasmus School of Law emerged from the process stronger. As dean of internationalization, he established strong and lasting contacts with leading universities in China and Indonesia. He strengthened cooperation with the academic world in the former colonies like the Netherlands Antilles. Many international students have found their way to Erasmus University Rotterdam through the many successful projects that he set up.

Professor De Zwaan is a true European, an idealist who could be seen building bridges between different countries and peoples. He focused in this regard mainly on the new and candidate Member States of the European Union, many of them in Eastern Europe. He established special partnerships with a number of prestigious universities, such as the Moscow State Institute of International Relations (MGIMO University) and Comenius University in Bratislava. As a member of the board of the European Studies Institute (ESI) of MGIMO University, he made a special contribution to Russo–European cooperation in higher education. Through his personality and academic qualities, Professor De Zwaan played a significant part in establishing a relationship of trust and commitment between Russia and the European Union.

As a scholar, a diplomat and an administrator, Professor De Zwaan has contributed in significant ways to the development of European law and thus European integration. He played a leading role in the Certificate of European Law and Economics (CELE) project. The purpose of this project was to disseminate knowledge about the key processes in European integration, not only in legal and economic terms but in an interdisciplinary way, mainly in Eastern Europe. As a token of appreciation for his outstanding services and the high quality of his work, Comenius University in Bratislava awarded him a Gold Medal of Merit. He had already been awarded the Imrich Karvas Medal by the same university in 2004 and received the Award of Excellence from the Romanian ambassador to the Netherlands in 2009. Professor De Zwaan also showed his qualities in other positions. These included Substitute Judge in the District Court of The Hague from 1979, Vice-President of the Executive Board and member of the Governing Board of the Asser Insituut from 2002 to 2005 and, from 2005 to 2011, Director of the Clingendael Netherlands Institute of International Relations. Moreover, he performed charitable administrative work. In recognition of his achievements, Professor De Zwaan was appointed an Officer in the Order of Orange-Nassau on the occasion of his retirement from Erasmus School of Law in March 2014.

Professor De Zwaan was a highly valued colleague in both personal and professional terms. He was a real team player and builder of bridges who truly justified his nickname, "The Diplomatic Dean", on a daily basis. The Erasmus School of Law is sincerely grateful for his services and wishes him all the best as a professor emeritus.

Rotterdam
Summer 2015

Professor Suzan Stoter
Dean of Erasmus School of Law
Professor Fabian Amtenbrink
Vice-Dean of Erasmus School of Law

Contents

List of Publications by Jaap W. de Zwaan

The Single European Act: conclusion of a unique document, Common Market Law Review 1986, pp. 747–765

Le Collège d'Europe, pionnier de l'éducation européenne, Septentrion, Revue de culture néerlandaise, Rekkem België, 20e année, numéro 4 1991, pp. 17–22

Eindredacteur van de bijdrage van de Nederlandse Vereniging Europees Recht voor het FIDE-Congres te Lissabon 1992 inzake het onderwerp: 'The imposition of sanctions for breaches of Community Law' (redacteuren: J.C.M. Montijn-Swinkels, K. Sevinga, T.M. Snoep en G. van der Wal), gepubliceerd in SEW april 1992, 40e jaargang no. 4, pp. 256–276

Institutional problems and free movement of persons, the legal and political framework for cooperation, in: Free movement of persons in Europe, Legal problems and experiences, Asser Instituut, The Hague 1993, pp. 335–352.

Het Comité van Permanente Vertegenwoordigers, ontstaan, werkwijze en rol in de besluitvorming van de Europese Gemeenschappen, Europese Monografieën nr 42, Kluwer Deventer 1993 (proefschrift)

Europees Parlement en uitbreiding: de ontwikkeling van het democratisch karakter van het besluitvormingsproces van de Unie. Het belang van Nederland, in: Institutionele toekomstverkenningen, de plaats van Nederland in de Europese Gemeenschap (EG) bij de toetreding van nieuwe leden, Sdu Uitgeverij, Den Haag 1993, pp. 29–36

The configuration of the European Union, The Community dimensions of institutional interaction (co-auteur Prof. Dr. T. Heukels), in: Institutional Dynamics of European Integration, Essays in Honour of Henry G. Schermers, Volume II, Martinus Nijhoff Publishers, Dordrecht Boston London 1994, pp. 195–228

Het voorstel van de European Constitutional Group voor een Europese grondwet: blauwdruk voor een intergouvernementeel Europa, SEW april 1995, 43e jaargang no. 4, pp. 252–267

Diversiteit van besluitvormingsprocedures in de Europese Unie: de Raad en het Comité van Permanente Vertegenwoordigers, in: Diversiteit van de besluitvorming van de Europese Unie. Enkele suggesties voor de IGC 1996, T.M.C. Asser Instituut, Den Haag 1995, pp. 17–33

The Permanent Representatives Committee: Its role in the decision-making of the European Union, T.M.C. Asser Institute—The Hague, Elsevier—North Holland, 1995 (Engelse vertaling/bewerking van het proefschrift van 1993)

De Intergouvernementele Conferentie van 1996, Nederlands Tijdschrift voor Europees Recht, maart 1996, nr 3, pp. 29–33

Het Verdrag van Amsterdam: een overzicht, Nederlands Tijdschrift voor Europees Recht, januari/februari 1998, nr 1/2, pp. 30–40

Een ruimte van vrijheid, veiligheid en rechtvaardigheid, en het Europese Burgerschap, Contribution to the Colloquium 'The European Union after Amsterdam' organised by the International Foundation 'Christians for Europe', 25 September 1997, Brussels, published by the Christians for Europe Foundation, 1998

Negotiating the Amsterdam Treaty, Contribution to the Seminar 'Legal and Constitutional Implications of the Amsterdam Treaty', 27 November 1997, published by Institute of European Studies, Dublin, Ireland, 1998

The future of the Third Pillar and the fight against EU fraud: Evaluation of the IGC and the Treaty of Amsterdam, Contribution to the 'Conference on Legal Instruments against EU Fraud in the Post-Maastricht Period', 23–24 October 1997, published in: J.A.E. Vervaele (ed.), Transnational enforcement of the financial interests of the European Union, developments in the Treaty of Amsterdam and the Corpus Juris, Intersentia Law Publishers, Antwerpen-Groningen-Oxford, 1999, pp. 13–28

Community dimensions of the Second Pillar, Contribution to the 40th Anniversary Colloquium of the Europa Institute of the University of Leiden 'Institutional and Constitutional Dimensions of European Integration: the legal Debate after Amsterdam', 6–7 November 1997, The Hague, published by the Europa Institute: T. Heukels, N. Blokker and M. Brus (Eds), The European Union after Amsterdam, A legal analysis, Kluwer Law International 1998, pp. 179–193

The future of the Third Pillar: an evaluation of the Treaty of Amsterdam (co-author M. Vrouenraets), Contribution to the 40th Anniversary Colloquium of the Europa Institute of the University of Leiden 'Institutional and Constitutional Dimensions of European Integration: the legal Debate after Amsterdam', 6–7 November 1997, The Hague, published by the Europa Institute: T. Heukels, N. Blokker and M. Brus (Eds), The European Union after Amsterdam, A legal analysis, Kluwer Law International 1998, pp. 203–214

Schengen and its incorporation into the new Treaty: the negotiating process, contribution to the Sixth Colloquium of the European Institute of Public Administration (EIPA) "Schengen's final days? Incorporation in the New TEU, External Borders and Information Systems", 5–6 February 1998, published by EIPA, Maastricht, 1998, pp. 13–25

Wat betekent Europees burgerschap voor gemeenteraadsverkiezingen?, Staatscourant 39 van 26 februari 1998, pp. 6–7

Het recht als fundament van de Europese Unie, Schets van belangrijke beginselen en recente vernieuwingen, rede uitgesproken bij de aanvaarding van het ambt van gewoon hoogleraar in het recht van de Europese Unie aan de Faculteit der Rechtsgeleerdheid van de Erasmus Universiteit Rotterdam op vrijdag 8 mei 1998, Kluwer Deventer 1998

Opting out and opting in: problems and practical arrangements, Contribution to the Conference Implementing Schengen, organised by the Centre for European Legal Studies (CELS) of the Faculty of Law of the University of Cambridge, 20 June 1998, published in the A. Dashwood and A. Ward (eds), Cambridge Yearbook of European Legal Studies, Volume 1 1998, Hart Publishing 1999

Haagse Post-Securitel coördinatie, De doorwerking van de Securitel-affaire op de Haagse coördinatie met betrekking tot Europees recht, SEW oktober 1998, 46e jaargang no. 10, pp. 362–367

Gavin Barrett (Ed.), Justice cooperation in the European Union, Institute of European Affairs, Dublin, Ireland, 1997, 237 pages (bookreview), Common Market Law Review, Vol. 36 No. 1 February 1999, pp. 249–250

Kroniek Europees Recht, verslagperiode januari-augustus 1998 (co-author Mr A.J. Bultena), NJB 11 september 1998, afl. 32, pp. 1441–1447

Flexibiliteit en het Verdrag van Amsterdam, contribution to the Asser Instituut Colloquium Europees Recht -28th Session- 'Flexibiliteit en het Verdrag van Amsterdam,' 4 September 1998, 1999 T.M.C. Asser Press The Hague

Martti Koskenniemi (Ed.), International law aspects of the European Union, Kluwer International Law, 1998, The Hague/London/Boston, ISBN 10: 9041104887 (bookreview), Maastricht Journal of European and Comparative Law 1998, Volume 5 Number 4, pp. 415–419

Case note on C-345/95 French Republic v. European Parliament, Judgment of 1 October 1997 [1997] I-5215 (seat of the European Parliament—European Parliament—part-sessions), Common Market Law Review, Vol. 36 No. 2 April 1999, pp. 463–470

Het Verdrag van Amsterdam, Etappe in het proces van Europese integratie, NJB 19 maart 1999, afl. 11, pp. 492–500

Rechtsvraag (276) Europees recht, Sancties tegen Moldonië, Ars Aequi 1999, Jaargang 48 - 3, maart 1999, pp. 194–195

De publieke en private verantwoordelijkheid van de overheid; een aantal Europeesrechtelijke beschouwingen, in: Derksen e.a. (red.), Over publieke en private verantwoordelijkheden, voorstudies and achtergronden, Wetenschappelijke Raad voor het Regeringsbeleid, Sdu Uitgevers Den Haag 1999, pp. 175–204

Annotatie arrest EG-Hof van Justitie van 17 september 1997 in de Zaak C-54/96, Dorsch Consult, Jur. 1997 I-4961, SEW november 1999, 47e jaargang no. 11, pp. 423–426

Beantwoording Rechtsvraag (276) Europees recht, De sancties tegen Moldonië, Jaargang 48 - 12/december 1999, pp. 949–954

De totstandkoming van Artikel 95 EG-Verdrag: de onderhandelingen van het Verdrag van Amsterdam, in: Artikel 95 EG-Verdrag, De (on)mogelijkheden voor lidstaten om af te wijken van geharmoniseerd EG-beleid, Publicaties van de Vereniging voor Milieurecht, Boom Juridische uitgevers, Den Haag 2000, pp. 11–25

Boekbespreking 'J.W. van de Gronden, De implementatie van het EG-milieurecht door Nederlandse decentrale overheden', Rechtsgeleerd Magazijn Themis, Jaargang 161 maart 2000, pp. 118–120

The Netherlands (judiciary and authorities) and Article 10 of the EC-Treaty, contribution to the FIDE-Congress in Helsinki of June 2000, SEW April 2000, 48e jaargang no. 4, pp. 132–154

The legal personality of the European Communities and the European Union, in: Netherlands Yearbook of International Law, Volume XXX 1999, Martinus Nijhoff Publishers 2000, pp. 75–113

Het Comité van Permanente Vertegenwoordigers, Onmisbare schakel in de Raadsorganisatie, in: M. Krop en H. Swarttouw (red.), De Groothoeklens, Europa in dertien bedrijven, Liber amicorum Ronald van Beuge, Scorpio Eckelrade 2001, pp. 81–92

De toekomst van de Derde Pijler: intergouvernementele of communautaire samenwerking?, in: Grensverkenningen in het recht, SI-EUR reeks deel 26, Sanders Instituut 2001, pp. 101–108

Het Verdrag van Nice, Een bescheiden stap in het proces van Europese Integratie, SEW februari 2001, 49e jaargang no. 2, pp. 42–52

De toekomst van de Europese Unie, Een aantal constitutionele kanttekeningen, Ars Aequi 2001, Jaargang 50 - 3/mei 2001 (Bijzonder nummer 'De toekomst van de Europese Integratie'), pp. 5–15

Alfred E. Kellermann, Jaap W. de Zwaan, Jenö Czuczai (eds.), EU Enlargement, The constitutional impact at EU and national level, T.M.C. Asser Press, The Hague 2001. In this book also: Foreword, pp. V–VI as well as Summing-up and Conclusions, pp. 481–498

J.W. de Zwaan en A.J. Bultena, Ruimte van vrijheid, veiligheid en rechtvaardigheid, De samenwerking op het gebied van Justitie en Binnenlandse Zaken in de Europese Unie, Sdu Den Haag 2002, 545 pagina's, ISBN 10: 9012096987

The Common Foreign and Security Policy of the European Union, Characteristics and prospects, in: A. Petchsiri, P. Sutthisripok, P. Thontiravong (eds), Comparative regional integration: ASEAN and the EU, Monographs Series Vol. 2 (2002), Chulalongkorn University, Bangkok, Thailand, pp. 185–194

Annotatie bij: Hoge Raad 10 september 1999, nr C98/012HR, Emesa Sugar (Free Zone) NV tegen de Staat der Nederlanden; en Hoge Raad 10 september 1999, nr C98/013HR, De Nederlandse Antillen tegen 1. de Staat der Nederlanden en 2. Emesa Sugar (Free Zone) NV, Nederlandse Jurisprudentie, Jaargang 2003—15 februari 2003, Aflevering 7, nrs. 94 en 95. Annotatie afgedrukt op pp. 652–655

Nederlandse Staatscourant, Officiële uitgave van het Koninkrijk der Nederlanden sinds 1814.

Bijdragen aan de rubriek 'Staat van de Unie':

- Kwestie Oostenrijk toont aan dat EU worstelt met mensenrechten, dinsdag 15 februari 2000, nr 32, p. 6
- Gezond verstand volstaat om de Europese Gemeenschap te behouden, vrijdag 31 maart 2000, nr 65, p. 6
- Het Europese Hof van Justitie en het Verdrag van Nice, vrijdag 1 december 2000, nr 234, p. 5

- Het Nederlandse parlement en zijn recht van instemming met Europese besluitvorming, vrijdag 23 maart 2001, nr 59, p. 5
- Nationale parlementen en de Europese Unie, maandag 23 april 2001, nr 78, p. 5
- Unie zonder gekozen Commissievoorzitter, maandag 18 juni 2001, nr 114, p. 5
- De toetreding: nieuwe kansen voor een 'Europa van de burger', maandag 16 juli 2001, nr 134, p. 5
- Een forum voor de Europese Unie, vrijdag 7 september 2001, nr 173, p. 5
- Terrorismebestrijding vereist coherent beleid, dinsdag 2 oktober 2001, nr 190, p. 5
- De 'rule of law' in een uitgebreide Unie, vrijdag 2 november 2001, nr 213, p. 4
- Unie na 2004 op weg naar een federatie?, dinsdag 27 november 2001, nr 230, p. 6
- Europese Raad als 'schakel', maandag 7 januari 2002, nr 4, p. 5
- Supranationaal of intergouvernementeel, dinsdag 29 januari 2002, nr 20, p. 6
- Het halfjaarlijks roulerend voorzitterschap, dinsdag 26 februari 2002, nr 40, p. 5
- Randvoorwaarden voor Europese Unie, dinsdag 26 maart 2002, nr 60, p. 5
- Srebrenica en het GBVB, dinsdag 23 april 2002, nr 78, p. 5
- Een ontwerp voor de Europese Unie, dinsdag 4 juni 2002, nr 103, p. 6
- EU moet slagvaardiger en democratischer, maandag 9 september 2002, nr 172, p. 5
- Europa: een vitaal belang voor Nederland, maandag 21 oktober 2002, nr 202, p. 5
- Europese Grondwet is geen 'doel op zich', dinsdag 26 november 2002, nr 228, p. 7
- Wisselend voorzitterschap zo gek nog niet, donderdag 2 januari 2003, nr 1, p. 3
- Een president voor Europa?, vrijdag 31 januari 2003, nr 22, p. 5
- Ook gestuntel met 'grote' voorzitter, dinsdag 18 maart 2003, nr 54, p. 5
- Wordt de Europese Commissie overbodig?, dinsdag 10 juni 2003, nr. 108, p. 4

Na de Gemeenschap een Unie: Hoe verder?, in: I. de Jong, B.J. Drijber, D. Kopmels, C. Kole (red), Liber Amicorum Bernard Bot, Rêves européens face aux réalités quotidiennes, Opmeer/De Bink/TDS vof (OBT), maart 2003, pp. 81–95

J.W. de Zwaan en F.A.N.J. Goudappel, 'Een Europese Grondwet: het onderscheid tussen primaire en secundaire teksten in de Europese Unie', in: J. Pelkmans, M. Sie Dhian Ho en B. Limonard, Nederland en de Europese grondwet, uitgave van de Wetenschappelijke Raad voor het Regeringsbeleid (serie WRR Verkenningen nr 1), Amsterdam University Press 2003, pp. 19–49

De Europese Grondwet: bijdrage aan het Europa van de burger? Ars Aequi, Jaargang 53, April 2004, pp. 253–258

The effectiveness of European Union law: the role of the national judiciary, in: The Role of European Union Law in the internal legal order of Member States, International Conference on European Law, 2004, Warsaw, ISBN 10: 8374162686, pp. 127–139

Gemeenschappelijk asiel- en immigratiebeleid, De relevantie van het jaar 2004, Studie in opdracht van de Adviescommissie voor Vreemdelingenzaken en de Adviesraad voor Internationale Vraagstukken, 38 pagina's, uitgave van de Adviescommissie voor Vreemdelingenzaken, Den Haag 2004, ISBN 10: 9085210089, ook op website www.acvz.com

De bestuurbaarheid van de Europese Unie, Efficiency Voorop, Publiek Management jaargang 7 nummer 4/2004, p. 25

De Europese Unie en de Burger: Het belang van een hecht partnerschap, in: P.L. Meurs en M. Sie Dhian Ho (red.), Democraat met beleid, Liber Amicorum ter gelegenheid van het afscheid van Michiel Scheltema als Voorzitter van de WRR, Wetenschappelijke Raad voor het Regeringsbeleid, Den Haag 2004, ISBN 10: 9080899712, pp. 183–198

EU-wetgeving, rechtspraak en documentatie, deel 14 A en B: Strafrecht, Prof. R. Barents, SEW, 52e jaargang, nr 11 van november 2004, pp. 488–498

The role of the European Commission over the years: changes and challenges, in: Jaap W. de Zwaan, Jan H. Jans, Frans A. Nelissen and Steven Blockmans (eds), The European Union, An ongoing process of integration, Liber Amicorum Alfred A. Kellermann, T.M.C. Asser Press The Hague 2004, ISBN 10: 9067041874, pp. 53–70

Jaap W. de Zwaan, Jan H. Jans, Frans A. Nelissen and Steven Blockmans (eds), The European Union, An ongoing process of integration, Liber Amicorum Alfred A. Kellermann, T.M.C. Asser Press The Hague 2004, ISBN 10: 9067041874, 371 pages

European Citizenship: origin, contents and perspectives, in: Deirdre Curtin, Alfred E. Kellermann and Steven Blockmans (eds), The EU Constitution: the best way forward?, T.M.C. Asser Press The Hague 2005, ISBN 10: 9067042005, pp. 245–264

De Europese Grondwet, verantwoorde stap in het integratieproces, Internationale Spectator, Jaargang 59, nr 3, maart 2005, pp. 123–131

De samenwerking tussen de Nederlandse Antillen, Aruba en de Europese Unie, in: Rogier en Hoogers (redactie), 50 jaar Statuut voor het Koninkrijk der Nederlanden, uitgegeven door Ministerie van Binnenlandse Zaken en Koninkrijksrelaties in Den Haag, 2005, pp. 123–138

Grondwet verbetert samenwerking, NRC-Handelsblad, vrijdag 29 april 2005, p. 7

Even pauze, veel debat en wie weet toch nog een ja, De Verdieping, Trouw/Podium, zaterdag 18 juni 2005, p. 17

Europese Unie moet beter op de kaart, Internationale Spectator, Jaargang 59, nr 9, september 2005, pp. 448–451

De Europese Unie en het draagvlak bij de burger (column), Internationale Spectator, Jaargang 60, nr 1, januari 2006, pp. 1–2

CDA doet te moeilijk over uitbreiding EU. Hoe meer lidstaten, hoe meer welvaart, NRC.Next, maandag 20 maart 2006, p. 19

Jaap W. de Zwaan en Flora A.N.J. Goudappel (eds), Freedom, security and justice in the European Union, Implementation of the Hague Programme, TMC Asser Press—The Hague, 2006 ISBN 10: 9067042250, 280 pages

EU asylum and immigration law and policy: state of affairs in 2005, in: Jaap W. de Zwaan en Flora A.N.J. Goudappel (eds), Freedom, security and justice in the European Union, Implementation of the Hague Programme, TMC Asser Press—The Hague, 2006 ISBN 10: 9067042250, pp. 91–150

Trapsgewijs toetreden tot de Unie (column), Internationale Spectator, Jaargang 60, nr 6, juni 2006, pp. 289–290

Bij een jubileum, Ten geleide bij jubileumnummer Internationale Spectator, Jaargang 60, nr 11, november 2006, pp. 545–546

Ramen open naar 't buitenland, NRC-Handelsblad, woensdag 22 november 2006, p. 7

Nieuw elan voor het Europa-debat? (column), Internationale Spectator, Jaargang 61, nr 3, maart 2007, pp. 125–126

De toekomst van het gemeenschappelijk migratiebeleid, in: Nederland migratiesamenleving 2005, uitgave van de Adviescommissie voor Vreemdelingenzaken, Den Haag 2007, Hoofdstuk 3, pp. 41–54

Nederland moet zijn plaats in Europa snel hervinden, Volkskrant vrijdag 1 juni 2007, Rubriek Forum, p. 12

40 Years of European Law, in: Forty years of international law, on the occasion of 40 years T.M.C. Asser Instituut, T.M.C. Asser Press—The Hague, 2007, pp. 23–27

2003–2007 De Europese Unie, Uitgebreid en hervormd, ook voorbereid op de toekomst?, Internationale Spectator, Jaargang 62, nr 1, januari 2008, pp. 19–25

Security as an international phenomenon, How to deal with security at international and local level, contribution to: Vriesendorp, Nelissen and Wladimiroff (eds), The Hague Legal Capital? Liber in Honorem W.J. Deetman, Hague Academic Press—The Hague, 2008, pp. 171–177

The future of the European Union, limits of integration/l'Avenir de l'Union européenne, les limites de l'intégration, public lecture Sofia 7 June 2007, Bulgarian Diplomatic Institute, Ministry of Foreign Affairs, Sofia, 2008, pp. 71–79

Foreign policy and defence cooperation in the European Union: Legal soundations, in: S. Blockmans (Ed.), The European Union and crisis management, policy and legal aspects, TMC Asser Press—The Hague, 2008, pp. 17–36

EU moet relatie met Rusland koesteren, Volkskrant woensdag 20 augustus 2008, Rubriek Forum, p. 11

Nederland in de wereld: een agenda voor de toekomst (column), Internationale Spectator, Jaargang 63, nr 1, januari 2009, pp. 1–2

Jaap de Zwaan, Edwin Bakker and Sico van der Meer (Eds.), Challenges in a changing world, Clingendael views on global and regional issues, on the occasion of the twenty-fifth anniversary of the Netherlands Institute of International Relations 'Clingendael', TMC Asser Press—The Hague, 2009, ISBN 9789067042970

Reflecting the world: Impressions from a Dutch perspective, in: Jaap de Zwaan, Edwin Bakker and Sico van der Meer (Eds.), Challenges in a changing world, Clingendael views on global and regional issues, on the occasion of the twenty-fifth anniversary of the Netherlands Institute of International Relations 'Clingendael', TMC Asser Press—The Hague, 2009, pages 1–14

Turkey's EU accession and the European identity, in: Peter M.E. Volten (Ed.), Perceptions and misperceptions in the EU and Turkey: stumbling blocks on the road to accession, ISBN 9789076301259, Harmonie Papers, published by the Centre of European Security Studies (CESS) in Groningen, The Netherlands, 2009, pp. 179–188

Preface: The end of a divided Europe, in: Leon Marc, What's so eastern about Eastern Europe?, Twenty years after the fall of the Berlin wall, Oldcastle Books, ISBN 9781842433409, 2009, pp. 11–14

Burger wil best meer Europa (column), Internationale Spectator, Jaargang 63, nr 11, november 2009, pp. 545–546

De Europese Unie na Lissabon. Voldoende op haar toekomst voorbereid? Fiat Justitia, uitgegeven door Juridische Faculteitsvereniging Rotterdam, Jaargang 23, nummer 5, september 2010, pp. 20–24

Europese samenwerking buiten Europa. De geografische grenzen van de EU samenwerking, in: Doeko Bosscher en Yuri van Hoef (Ed), Koning Nobel, Liber Amicorum voor Prof. Dr. Hans Renner, Van Denderen-Groningen 2011, pp. 213–221

Sarah Wolff, Flora A.N.J. Goudappel en Jaap W. de Zwaan (Eds.), Freedom, security and justice after Lisbon and Stockholm, T.M.C. Asser Press—The Hague 2011, ISBN 9789067043175, 281 pages

Editorial—The area of freedom, security and justice after the Lisbon Treaty and the Stockholm Programme: From myth to reality (co-authors: Sarah Wolff and Flora Goudappel), in: Sarah Wolff, Flora A.N.J. Goudappel en Jaap W. de Zwaan (Eds.), Freedom, security and justice after Lisbon and Stockholm, Chapter 1, T.M.C. Asser Press—The Hague 2011, pp. 1–5

The new governance of Justice and Home Affairs: towards further supranationalism, in: Sarah Wolff, Flora A.N.J. Goudappel en Jaap W. de Zwaan (Eds.), Freedom, security and justice after Lisbon and Stockholm, Chapter 2, T.M.C. Asser Press—The Hague 2011, pp. 7–25

European citizenship and free movement of persons (co-author: Flora Goudappel), in: Sarah Wolff, Flora A.N.J. Goudappel en Jaap W. de Zwaan (Eds.), Freedom, security and justice after Lisbon and Stockholm, Chapter 3, T.M.C. Asser Press—The Hague 2011, pp. 27–39

The Treaty of Lisbon, Towards a more supranational legal order of the European Union, in: Marie-Claire Foblets, Mireille Hildebrandt, Jacques Steenbergen (Eds.), Liber Amicorum René Foqué, Larcier—Boom Juridische Uitgevers, 2012, ISBN 9782804449827, pp. 301–319

De toekomst van de Europese Unie-samenwerking, Op zoek naar een hervormd en duurzaam samenwerkingsmodel waaraan ook niet-Europese landen kunnen meedoen, SEW Tijdschrift voor Europees en economisch recht, Uitgeverij Paris, 60e Jaargang, nr 11 van november 2012, pp. 438–450

Europa en de Burger, Hoe verder met de Europese Unie-samenwerking? Intreerede De Haagse Hogeschool 24 januari 2013, 56 pagina's, ISBN 9789073077485

The new institutional balance of power in the European Union, in: Which way forward, Present challenges, strategic choices and future perspectives of the EU, Theseus publication, Fritz Thyssen Stiftung, September 2013, ISBN 9783487148311, pp. 32–38

Europese integratie en de beroepspraktijk, in: C.M.A. van der Meule (Ed.), Onderzoekend op weg, Een essaybundel over opdrachten voor de toekomst, bijdrage aan Liber Rob Brons, ter gelegenheid van zijn afscheid als voorzitter van het College van Bestuur van De Haagse Hogeschool te Den Haag, 2014, De Haagse Hogeschool 2014, ISBN 9789073077539, pp. 41–49

Editorial TEPSA Newsletter (Trans European Policy Studies Association) http://www.tepsa.eu/

- February 2014: European Union cooperation: The Art of Explaining
- April 2014: Democracy in the European Union: the importance of the European elections
- July 2014: TEPSA, new opportunities in spite of setback
- July 2014: The European Parliament, the winner takes it all (column)
- September 2014: The neighbouring policy of the European Union: it is Soft Power that is needed
- November 2014: European Parliament and National Parliaments; partners or competitors
- February 2015: Speaking with one voice
- April 2015: The tragedies in the Mediterranean and the European Neighbourhood Policy

De voortgang van de Europese Integratie, wisselwerking tussen recht en beleid ('Progress of the European integration process, interaction between law and policy'), valedictory lecture of 14 March 2014 at the Erasmus University Rotterdam, Erasmus Law lectures 35, Boom Juridische Uitgevers 2014, ISBN 9789089749963

The relationship European Union-Russia, A story of missed opportunities, april 2014-edition of the periodical International Affairs (Mezhdunarodnaya Zhizn) of the Russian Ministry of Foreign Affairs in Moscow

Europese verkiezingen, Heel belangrijk, Jaap de Zwaan en Chris Aalberts (Eds.) De Haagse Hogeschool, Lectoraat European Integration, mei 2014, ISBN/EAN 9789073077560, 92 pagina's

Inleiding: de relevantie van de Europese Verkiezingen, in: Europese verkiezingen, Heel belangrijk, Jaap de Zwaan en Chris Aalberts (Eds.) De Haagse Hogeschool, Lectoraat European Integration, mei 2014, pagina's 7–8

De Europese Unie-samenwerking: hoe leggen we het uit?, in: Europese Verkiezingen, Heel belangrijk, Jaap de Zwaan en Chris Aalberts (Eds.), De Haagse Hogeschool, Lectoraat European Integration, mei 2014, pagina's 31–37

European Integration and Democracy: A gradual process, with certain limits, contribution to the European Group of Public Law (EGPL) Conference of 13–14 September 2014 dedicated to issues regarding New Challenges of Democracy/ Nouveaux à la démocratie in Spetses, Greece, organised by the European Public Law Organisation (EPLO) in Athens, Greece (to be published)

Curriculum Vitae Jaap Willem de Zwaan

Born on 9 February 1949 in Amsterdam

Professional activities

2012–	Lector European Integration at the The Hague University of Applied Sciences (part-time)
2005–2011	Director of the Netherlands Institute of International Relations (Clingendael), The Hague
1998–2014	Professor of the Law of the European Union at the Law School of Erasmus University Rotterdam and holder of the EU Jean Monnet Chair 'Future developments of the European Union'. In the period 1998–2005 on a full-time basis, in the period 2005–2014 on a part-time basis Served also as: Dean of International Relations (1999–2001) Dean of the Law School (2001–2004)
1979–1998	Ministry of Foreign Affairs
1979–1981	Staff Member of the Department on European Integration, The Hague
1981–1983	Member of the Legal Service, The Hague
1983–1988	Legal Advisor of the Netherlands Permanent Representation to the European Communities, Brussels
1988–1995	Senior Member of the Legal Service, The Hague
1995–1998	Legal Advisor and Head of Division Justice and Home Affairs of the Netherlands Permanent Representation to the European Union, Brussels Acted during his work as member of the Legal Service of the Ministry of Foreign Affairs (1981–1983 and 1988–1995) as Agent for the Netherlands Government in numerous cases, covering all aspects of the institutional and substantive Law of the European Union, before the Court of Justice of the European Union in Luxembourg.

	Was involved as Legal Advisor of the Permanent Representation (1983–1988) in the negotiations on and the drafting of the Single European Act. Was furthermore involved in the negotiations on and the drafting of the Treaties of Accession of Spain and Portugal to the European Communities. Was involved as Legal Advisor of the Permanent Representation (1995–1998) in the negotiations on and the drafting of the Treaty of Amsterdam. Chaired during the Netherlands Presidency (first half of 1997) the Group 'Friends of the Presidency'/'Amis de la Présidence'. Was involved as Head of Division Justice and Home Affairs in the development of the Third Pillar cooperation.
1979–1985	Substitute Judge in the District Court of The Hague
1973–1979	Member of the Bar of The Hague (Office Pels Rijcken & Droogleever Fortuijn)

Education

1993–	Doctor's degree in Law at the University of Groningen ('The Permanent Representatives Committee, its role in European Union decision making')
1972–1973	Postgraduate studies at the College of Europe, Bruges in Belgium. Main courses in European Law (Institutional law, Substantive law, Legal protection, Competition law), optional courses: Political Sciences and Economy
1972–	Traineeship at the Commission of the EC, Brussels, Belgium (DG VI, Agriculture)
1967–1972	Study at the Law School of the University of Leiden. Main courses in Dutch Civil Law, optional courses: European Law and Public Finances
1961–1967	Secondary Education (Gymnasium B) at 'Het Amsterdams Lyceum' in Amsterdam

Other Activities

2015–	Member of the Dutch Helsinki Committee (OSCE, Organization for Security and Co-operation in Europe)
2014–	Member of the European Group of Public Law (EGPL) of the European Public Law Organisation (EPLO), having its seat in Athens, Greece
2014–	Secretary-general of the Trans European Policy Studies Association (TEPSA), a network organization for Institutes for European Studies in the Member States and candidate-Member States of the European Union, having its seat in Brussels, Belgium
2013–	Member of the Participation Council (Hogeschoolraad), of The Hague University of Applied Sciences, Chair of the Committee on Personal and Organizational matters (P&O)

2011–	Member of the Foresight Advisory Council of the Alfred Herrhausen Gesellschaft, the International Forum of Deutsche Bank, Berlin, Germany
2009–	Member of the Board of the Trans European Policy Studies Association (TEPSA), a network organization for Institutes for European Studies in the Member States and candidate Member States of the European Union, having its seat in Brussels, Belgium
2009–	Member of the Advisory Board ('Wissenschaftlichen Direktorium') of the Institut für Europäische Politik, Germany, Berlin
2008–2011	Chairman of the Board of the 'Haagse Academische Coalitie' (the 'Hague Academic Coalition'), a foundation serving as framework for cooperation between academic institutions in The Hague in the context of the profile of the city of The Hague as UN 'Legal Capital' of the World
2007–2015	Member of the Board of the Amsterdam Institute of German Studies in Amsterdam ('Duitsland Instituut Amsterdam')
2006–	Member of the Governing Board of the European Studies Institute, established by the European Union and the Russian Federation in the framework of the Partnership and Cooperation Agreement (PCA-cooperation), in Moscow, Russia As from April 2012 also Member of the Executive Committee of the Governing Board
2005–2010	Editor-in-chief of the 'Internationale Spectator', the monthly periodical for international affairs published on behalf of the Netherlands Institute of International Relations ('Clingendael') in The Hague
2005–	Member of the French–Dutch Cooperation Council ('Conseil de coopération franco-néerlandais')
2005–2010	Member of the Board of the Netherlands Association for European Law ('Nederlandse Vereniging voor Europees Recht')
2004–	Member of the Board of Directors of the European Public Law Organisation (EPLO), having its seat in Athens, Greece
2004–2008	Member of the General Board of the 'Europese Beweging Nederland' ('EBN'), European Movement, section of The Netherlands
2004–	Member of the Commission 'European Union' instituted in January 2004 by the Government of the Kingdom of the Netherlands to review the modalities of cooperation between the Dutch Antilles and Aruba on the one hand, and the European Union on the other
2002–	Member of the Board of the 'Rotterdams Juridisch Genootschap' (Rotterdam Law Association)
2002–2008	Member of the Board of the Foundation 'Nederland-Roemenië' (The Netherlands—Romania)
2002–2005	Vice President of the Executive Board ('Dagelijks Bestuur') of the T.M.C. Asser Instituut, Institute for International Private and Public Law and European Law, in The Hague

2002–2005	Member of the General Board ('Algemeen Bestuur') of the T.M.C. Asser Instituut, Institute for International Private and Public Law and European Law, in The Hague
2000–2012	Member of the Commission on European Integration (CEI), which is one of the committees of the Advisory Council on International Affairs (AIV) of the Minister of Foreign Affairs
1999–2002	President of the Scientific Council (Wetenschappelijke Raad) of the T.M.C. Asser Instituut, Institute for International Private and Public Law and European Law, in The Hague
1998–2000	Member of the Administrative Council of the Salvador Madariaga Foundation, research foundation for the College of Europe in Bruges (Belgium)
1997–2002	Member of the Advisory Board (Curatorium) of the Europa Institute of the Law School of the University of Leiden
1991–1994	Lecturer in the European Law courses of the Rijks Opleidingsinstituut ('State Training School') in The Hague. Main target group: members of the Legal and Legislative Departments of all Ministries of the Government in The Hague
1984–1988	President of the Association of Former Students of the College of Europe in Bruges (Belgium). In the period 1988–1995 regional representative of the Association in the Netherlands
1976–1978	Member respectively President of the Board of the Young Bar Association to the Supreme Court in The Hague
1967–1972	Several functions in student associations, such as President of the Liberal Student Association in Leiden (1969–1971)

Miscellaneous

2014–	Dutch Royal decoration 'Officier in de Orde van Oranje-Nassau'
2014–	'Ad Fontes'-medal of the Erasmus University Rotterdam
2010–	'Commemorative Medal' of the Faculty of Law of Comenius University Bratislava, Slovak Republic
2009–	Award of Excellence' of the Embassy of the Republic of Romania in recognition of the outstanding contribution to promoting Romanian values in The Netherlands and to supporting assistance projects for Romania throughout the 20 years after 1989
2004–	'Imrich Karvas' medal of the University of Economics in Bratislava, Slovak Republic
1998–	Officier dans l'Ordre national du mérite of the French Republic

Introduction

When Jaap de Zwaan retired in 2014 from his position as professor of European Union Law at Erasmus School of Law, he left a large legacy in research and lecturing. The contributions in this volume reflect not only the intellectual ties between the authors and their colleague and friend Jaap de Zwaan, but also his distinguishing approach to the development and enlargement of the European Union. Jaap de Zwaan viewed the European Communities and, later on, the European Union as a constitutional structure that should be characterized by the principles of democracy and the rule of law. And, most important, he developed this view at a time when most other specialists still concentrated on the four freedoms of the internal market: the free movement of goods, capital, services and people. This is not to say that the economic freedoms decline in importance. What we, following the traces of his work, think that should be emphasized is this: in the long run these freedoms can only retain their importance under the condition that they are rooted in a fuller realization of the constitutional principles of rule of law and democracy. Article 2 of the Treaty on the European Union states: "The Union is founded on the values of respect for human dignity, freedom, democracy, equality, the rule of law and respect for human rights, including the rights of persons belonging to minorities. These values are common to the Member States in a society in which pluralism, non-discrimination, tolerance, justice, solidarity and equality between women and men prevail".

Europhobic resistance against the freedoms of movement, especially that of persons, can only be counterbalanced by the inclusion of the persons in a shared

Flora A.N.J. Goudappel
Rotterdam, The Netherlands
e-mail: flora@floragoudappel.nl

Ernst M.H. Hirsch Ballin
T.M.C. Asser Instituut, The Hague, The Netherlands
e-mail: Ballin@asser.nl

Ernst M.H. Hirsch Ballin
Tilburg University, Tilburg, The Netherlands

public sphere, informed by these principles. This is why European citizenship, another topic that is consistent with his basic approach received Jaap de Zwaan's attention, and why he in his practical activities and teaching abroad rightly viewed adherence to these principles as essential, at a time when most politicians and civil still thought that economic liberalization in the new Member States was the only really important thing and rule of law merely its framework. Jaap was already advising and lecturing on this years before the adherence of new Member States in these Member States themselves. When the TFEU's preamble promises "an ever closer union", it is not the disappearance of socio-cultural differences between the Member States that we should have in mind, but a continuous growth in the shared acceptance of democracy and rule of law. In recent case law of the Court of Justice, we may even view how the fundamental rights of the Charter and the principle of the rule of law give direction for further development of the economic freedoms.

The contributions to this volume apply, step by step, this approach to the present and the future of the European Union. The *first part* deals with the "Constitutional Foundations" as such. The notion "rule of law" is differently interpreted among and within distinct legal traditions. In the common law tradition, it appears to state simply that the law, not men should govern relations between people, whereas the words "Rechtsstaat" and "État de droit" in the German and Dutch, respectively, French language versions, appear to have a more substantive connotation. In a historically underpinned account, Mortimer Sellers demonstrates that the principle of the rule of law is intrinsically defined by the absence of arbitrary power and the notion that "power should be regulated by law, to advance the common good".

This means that the rule of law is procedural as well as substantive, which justifies the emerging EU practice of assimilation between the notions derived from different legal traditions. The procedural and substantive dimensions of the rule of law cannot be separated from each other, since procedures are needed in order to substantiate the values. These procedures ought to be democratic, since democracy is the political decision-making process in which all political views have to be treated equally and in a democratic debate have to compete with each other. The democratic legitimacy of the European Union is however under pressure, especially as far as the political culture continues to concentrate on the national sources of legitimation. Ton van den Brink demonstrates that this is especially visible with respect to the new EU Economic Governance Model, which coordinates public finance and macroeconomic policies of Member States. In a realistic analysis he recommends national parliaments to redefine their own role with respect to these policies in the actual European context, instead of merely complaining about an alleged loss of sovereignty.

It is only through the interaction between the EU political level and that of the Member States that the aspirations of Article 2 TEU can be brought to life. Helena Raulus concentrates on the ultimate sanction for policies of the Member States that do not comply with Article 2, and how to prevent such a situation. In the Hungarian situation the Article 7 has even not been initiated. After having discussed recent initiatives from the Dutch and other governments as well as from the Commission, Helena Raulus recommends going one step further and enhancing the role of the Fundamental Rights Agency under the treaties.

Contrary to the state-centred approach that the development of European law has inherited from its constitutional origination from treaties, a constitutional adherence to the principles of democracy and rule of law brings the citizens to the forefront. This has been confirmed in the emphasis on human rights in Articles 2 and 6 TEU and the adoption of the Charter of Fundamental Rights, which includes a title on citizens' rights, as a part of the treaty framework. European citizenship is the legal institution that completes the principles of democracy and rule of law. Fiona Murray elucidates how European citizenship has broadened and deepened since 1993 and how the way ahead is connected with the rule of law and democratic participation.

When the notion of rule of law is discussed, one of the most obvious elements is the right of citizens to invoke the decision of an independent court in a dispute with the administration. Since national courts are the first in line to respond, the rule of law in the European Union depends primarily on them. Urszula Jaremba argues that the entry into force of the Charter of Fundamental Rights as EU primary law has contributed to the importance of the role of national courts. The protection of the rights of individuals under the Charter when Member States implement EU law, might increase the number of requests for a preliminary ruling from the Court of Justice by national courts. At the same time, lack of time, resources and knowledge might hamper the fulfilment of this important role by national courts.

Marc van der Woude draws our attention to the fact that at the same time, the court system of the European Union itself, especially the General Court and the Court of Justice, are confronted with a huge workload. The administration of the court is such a demanding task that improvements while maintaining the independence of the courts is urgently needed. This chapter includes a vintage description of the internal management and governance of the European courts. The vital importance of truly independent courts in any constitutional set-up that aims at full compliance with the principle of the rule of law, has been the reason in several EU Member States for the instruction of a Council for the Judiciary. The Netherlands has followed this example, in 2002. Marc van der Woude recommends the establishment of a High Council for the Judiciary at the European level, a recommendation that deserves the attention of anyone who understands that the quality and effectiveness of both political and judicial decision-making are key factors in the future of the European project.

Part I of the book concludes with a thought-provoking reflection by Christiaan Timmermans on the constitutional identity of the European Union. Many avoid this subject after the demise of the Treaty establishing a Constitution for Europe, but Timmermans demonstrates that the subject continues to be politically and—given the outplacement of certain procedures, e.g. concerning the monetary stability, as well as the ongoing debate on the relation with German Constitutional Law—judicially relevant. Qualifying the European Union as a "Union of States and Citizens" (a proposal from J. Hoeksma) would in Timmermans' view be appropriate because of the required strengthening of European citizenship.

Part II of the book concentrates on "Procedures". The contributions to this part of the book demonstrate how the relation between procedure and substance in the European Union works out in legislative and treaty making practice. Anita Bultena elucidates the overwhelmingly important role of negotiations in the European legislative process. This feature distinguishes it from dominant practices in domestic legislative processes. Of course, negotiations play a role there as well, but not to the same extent as in the European Union. Maybe this is an (overlooked) explanation for the fact that notwithstanding the democratization of the European legislative processes, most people still experience a feeling of alienation vis-à-vis European legislation that is usually described as its "democratic deficit". A never-ending sequence of negotiations can indeed hardly be viewed as an expression of the political will of the European citizenry yet it is part of the European Union's everyday system.

The processes through which the European Union affirms its adherence to the principles of rule of law and democracy include the external action of the Union. Consistency of internal and external with respect to these principles is not only a question of effectiveness, but also of credibility. Cornelius James deals in his contribution with the extent to which these principles inform the European Union's development cooperation policies. The Union's agreements with third countries (be it bilateral or multilateral, like the Cotonou agreement) on financial and technical support usually, include, like trade agreements, a "human rights clause". Through the promotion of "good governance" in its political, economic, social and environmental terms, the European Union gives "sustainable development" a meaning that is related to the rule of law and democracy. The relevance of this chapter surpasses its focus on developing countries. Developed countries, including the Union's Member States themselves, also ought to review their policies and decision-making processes keeping in mind that we all need a wider understanding of sustainability.

Accession treaties to the European Union have to be preceded by an assessment procedure concerning the candidate Member State's ability to comply with European Union law and policies. Here we can view a change in approach that reflects the profound change that we described at the beginning of this introduction. After the fall of the Berlin Wall, the enlargement process initially (over) emphasized the economic adaptation of the candidate Member State to the EC standards. In the view of many politicians at that time, who even belittled the lawyers with their concerns about reform of the judiciary and law enforcement, the most important thing was the privatization of the state owned companies. By now, we know how the privatization was turned into a grab bag for shrewd investors who consolidated their newly acquired wealth through financial support for their political benefactors. The failure of the one-sided privatization was the learning fee European politics had to pay before due priority was given to fighting fraud and corruption and strengthening the rule of law institutions in candidate Member States.

The author of the final chapter of this part, Alfred Kellermann, reflects on his active participation in Albania's preparations for the accession procedure. The story of this contribution may be something of the past—developments in Albania have meanwhile taken a turn for the good—but it helps us to understand how difficult transition processes can be and how much effort is needed before one can confirm that a state has effectively adopted and implemented the principles of rule of law and democracy.

Part III of the book deals with a number of policies in which the importance of the EU's adherence to the principles of rule of law and democracy emerges. Hans van Meerten discusses recent ECJ case law on pensions. State liability is a real-life rule of law guarantee in situations when workers risk to lose their pension entitlements.

Monica den Boer illustrates the unavoidable interconnectedness of experiences of injustice "inside" and "outside" the rule of law. Her examples are compelling: terrorism, human trafficking and other forms of criminal behaviour require action at the European level. It is part of the nature of such public tasks that they require actions at different levels. It is not easy, though, to live up to the standards of European principles when the European Union has to face areas with completely different standards, e.g. the countries in Africa from which asylum seekers crossing the Mediterranean border try to get to the EU. Specific subjects related to the Area of Freedom Security and Justice are discussed in the following chapters: the confiscation of proceeds from crime, by Ladislav Hamran and efforts to widen readmission of migrants in their countries of origin, by Türkan Ertuna Lagrand. The latter subject deals with the strict side of migration policy. Lagrand rightly emphasizes that this policy should also be guided by *respect for human dignity and freedom and by respect for human rights*. These contributions reconfirm indeed that internal and external commitment to the principles of rule of law and democracy have become more and more intertwined.

Finally, two chapters deal with policies related to the working of the rule of law across state borders. Viola Heutger discusses the relation between the EU's sphere of competence with respect to private international law and the attempts to make room for sub-national regional law. Gerhard Hafner elaborates on the relation between the European Union and the International Criminal Court, the first global court that deals with crimes against human dignity and international humanitarian law. Important practical questions concerning cooperation between the EU and the ICC, with respect to information and the position of the EU's civil and military personnel, have become the subject of a separate agreement that is analysed in this chapter.

An essay annexed at the end of the book by one of Jaap de Zwaan's fellow-travellers in EU Law and diplomacy, former deputy Prime Minister Laurens-Jan Brinkhorst, concludes with a forward-looking view on the close relationship between the European integration and democracy, and the need to translate the legal debate into a constructive political discourse, inside and outside parliaments.

Part I
Constitutional Foundations

What Is the Rule of Law and Why Is It So Important?

Mortimer Sellers

Abstract A state governed by the rule of law describes a state where both private and public powers are removed from the administration of justice and are regulated by law. The rule of law serves the public good of the community as a whole. It is a system where laws rule and not men. The law determines what is necessary in a society to prevent domination and oppression and to promote the common good. As people seek justice through law, the rule of law comes at first from men itself, because men obey rules they believe to be just and arise against ones they consider unjust. The value of the rule of law lies in the fact that it prevents arbitrary judgments, secures justice, and prevents tyranny and oppression. It limits the power of those who have authority. The government must first control the people and then it must be obliged to control itself. It must therefore be stable and constitutional and it can therefore be implied that some states are not ready to implement the rule of law, because the governments cannot be trusted. The author argues that the most important step towards the rule of law is when judges are independent of executive and legislative powers. Constant attention to the combination of powers in a state is required, because only in this way can laws be created for the common good. Law must be separated from arbitrary power.

Contents

M. Sellers (✉)
University System of Maryland, Adelphi, MD, USA
e-mail: msellers@ubalt.edu

M. Sellers
Center for International and Comparative Law, University of Baltimore, Baltimore, USA

F.A.N.J. Goudappel and E.M.H. Hirsch Ballin (eds.), *Democracy and Rule of Law in the European Union*, DOI 10.1007/978-94-6265-066-4_1

1 Introduction

These reflections on the rule of law consider the concept of the rule of law from within the rule of law tradition. This contribution clarifies: (i) what the rule of law is; (ii) what the rule of law requires from us; (iii) where the rule of law comes from; (iv) why it is so valuable; and (v) how we can secure it. Let there be no confusion about the subject matter of this inquiry. The rule of law in its original, best, and most useful sense signifies the "*imperium legum*" of the ancients, "the empire of laws and not of men" pursued by the early humanists, by the partisans of liberal Enlightenment, and republican revolutions across the globe. This is not the later, positivist, more limited understanding of the rule of law as "*Rechtsstaat*," which has sapped the rule of law everywhere and caused so much confusion. The rule of law in its original and most natural sense is a pure social good, in which the legalism of the *Rechtsstaat* plays only a partial and supporting role. Societies that enjoy the rule of law are vastly better situated than those that do not. This makes the real rule of law (or its absence) the central measure dividing good from bad government everywhere. All law and political institutions can and should be evaluated to determine whether it or they advance the rule of law—or do not.[1]

Five main points should be made as plainly as possible at the outset. First, the definition: "rule of law" is the English translation of the Latin phrase "*imperium legum*," more literally "the empire of laws and not of men." This goes beyond the mere legalism of a "rule *by* law" or "*Rechtsstaat*," through which one man, or a faction, or a party rules through positive law to impose his or her or their will on others. Second, the rule of law—the *imperium legum*—requires of us that we remove the will of public officials as much as possible from the administration of justice in society. No executive, legislator, judge, or citizen should enjoy arbitrary power to act against the public welfare. Third, the rule of law ideal arises from human nature, because all people seek justice through law and all law and governments claim—explicitly or implicitly—that the laws they promulgate serve justice in fact. From this it follows (fourth) that only the rule of law can secure stable justice in society, which makes the rule of law vastly important. So the fifth and greatest question is how to discover, create, interpret, and enforce the rule of law in such a way that law controls and governs the various private interests, not only

[1]This chapter was first published in Barenboim et al. 2014, and elaborates (from a slightly different perspective) arguments also presented in Sellers 2010.

of ordinary citizens, but also of the public officials who administer the state. All this follows from the original, once pervasive, and still the most useful understanding of the "rule of law" as "the empire of laws and not of men"—not simply the rule of men through law.

2 What the Rule of Law Is

The rule of law signifies "the empire of laws and not of men": the subordination of arbitrary power and the will of public officials as much as possible to the guidance of laws made and enforced to serve their proper purpose, which is the public good ("*res publica*") of the community as a whole. When positive laws or their interpretation or enforcement serve other purposes, there is no rule of law, in its fullest sense, but rather "rule *by* law"—mere legalism—in service of arbitrary power. The vocabulary here is important, because the concept of the rule of law enjoyed its fullest elaboration in tandem with related struggles for "liberty" and "republican government" against tyranny and oppression. The liberty ("*libertas*") of the ancients, the Enlightenment, and the republican revolutions of emergent modernity signified protection by the law and government of all members of society against domination by other persons, or by states, or by the governments of states (where "domination" consists in the arbitrary control by one person or faction of another, without reference to the common good). The key here is the purposes for which positive laws and state action are created, interpreted, or enforced. The law may legitimately control us, but public officials must respect law's proper purpose, which is the common good of society as a whole, and not their own private interests.

When we have and maintain a legal system that serves the common good of society as a whole, then we have the rule of law (because the laws rule and not men), we have liberty (because the law prevents oppression), and we live in a republic (because government advances the "*res publica*" or "common good" of its subjects). The rule of law, liberty, and republican government are three facets of the same substantive good, secured only where the laws rule and protect us from tyranny and oppression. When positive laws and their interpretation and enforcement serve the public good, and prevent domination by any person or group of persons, then we have the "*imperium legum,*" the rule of law in its fullest and best sense: "the empire of laws and not of men."

Persons may, of course, disagree on what serves the common good best. Nor should we forget that the "common good" ("*res publica*") also includes and protects the legitimate private goods and interests ("*res privata*") of separate individuals and groups. This raises the second-order question, how best to discover and preserve the common good through law: "What combination of powers in society, or what form of government, will compel the formation of good and equal laws, an impartial execution, and faithful interpretation of them, so that citizens may constantly enjoy the benefit of them, and be sure of their continuance."[2] The difficulty of answering this question should not obscure the central importance of the value that it seeks to advance. The rule of law is not simply one or a few or the most important of the techniques sometimes used to secure the "empire of laws and not of men," but rather the "*imperium legum*" itself. There is no rule of law unless the law itself rules, and regulates the private interests of those with power, so that they cannot act against the common good of society as a whole.

3 What the Rule of Law Requires from Us

The rule of law requires that we remove the private will of public officials as much as possible from the administration of justice in society. Private as well as public power should be regulated by law, to advance the common good. When acting in a public capacity our only concern should be the public good. When acting in a private capacity, the law should also limit our self-interest to protect the community as a whole. The concept of law embodied in the rule of law tradition therefore includes an element of impartiality that regulates the scope of public power. Legislators should legislate for the common good. To do otherwise would be "corrupt" (a term of art) and undermine the rule of law. Public officials should execute the laws in the light of the common good. To do otherwise would be "tyranny"(another term of art) and violate the rule of law. Judges should interpret the law to advance the common good. To do otherwise would be "arbitrary" (a third term of art) and violate their duty to society. The rule of law constrains the guardians of the law to serve the interests of the law, which is the interest of the whole, rather than any particular party or faction.

The rule of law requires fidelity to one overarching value, sometimes called "liberty," the state that obtains when law prevents domination by powerful interests, public or private. Note the limits of this requirement. The rule of law does not require that citizens always act in the public interest, but rather, that they do so when the law determines such deference to be necessary, in the light of the common good. Citizens may and properly should have and pursue private interests, but not at the expense of their public duties (which increase as they gain more authority). There can be a significant gap between the requirements of law and morality. The law determines what is *necessary* and therefore required to prevent domination and promote the public good. Morality reflects what is *useful* in advancing the good of society as a whole, but may not be required. Law has much the narrower jurisdiction.

The rule of law requires that laws be made and enforced only to serve their proper purpose, which is the common good or *res publica* of society as a whole. From this many other requirements follow, but always limited by the central purpose of the enterprise. For example, legal certainty is a great friend of liberty. Well-known and easily understood laws can be significant constraints on

[2] Adams 1787, p. 128.

self-serving power. But legal certainty at the expense of the common good would defeat the purpose of law. Advocates of rule *by* law sometimes undermine the rule *of* law by legitimating the enactments of tyrants. Positive laws promulgated in the private interest do not satisfy the rule of law—although they may sometimes be an advance on otherwise unregulated tyranny. Promulgation and the other virtues of legal formalism often advance the empire of laws. But they are only secondary and contingent requirements of the rule of law, and not the thing itself.

4 Where the Rule of Law Comes From

The rule of law ideally arises in the first instance from human nature, because all people and all nations seek—or claim to seek—the rule of justice through law. All legal systems claim to be actually and normatively "legitimate," in the sense that they have the moral right to rule. This does not suggest that all such claims are true or sincere, but rather that they are made—implicitly or explicitly—by every existing system of law. The law's universal claim to obedience is dependent upon a prior claim to serve justice. Note the vagueness and procedural ambiguity of the first-order claim to legitimacy. Rulers may claim to find the law through sortition, or by virtue of their own infallibility, or (as Numa did) by direct consultation with God. The veracity (or not) of such claims is less significant than their unanimity. All legal systems depend on the assertion (explicit or implicit) that the laws do and should rule, and not men. All claim to implement the rule of law.

The law's claim to serve justice, rather than the interests of those in authority, arises from human nature and the realities of social power. People more readily submit to laws they perceive to be just, therefore all legal systems claim to realize justice in fact. These natural and universal origins of the rule of law explain the concept's latent appeal, but not its actual success. Besides, the universal human desire for the rule of law is the historical rule of law tradition, through which lawyers, governments, and nations have sought to specify, implement, and ultimately to realize the rule of law in practice. This gives the world a basis for evaluating existing legal systems. It is not enough to simply assert the primacy of law. States must actually advance it. If "law" in practice were reduced to the simple self-interested commands of those in power, then the "*Rechtsstaat*" would be an instrument of oppression, and law itself no more than a weapon, to be wielded for good or ill by whosoever holds the scepter of the state.[3]

The American John Adams,[4] followed the Englishman James Harrington,[5] in quoting the Florentine Donato Giannotti,[6] who divided the whole history of law

[3]See Raz 1985, pp. 285 and 299.

[4]Adams 1787, p. 126.

[5]Harrington 1992, p. 6.

[6]Giannotti 1974.

and politics into a battle between two parties: those fighting for the rule of law (or government "*de jure*") and those fighting for the rule of certain particular men (or government "de facto").[7] This descent of authority, back from America and France to England, Venice, Florence, and ultimately Rome, illustrates the high points of the modern rule of law tradition, which sought to work out in practice what the rule of law requires in principle. The conflict between the "de facto" theory of law as the instrument of power, and the "*de jure*" conception of law as the product of reason and justice, has been the driving force of legal modernity, and the development of constitutional government throughout the world.[8]

5 Why the Rule of Law Is so Valuable

The rule of law is of vast and permanent value to any society, because only the rule of law can secure justice, by preventing tyranny and oppression. The Universal Declaration of Human Rights, approved by the General Assembly of the United Nations without dissent, recognized that "it is essential, if man is not to be compelled to have recourse, as a last resort, to rebellion against tyranny and oppression, that human rights should be protected by the Rule of Law."[9] More recently, the General Assembly identified "human rights, the rule of law and democracy" as "universal and indivisible core principles of the United Nations."[10] These ringing assertions, repeated or paraphrased by the European Convention on Human Rights,[11] the American Convention on Human Rights,[12] the African Charter on Human and Peoples Rights,[13] and numerous other regional agreements and national constitutions[14] illustrate the substantive moral component always present in appeals to the "rule of law." The 'rule of law" in its best and usual sense implies the fulfillment of justice through law and the negation of arbitrary government.

The battle of the rule of law against arbitrary government takes place in every human society when those with power seek to expand their discretion, and their subjects resist. Nor are the advocates of unfettered power without arguments in their favor. The most learned apostle of despotism, Thomas Hobbes, denied any distinction between "right and wrong," "good and evil," "justice and injustice,"

[7]*Cf.* Tacitus, at I.2.

[8]See Sellers 1998.

[9]*Universal Declaration of Human Rights* (December 10, 1948), Preamble.

[10]See U.N.G.A./RES/61/39, 18 December, 2006, on "The rule of law at the national and international levels". *Cf.* U.N.G.A./RES/62/70; U.N.G.A./RES/63/128.

[11]*European Convention on Human Rights* (4 November, 1950), Preamble.

[12]*American Convention on Human Rights* (22 November, 1969), Articles 8 and 9.

[13]*The African Charter on Human and Peoples Rights* (27 June, 1981), Articles 3, 6, and 7.

[14]See, for example, *Constitution of Russia* (12 December, 1993), Article 1; *Constitution of the Peoples Republic of China* (4 December, 1982), Article 5.

beyond our separate and conflicting desires.[15] Hobbes had seen in the horrors of England's Civil War the indiscriminate misery of anarchy, "which is the greatest evil that can happen in this life."[16] From this it follows (he suggested) that we need an absolute and uncontested sovereign power to rule us and keep us safe.[17]The fear of anarchy is a powerful and compelling argument for despotism, and as a result the struggle for freedom usually begins with small and incremental advances, beginning with the simple call for written laws, to contain the discretion of those in authority, and only later attempting to secure just and impartial laws, a much more difficult undertaking.[18]

The rule of law is so valuable precisely because it limits the arbitrary power of those in authority. Public authority is necessary, as Thomas Hobbes rightly observed, to protect against private power, but the rule of law keeps public authorities honest. The rule of law implies constitutionalism, and all states or societies that struggle towards the rule of law are also working towards constitutional government, to control power with reason, or (more prosaically) make "ambition counteract ambition,"[19] with the constant aim to "divide and arrange the offices in such a manner as that each may be a check upon the other–that the private interest of every individual may be a sentinel over the public rights."[20] The rule of law is valuable, because only the rule of law compels "the formation of good and equal laws, an impartial execution, and faithful interpretation of them, so that citizens may constantly enjoy the benefits of them, and be sure of their continuance."[21]

6 How to Secure the Rule of Law

The fundamental principle of the rule of law is so widely and universally accepted as to be almost a truism. The laws should rule, and not arbitrary power. The real difficulty arises in securing the rule of law in practice. The great constitutionalist, John Adams, observed that "in establishing a government which is to be administered by men over men," the greatest difficulty "lies in this: you must first enable the government to control the governed; and in the next place oblige it to control itself." This requires a "well-ordered constitution" so that justice could prevail "even among highwaymen," by "setting one rogue to watch another," so that "the

---

[15]Hobbes 1651, I.vi.24; I.xiii.63.

[16]Id. at II.xxx.175.

[17]Id. at II.xviii.90.

[18]The famous story of the *decemviri* and the struggle for the rule of law in Rome was told by Livy in the third book of his history (*aburbe condita libri* III.33ff). For similar developments in Athens, see Ostwald 1986.

[19]Madison 1788a, b.

[20]Id.

[21]Adams 1787, p. 128.

knaves themselves may in time, be made honest men by the struggle."[22] Many of these necessary legal and political controls were as well known (as John Adams expressed it) "at the time of the neighing of the horse of Darius" as they are today.[23] The basic guarantors of the rule of law include representative government, a divided legislature, an elected executive, and above all, an independent judiciary serving for extremely long and nonrenewable terms in office.[24]

To recognize the necessary connection between the rule of law as an ideal and well-constructed constitutional government does not and should not be taken to imply that all states can or should maintain the same constitutional structures in practice. The social, historical, geographical, and other circumstances in different societies will always differ, limiting what is appropriate, prudent, and possible. Certain practices will never be justified, however, and certain standards and basic institutions will be shared by every society that aspires to attain "the government of laws and not of men." This brief investigation cannot and should not presume to offer a detailed formula for securing the real rule of law, but it can help to establish a basic outline of the common elements necessary to any rule-of-law polity, including some of the exceptions and allowances that may be needed to establish the rule of law in fact, when history and governments are deeply set against it.

The rule of law will be best secured by stable constitutional government, because well-constructed constitutions alone hold out the hope of controlling the governors themselves. If the only legitimate purpose of government is to advance the common good, and to establish justice (which follows from the common good), then procedures will be needed to determine what the common good requires in practice, and adjudicate between rival conceptions of the public welfare. A rule of law constitution does this by so structuring public institutions and civic debate that private interests cannot usurp public power. This civic architecture of law and government has two main purposes: first, to secure good public officials, second, to make them rule well. The two are related, but one does not always follow from the other. Constitutionalism and the rule of law tradition recognize the inevitable fallibility of human judgment. No person is so well-placed or well-intentioned that she or he will not benefit from the checks and balances of a stable and constitutional rule of law.

7 Some Practical Requirements

The first necessary and inescapable desideratum of the rule of law is an independent judiciary. Judges must be secure and well-paid, so that they can apply the law without fear or favor. The great breakthrough in securing the rule of law in most

---

[22] Adams 1788, p. 505 (Letter VII, December 26, 1787).

[23] Id., Preface, p. I.ii.

[24] Id.

societies occurs when judges attain tenure "quam diu se bene gesserint" (or during good behavior) rather than "durante bene placito" (at the whim of those in authority). This transition took place in England with the "Glorious Revolution" of 1688, confirmed by the Act of Settlement in 1701, which also prevented the executive from diminishing judicial salaries, once they had been established by law.[25] The Act of Settlement was a turning point in the progress of the rule of law, which made Britain the envy of other European nations.[26] Wherever judges do not enjoy secure tenure in their offices, their rulings are subject to improper influence and coercion.[27]

Judges secure in their salaries and tenure in office, who believe the law to be just, will do their best to uphold law's empire, not least because their own status and prestige depends upon the legal system's standing in society. This confirms the second great basis of the rule of law, which is that laws themselves should seek justice. Not only must judges apply the laws fairly, but the process of legislation must also attempt to advance justice, for its products properly to attain the status of "law." This is a complicated point. The concepts of law and fidelity to law imply a claim to justice.[28] The rule of law assumes a theory of law that separates law from the volition of those who serve it. Thus, pursuit of the rule of law also requires the maintenance of legislative procedures that will generate legislation for the public good, and not to promote the private interests of those with power.

This link between the rule of law and a "common good" theory of justice is profound and essential. The "empire of laws and not of men" seeks a world of "equal" laws that serve all those subject to their control.[29] This absence of partiality is what sets government "*de jure*" apart from government "de facto" (to use the old terminology) and distinguishes "the empire of laws" from "the government of men."[30] But the question remains how to find "good and equal laws."[31] "Representative government" and "checks and balances" in the legislature (and the separation of both from the actual administration of justice) seem necessary precursors to "good and equal laws"[32]—and here we begin to reach the limits of the "essential" or "necessary" rule of law.[33]

[25]*Statutes of the Realm* VII, 636f.; 12–13 William III, c.2.

[26]See, for example, Voltaire 1734, *Lettre* 8, *Lettre* 9.

[27]See, for example, de Tocqueville 1835, 1840 volume I, part 2, Chap. 8, for how even the elections of judges by the people poses a threat to the rule of law.

[28]See Sellers 2004, p. 145.

[29]See the citations to John Adams and Voltaire above; *Cf.* Rawls 1999, p. 71.

[30]*Supra,* notes 25–28.

[31]To use John Adams' felicitous description *supra,* text accompanying note 2.

[32]Id. at I.1.

[33]For the concept of "necessary" law, see de Vattel 1758 Preface pp. xx–xxi. His "voluntary" law is also "necessary," in the more natural sense of the terminology; *cf.* Wolff 1764.

8 Exceptions to the Rule of Law

John Stuart Mill advanced a theory of liberty and government, still extremely popular among statesmen, according to which some societies may not yet be sufficiently developed in their institutions and culture to support even such simple requirements of just government as the separation of powers between the executive and legislative powers, checks and balances in the legislature and administration of justice, or representative institutions in any branch of the government.[34] In circumstances such as these, perhaps "a ruler full of the spirit of improvement" may be "warranted in the use of any expedients that will attain an end perhaps otherwise unattainable."[35] But, there are offensive implications in making the judgment that certain peoples or nations are not yet capable of being trusted with political freedom and equality.[36] Despotism in the common interest, even when pursued with a view to developing the higher faculties of those subject to its rule, is still despotism, and vulnerable to abuse.[37]

The dependence of the rule of law upon the institutions of representative government arises from the observation that government *by* any subgroup within the larger society will inevitably become government *for* the interests of that subgroup, above the others.[38] And even were the natural effects of self-interest somehow avoided, the laws of a benevolent despot would suffer from a very incomplete knowledge of the actual needs and circumstances of the citizens that all laws must actually serve, to be worthy of the name.[39] So, the concept of the rule of law implies an attempt to establish just laws, which, in turn, implies representative government, in order to achieve the degree of general knowledge and commitment to the common good necessary for an impartial legal system.[40] The rule of law entails the impartial pursuit of justice, which requires an equal concern for the welfare of all members of society.

While the rule of law without representative government may be a near impossibility, due to the fallibility of human nature, representative government by itself does not assure the rule of law, and may sometimes impede it. The earliest recorded musings about law and justice already distinguish "tyranny" from the rule of law, and contemplate the dangers of the tyranny of the majority, as well as by smaller factions.[41] The word "democracy" implied a sort of popular despotism

[34]Mill 1859 referred to "backward states of society in which the race itself may be considered as in its nonage.".

[35]Id.

[36]And Mill was not shy in spelling these out. Id.: "Despotism is a legitimate mode of government in dealing with barbarians.".

[37]See Pettit 1997.

[38]Mill 1861, Chap. III.

[39]See Bohman 1996.

[40]See Sellers 1991, p. 273.

[41]See, for example, Aristoteles, p. 1289 a 26 ff.

for most of its history,[42] and the concept of "representative" government was developed to distinguish elected deliberative assemblies from more narrowly "democratic" governments.[43] Representative legislatures must be constructed to respect the rights of minorities, and will require the checks and balances of divided power to guide them away from populism and oppression.[44]

9 Conclusion

This short review of the primary attributes of the rule of law provides a brief reminder of the principles and institutions towards which nations and their peoples struggle, as they seek to create "an empire of laws and not of men." Establishing the rule of law requires constant attention to the "combination of powers in society" that will form the most impartial laws, for the benefit of everyone, without regard to the interests of those in power. These include representative government, a divided legislature, an elected executive, the separation of powers, and an independent and self-confident judiciary, with the power to interpret and apply the laws impartially, without interference (or influence) over actual cases by executive or legislative power.

The greatest threats to the rule of law differ at different times and places, but the underlying principle remains the same: to separate the law from arbitrary power. In many societies, custom and public opinion are the best and only constraints against despotism. More developed polities create written statutes to constrain those in authority. The single greatest advance towards the rule of law occurs when judges secure their independence from executive and legislative power. "Rule of law" states finally come into being with the emergence of constitutional government, provided that the constitution seeks justice and the common good through the checks and balances of divided governmental power, under the ultimate review of independent judges. These fundamental preconditions of an impartial legal system can be vastly improved upon and infinitely refined—but they are hard enough to achieve in themselves and do not entirely prevail under any existing polity.[45]

The rule of law may be difficult to obtain, but its absence is never hard to perceive. Whenever power and naked self-interest can prevail against reason and the common good, the rule of law is not complete. Government will always be needed to protect liberty against aggression and secure the many social goods that require large-scale collective action, but the rule of law constrains those in power to the purposes that justify their authority. Scholars may sometimes advocate partial departures from the rule of law, or its incomplete realization, or its different

---

[42]So much so that Kant baldly stated that democracy was "*im eigentlichen Verstande des Worts notwendig ein Despotismus*." In: Kant 1795.

[43]Madison 1788a, b.

[44]This necessity is well expressed by Madison 1787.

[45]To give just one example, the United States still retains popular elections of sitting judges in many States of the Union.

application in different societies, because of transient or unfortunate circumstances, but no one can deny that every departure from the rule of law is a denial of justice. The ultimate goal of every society and every legal system should be equal and impartial justice for all, free from oppression by arbitrary power.

References

Adams J (1787) A Defence of the Constitutions of Government of the United States of America, vol I. London

Adams J (1788) A Defence of the Constitutions of Government of the United States of America, vol III. London

Aristoteles (350 B.C.) Politika. http://classics.mit.edu/Aristotle/politics.html

Barenboim P, Hickey J, Silkenat J (eds) (2014) The Legal Doctrines of the Rule of Law and the Legal State. Springer

Bohman J (1996) Public Deliberation: Pluralism, Complexity, and Democracy. MIT Press

de Tocqueville A (1835) De la démocratie en Amérique. Paris

de Vattel E (1758) Le droit des gens ou principes de la loi naturelle appliqués à la conduite et aux affaires des nations et des souverains. http://lf-oll.s3.amazonaws.com/titles/1051/0586-01_Bk.pdf

Giannotti G (1974) Libro della Republica de' Viniziani (1540). In: Diaz F (ed) Opere politiche. Marzorati, Milan

Harrington J (1992) The Commonwealth of Oceana (1659). In: Pocock JGA (ed) Harrington, The Commonwealth of Oceana and a system of politics. Cambridge University Press, Cambridge

Hobbes T (1651) Leviathan

Kant I (1795) Zum ewigen Frieden

Madison J ["Publius"] (1787) in The Federalist No. 10, 22 Nov 1787

Madison J ["Publius"] (1788) in The Federalist LI, 6 Feb 1788

Madison J ["Publius"] (1788) in The Federalist LXIII, 1 March 1788

Mill JS (1859) On Liberty

Mill JS (1861) Considerations on Representative Government. London

Ostwald M (1986) From Popular Sovereignty to the Sovereignty of Law. University of California Press

Pettit P (1997) Republicanism: a Theory of Freedom and Government. Oxford University Press, Oxford

Rawls J (1999) The Law of Peoples: With, "The Idea of Public Reason Revisited". Harvard University Press

Raz J (1985) Authority, Law and Morality. The Monist 68(3):295–324

Sellers MNS (1991) Republican Impartiality. Oxf J Legal Stud 11(2):273–282

Sellers MNS (1998) The Sacred Fire of Liberty: Republicanism, Liberalism, and the Law. Palgrave MacMillan, London

Sellers MNS (2004) The Value and Purpose of Law. Baltimore Law J 33:145 et seq

Sellers MNS (2010) An Introduction to the Rule of Law in Comparative Perspective. In Sellers MNS, Tomaszewski T (eds) The Rule of Law in Comparative Perspective. Springer, Heidelberg, pp 1–9

Tacitus C Annalium ab excessu divi Augusti libri. https://archive.org/stream/annaliumabexces02tacigoog#page/n6/mode/2up

Voltaire (1734) Lettres philosophiques. http://www.ebooksgratuits.com/blackmask/voltaire_lettres_philosophiques.pdf

Wolff C (1764) Jus gentium methodo scientifica pertractatum

National Parliaments and EU Economic Governance. In Search of New Ways to Enhance Democratic Legitimacy

Ton van den Brink

Abstract The current economic crisis has challenged the democratic model of representation within the European Union. The author mentions three fundamental tensions that characterize the legal position of EU states: First, the tension between national sovereignty and economic stability; second, the tension between executive and legislative powers; third, the tension of the gradual introduction and development of redistributive policies at the European level. According to the author, the debate on the 'democratic deficit' is still alive. One of the strongest points of critique on the entire EU has been that there is no concrete democratic path for the national governments. Many measures have been taken to address the economic crisis, such as treaties and soft law instruments. These have led to a new EU Economic Governance Model, where public finance and macroeconomic policies of member states are being coordinated. EU institutions are, on one hand, involved via the European Semester and on the other hand via special procedures in case of problems. The author considers the role of the European Parliament still weak in this issue, as it has no real powers. Arguments therefore arise for stronger national parliaments, for example to compensate this lack of power. The author reminds that national governments are still the key players in defining national economic policies. Although the procedural role of national parliaments in the EU dominates, the author claims that the essential issue is which substantive roles they must pursue in the field of economics.

Associate professor of European Law at the Europa Institute of Utrecht University. Member of the management board of the Europa Institute and the Management team of the Utrecht Centre for Regulation and Enforcement in Europe (RENFORCE).

T. van den Brink (✉)
Europa Institute of Utrecht University, Utrecht, The Netherlands
e-mail: a.vandenbrink1@uu.nl

F.A.N.J. Goudappel and E.M.H. Hirsch Ballin (eds.), *Democracy and Rule of Law in the European Union*, DOI 10.1007/978-94-6265-066-4_2

Contents

1 Introduction

Democratic legitimacy has long been a concern in the European Union. The issue has been addressed by scholars from various disciplines and at various levels (from the conceptual to the concrete level of the actual functioning of the EU). But also in political circles and society at large the issue has featured high on the agenda.

The Treaty of Lisbon constituted a consolidation of this constitutional model of EU democracy. The representative democracy has explicitly been designed as the foundation of the Union (Article 10 TEU), supplemented with elements from other democratic models. Article 12 TEU establishes a dual model of democracy which is vested in the European Parliament and national parliaments jointly. This democratic model is currently severely challenged by the economic crisis and the measures that have been adopted to combat it. But the crisis has also highlighted that the democratic model lacks elaboration and precision. Efforts to further clarify the model have been limitedly successful. European Council President Van Rompuy—who has actually been one of the few to make a serious attempt—has come not much further than to link democratic control to the level at which decisions are made.[1] And even this claim is problematic as is proves increasingly difficult to assign measures adopted to combat the economic crisis to a specific level of government. But more about that later. Suffice it for now to conclude that the democratic model introduced by the Treaty of Lisbon has come at a crossroads. Being far from complete and greatly challenged in the current economic crisis, the democratic model is transforming and will need to do so in such a way as to respect the democratic values formulated in the Basic Treaties. I will focus on the role of national parliaments in the current crisis. First, I will set out three major tensions that define the role of national parliaments in both substantive and procedural terms. After this, I will consider the constitutional developments that shaped national parliaments' position in the European Union up until now, including some of the most important trends and positions in scholarly debates. Subsequently, I will analyze the necessity of national parliaments' involvement in the emerging

[1] http://www.consilium.europa.eu/uedocs/cms_data/docs/pressdata/en/ec/132809.pdf (last accessed 21 February 2014).

system of economic governance. Lastly, I will make some observation on how such involvement could be shaped.

2 Fundamental Tensions

The legal position of national parliaments is characterized by at least three fundamental tensions. The first is the tension between national sovereignty and economic stability. Arguably, the principle of national sovereignty favors national decision making, whereas the interconnectedness of European economies requires the European level as the most appropriate for effective decision making aimed at economic stability. A dominant 'frame' is, thus, that of the transfer of sovereignty from national to European levels. In this sense, national sovereignty becomes a synonym to the—independent—exercise of powers. The European Union's 'translation' is the principle of conferral (Article 5 TEU) which establishes the ultimate locus of powers at the national level and the Member States' conferral as the mechanism of empowerment of the EU. The discussion on the EMU illustrates the dominance of this frame as well as the problems related to it. As regards the further strengthening of the EU economic governance, the Dutch Prime Minister Rutte has argued that national sovereignty has not been at stake, since the actual transfer of power in the field of monetary and economic policies had already taken place by the entry into force of the Treaty of Maastricht (the establishment of the EMU itself). Yet, the further shaping of the EMU highlights other aspects related to national sovereignty. The decreased importance of the Council in EMU decision-making processes and the possibility for automatic imposition of sanctions also touch upon national sovereignty. More importantly, economic policy coordination affects national parliament's budget rights. Thus, when viewed in light of national sovereignty, the issue of transfer of powers only seems to cover part of the legal developments.

Another tension that shapes the legal framework in the field of economic policies relates to the tension between executive and legislative powers. Institutions currently taking the lead in combating the economic crisis include the European Council, the Council, the Eurogroup, the Commission, and national governments. We thus witness 'executive dominance' both at the European and national levels. Parliaments are struggling to ensure democratic control over these executive decisions. Budget rights of national parliaments are at stake, but their position also deserves attention in light of the position of the European Parliament. The latter institution still has a rather weak position in the framework. This may be explained from various reasons. No substantive powers are included for the European Parliament under the ESM treaty, but also the Treaty on Stability, Coordination and Governance (the "Fiscal Compact") does not include substantive powers for the European Parliament. But also within the EU basic treaties the powers of the European Parliament in economic policies (e.g., within the European semester) are limited.

The third tension regards the gradual introduction and development of redistributive policies at the European level. New issues of solidarity are raised, between and inside the Member States.[2] The ESM is a key instrument here, but the euro crisis measures also affect the balance between the state and the market, and between the public and private domain in fundamental ways. As such, these measures highlight tensions that have defined political landscapes in the Member States. The creation of the Banking union is the prime example here. The key issue is the scope of discretion which will be left to banks and other financial institutions. This touches upon political choices that were previously reserved for the national political arena. Thus, the interplay between tensions (national/European; state/market) further exacerbates the complexities.

3 National Parliaments and Democratic Legitimacy in the European Union

The first strand of strengthening democratic legitimacy has focused on the European Parliament. The introduction of the term "institutional balance" has confirmed the 'coming of age' of the institution.[3] The Treaty of Lisbon has marked a further—but arguably only intermediate—step in this process of a gradual strengthening of the European Parliament's powers.[4] Nevertheless, the debate on what has been coined the 'democratic legitimacy deficit' is still a vivid one. Fundamental questions include the lack of a European *demos*[5] which is seen by some as an obstacle to the emergence of a real, functioning democracy at the European level. The decision of the German constitutional court on the legality of the Treaty of Lisbon may be seen as an example of that reasoning.[6] Thus, the very foundations of democracy in the European Union are being challenged. Constitutional scholars have responded to the democratic challenges by creating new constitutional theories that accommodate the wish to seek democratic legitimacy of the EU at levels other than that of the EU itself.[7]

---

[2]In her Conclusion to the Pringle case A-G Kokott discussed the emergence of inter-state financial solidarity: Conclusion of 26 October 2012, Case C-370/12, nyr. Borger has further developed this idea in: Borger 2013, pp. 7–36.

[3]Corbett et al. 2007, p. 245.

[4]See for an overview of the European Parliament's new powers under the Treaty of Lisbon: Piris 2010, p. 118 ff.

[5]See critically on this e.g. Weiler 1995, pp. 219–258.

[6]Lisbon Case, BVerfG, 2 BvE 2/08 from 30 June 2009, available at: http://www.bundesverfassungsgericht.de/entscheidungen/es20090630_2bve000208.html.

[7]These include the constitutional theories of Multilevel constitutionalism (coined by Pernice 2002, p. 511) and legal pluralism (coined by Walker 2002, pp. 317–359).

Although one of the first comparative analyses of the role of national parliament dates back to the early 1970s,[8] only in the 1990s did the theme actually gain greater wings. Normative and conceptual analyses have been carried out, but also institutional, administrative, and organizational issues have been studied (e.g., information dependencies and flows, the parliamentary procedures for selection of EU legislative proposals for scrutiny, the scrutiny procedures themselves and inter-parliamentary cooperation).[9] In the new century, new impetus has been given to the theme. Following the European Council Laeken Declaration, the European Convention that presented a proposal for a European Constitution, had included both a working group on national parliaments and one on subsidiarity which presented their findings. The option suggested already by the European Council to empower national parliaments to scrutinize EU legislative proposals on compliance with the principle of subsidiarity, eventually made it into the Treaty of Lisbon.[10]

The 'coming of age' of national parliaments as constitutional actors in the European Union has not escaped criticism, however.[11] One of the fundamental points of critique has been that the EU constitutional architecture lacks a clear choice for a particular democratic model, which leads to diverging expectations on what the role of national parliaments should entail.[12] Also, the new mechanism for subsidiarity scrutiny has been criticized. It has been questioned whether this mechanism may actually contribute to EU legitimacy and whether it actually enables national parliaments to influence EU decision making (especially in light of the necessary cooperation between national parliaments.[13] Another issue has been whether national parliaments would actually limit themselves to the application of the subsidiarity principle. It might perhaps be expected that national parliaments would extend scrutiny of EU legislative proposals to issues such as the legal basis and proportionality of the measure at hand and even political expediency in general.

However, on the basis of the actual functioning of the Early Warning Mechanism (as introduced by the Subsidiarity Protocol), substantial parts of this critique must be rebutted. Subsidiarity scrutiny may effectively lead to 'yellow cards' being raised, as a result of which the European Commission must reconsider its proposal. National parliaments' rejection of the so-called 'Monti-II' Regulation[14] was the first example, to be followed in the Fall of 2013 with the rejection of the Regulation of the Council on the establishment of the European

[8]Niblock 1971.

[9]See *inter alia* Cygan 2001; Smith 1996; Norton 1996 and Laursen and Pappas 1995.

[10]Protocol no. 2.

[11]See e.g. Kiiver 2006 and Cygan 2001, pp. 478–497.

[12]Nettesheim 2005, p. 358.

[13]Cygan 2012a, pp. 55–73, b, pp. 517–533.

[14]Proposal of 21 March 2012 of the Commission for a Council Regulation on the exercise of the right to take collective action within the context of the freedom of establishment and the freedom to provide services, COM(2012) 130 fin.

Public Prosecutor's Office (EPPO).[15] Undeniably, it has proved unrealistic to expect national parliaments to focus on the subsidiarity aspects of proposed legislation. Still, the analysis of subsidiarity aspects constitutes the central element of national parliaments' scrutiny procedures.[16]

4 National Parliaments in EU Economic Governance: Why?

The aggregate of measures to address the economic crisis constitutes a legal patchwork. Some measures have been adopted in the form of a treaty (the Treaty on Stability, Coordination and Governance—TSCG and the Treaty establishing the European Stability Mechanism—ESM). Other measures take the form of EU secondary law such as the so-called legislative 'six-pack' (2011) and 'two-pack' (2013). Also, soft law instruments such as the 'Euro-plus pact' have been adopted. Furthermore, the Treaty on the Functioning of the EU (TFEU) has been amended by the decision of the European Council to amend Article 136 TFEU to allow the setting up of the stability mechanism. This was one of the first occasions when the simplified treaty revision procedure was applied.[17] The effectiveness and the legality of these measures have been heavily analyzed and debated, by scholars, courts, and politicians alike.[18] The need to ensure democratic accountability of EU economic governance has been voiced quite widely as well, but this has—as yet—not resulted in concrete plans of how to shape this.

Arguably, democratic accountability depends on the nature and type of decision making. The legal acts mentioned above have all been adopted and entered into force, which has resulted in a renewed EU economic governance model. The cornerstone of that model is the system of coordination of public finance policies of the Member States and coordination of their macroeconomic policies. Since the entry into force of the legislative six-pack, for both parts of these economic policies financial sanctions may be imposed on Member States that fail to fulfill the requirements, albeit many procedural steps must be taken before such sanctions may actually be imposed. The involvement of EU institutions in national economic policies is twofold.[19] The regular system involves a procedure that is called

---

[15]COM (2013) 534 fin.

[16]van den Brink 2011, pp. 160–180.

[17]Article 48(6) TEU.

[18]To mention just a selection of contributions: the Pringle case in which the ECJ reviewed the legality of use of the simplified treaty revision procedure: C-370/12. Craig has analyzed the legality of the Fiscal Compact in: Craig 2012, p. 231.

[19]In fact, a third type of involvement may be identified for countries that have received financial assistance on the basis of the European Stability Mechanism (ESM). This is actually the most far reaching form of EU involvement. The ESM will, however, be excluded from the scope of this contribution.

the European Semester, which is a yearly cycle of economic policy coordination and which essentially boils down to a policy dialogue between European and national institutions. This regular system is supplemented with special procedures which apply in case of problems: the Excessive Deficit Procedure (EDP) and the Excessive (macroeconomic) Imbalances Procedure (EIP).

The role of the European Parliament in the system of economic governance is still weak. An 'Economic Dialogue' has been set up, but this involves no real powers for the European Parliament. The position of the European Parliament is equally weak in ESM decision making. Thus, a strong argument for greater national parliaments' involvement emerges, especially for those that see a primary role for national parliaments in areas in which the EPs' lack of powers needs to be compensated for.

Another argument would be that the European Semester directly affects national parliamentary budget rights.[20] These rights, often enforced only after fierce struggles, have enabled parliaments to influence national economic policies but also to claim influence far beyond the economic domain.[21]

Thirdly, economic policy coordination in the EU becomes increasingly political in nature. This may come as a surprise in light of efforts to 'de-politicize' some of the substantive norms of the SGP, e.g., by obliging the Member States to implement them in provisions of national law, 'preferably of a constitutional nature' (Article 3(2) TSCG). The reality of EU economic policy coordination reveals a far more political picture, however. The coordination of macroeconomic policies is political in nature and has—now that a macroeconomic imbalances procedure has been included—been strengthened significantly. But also the coordination of national public finance policies has become more political in nature. Notably the Commission disposes of more policy discretion than before. The reason is the Commission's application of the exception it may grant to comply with the budgetary objectives.[22] In the current crisis in which many Member States have difficulties in meeting these objectives, the exemptions and the conditions the

[20]More in detail on this issue for the Dutch context: Report W01.12.0457/I of the Dutch Council of State of 18 January 2013 on the embedding of democratic control in the reform of economic governance in Europe to combat the economic and financial crisis; also Emmerik and Diamant 2013, pp. 94–129.

[21]The Dutch Council of State made a distinction between formal and substantive budget rights with the latter concept referring to this further-reaching influence, *infra* nt. 20, p. 4.

[22]Article 5 Regulation 1466/97/EC as amended by Regulation 1175/2011/EU on the strengthening of the surveillance of budgetary positions and the surveillance and coordination of economic policies. This provision reads as follows: "In the case of an unusual event outside the control of the Member State concerned which has a major impact on the financial position of the general government or in periods of severe economic downturn for the euro area or the Union as a whole, Member States may be allowed temporarily to depart from the adjustment path towards the medium-term budgetary objective referred to in the third subparagraph, provided that this does not endanger fiscal sustainability in the medium term."

Commission attaches to these exemptions greatly enhance the political nature of the decision making, thereby calling for democratic control.

Lastly, a stronger involvement of national parliaments is warranted in light of the 'country-specific' nature of a large part of the decision-making process. The European Semester encompasses several general elements (i.e., elements that apply to all Member States). Substantial parts, however, deal with the evaluation of national economic policies. As such, they involve a policy dialogue between the Commission, the Council (and the European Council) on the one hand and national institutions, most notably national governments, on the other. Thus, it would be more of a rational choice to involve national parliaments in these country-specific parts of the European semester than it would to turn to the European Parliament to ensure democratic control.

5 National Parliaments in EU Economic Governance: How?

The role of national parliaments has a procedural and a substantive dimension. However, the procedural dimension often dominates in this discussion. Apparently, the idea is that by creating effective procedures democratic legitimacy by national parliaments will be ensured. Yet, the substantive dimension is relevant as well. A lot of the discussion on the introduction of the Early Warning System on subsidiarity scrutiny indeed focused on procedural aspects of subsidiarity. The substantive role of national parliaments in this new mechanism has thus largely been neglected, although the substantive dimension was indicated by the subsidiarity principle. The risk of focusing too much on procedural aspects is what the Dutch Council of State has called 'democratic alienation'.[23] Despite stronger parliamentary powers, the distance between citizens and parliaments still increases, and the former feel neither represented by politicians nor responsible for the measures they adopt.

But is the mechanism set up by the Treaty of Lisbon suitable for application to EU economic governance? Although subsidiarity is a general principle, applicable to all institutions and to all their actions,[24] it is undeniably geared to *legislative* measures of the European Union. The Early Warning Mechanism is limited to scrutiny of draft legislative acts. This may well be explained by the fact that at the European level the adoption of legislation outweighs executive measures by far (as the latter are to a great extent reserved for national and subnational authorities). Arguably, with the Early Warning Mechanism, national parliaments have claimed a co-legislative role at the European level. In EU economic governance, however,

[23] P. 6 of its report.

[24] Article 1 of Protocol no. 2 attached to the Treaty of Lisbon on the application of the Principles of Subsidiarity and Proportionality.

measures are mostly executive in nature. Thus, rather than legislative powers and procedures, mechanisms of democratic control and accountability are called for.

Also, unlike most other areas of EU activity, EU economic governance challenges national parliaments' positions as representatives of tax payers. Decisions to grant financial aid to economically troubled Member States directly affect tax payers' interests and the same is true for the European semester—especially since it now involves prior involvement in national budget setting procedures.

The subsidiarity Early Warning System would, thus, not be an appropriate instrument. However, the so-called 'Barroso-initiative' does provide for useful inspiration here.[25] This initiative involved sending all Commission proposals to national parliaments and an invitation to them to react to these proposals. As such, it was meant as a mechanism that should precede the activation of possible Early Warning Mechanisms. Thus, a direct institutional link was created between national parliaments and the European Commission.

Such a direct link between national parliaments and the European Commission should also be activated within the system of EU economic governance. Especially the increasing political role of the Commission (as was argued above) is an important reason for such a direct link. National parliaments have been experimented somewhat with establishing such a link (e.g., by inviting 'EMU-commissioner' Rehn to attend parliamentary sessions). Such experiments should result in a stable institutional arrangement. As such, this proposal differs from the model European Council President Van Rompuy has put forward. In his October interim report on the Future of the Economic and Monetary Union[26] he formulated the principle that democratic control should be exercised at the level at which decisions are taken. Fundamentally, the 'Van Rompuy' principle presupposes that levels of government in the European Union are still clearly separable, but this is less and less so. A direct institutional link between national parliaments and the European Commission would be an acknowledgement of the increased intertwining and interconnectedness of levels of governance.

But also the relations between national governments and national parliaments need to be adjusted to the changed realities. Despite EU involvement, national governments are still key players in defining national economic policies. National parliaments need new powers and mechanisms of control over their national parliaments. Again, the German Constitutional Court may serve as an example. It has *inter alia* prescribed that the national parliament should have a—prior—say on issues such as decisions on the national contribution to the authorized capital stock of the ESM. Essentially, however, this is an internal situation and much depends on the actual position of national parliaments within their respective national constitutional systems.

[25]See Jancic 2012.

[26]'Towards a Genuine Economic and Monetary Union' of 12 October 2012, available at: http://www.consilium.europa.eu/uedocs/cms_data/docs/pressdata/en/ec/132809.pdf (last accessed: 21 February 2013).

The above observations may seem to focus—again—on the procedural aspects rather than on substance. But the essential issue is in my view what substantive roles national parliaments need to pursue and which roles they themselves wish to pursue. If such roles include the exercise of fiscal sovereignty, they should not remain passive and deplore the alleged loss thereof, but seek new ways to pursue it. As has been shown, there are certainly ways available to do so.

References

Borger V (2013) How the Debt Crisis Exposes the Development of Solidarity in the Euro Area. Eur Const Law Rev 9(1):7–36

Corbett R, Jacobs F, Shackleton M (2007) The European Parliament, 7th edn. Harper, London

Craig PP (2012) The Stability, Coordination and Governance Treaty: Principle, Politics and Pragmatism. Eur Law Rev 37:231–248

Cygan A (2001) National Parliaments in an Integrated Europe: an Anglo-German perspective. Kluwer International, The Hague

Cygan A (2011) The Parliamentarisation of EU Decision-Making? The Impact of the Treaty of Lisbon on National Parliaments. Eur Law Rev 36:478–497

Cygan A (2012a) Collective Subsidiarity Monitoring by National Parliaments after Lisbon—The Operation of the Early Warning Mechanism. In: Trybus M, Rubini L (eds) After Lisbon: The Future of European Law and Policy. Edward Elgar, Cheltenham, pp 55–73

Cygan A (2012b) National Parliaments within the EU Polity—no Longer Losers but Hardly Victorious. ERA Forum 12(4):517–533

Emmerik ML, Diamant M (2013) Het Nederlandse budgetrecht in Europees perspectief. Tijdschrift voor Constitutioneel Recht 4(2):115

Jancic D (2012) The Barroso Initiative: Window Dressing or Democracy Boost? Utrecht Law Rev 8(1):78

Kiiver Ph (2006) National Parliaments in the European Union. Kluwer, Deventer

Laursen F, Pappas SA (eds) (1995) The changing Role of Parliaments in Europe, EIPA

Nettesheim M (2005) Developing a Theory of Democracy for the European Union. Berkeley J Int Law 23:358

Niblock M (1971) The EEC: National Parliaments in Community Decision-making. Chatham House, London

Norton Ph (ed) (1996) National Parliaments and the European Union. Frank Gass, London

Pernice I (2002) Multilevel Constitutionalism in the European Union. Eur Law Rev 2002:511

Piris JC (2010) The Treaty of Lisbon. A legal and political analysis. Cambridge University Press, Cambridge

Smith E (ed) (1996) National parliaments as cornerstones of European integration. Kluwer Law International, The Hague

van den Brink A (2011) Substantiating Subsidiarity. The Interpretation and Meaning of the Principle after Lisbon. In: Trybus M, Rubini L (eds) The Future of European law after Lisbon. Edward Elger Publishers, Birmingham, pp 160–178

Walker N (2002) The Idea of Constitutional Pluralism. Modern Law Rev 65(3):317–359

Weiler JHH (1995) Does Europe need a Constitution? Demos, Telos and the German Maastricht Decision. Eur Law J 1(3):219–258

The Growing Role of the Union in Protection of Rule of Law

Helena Raulus

Abstract The central focus of this contribution is the discussion of the limited options available under Article 7 TEU mechanism. Especially the developments in Hungary have alerted the Union institutions and the Member States that the Union's role in the protection of rule of law needs to be strengthened, and there are proposals on how to get this done. These proposals are assessed and analyzed.

Contents

1 Introduction—Union or the Member States as Protector of Rule of Law and Democracy

The European Union has gained step-by-step very wide competences and its operation encompasses from the core Single Market to Area of Freedom, Justice, and even cooperation in the Common Foreign and Security Policy. Yet, there is an area that is less well developed, which could be described as having been fenced off

H. Raulus (✉)
European Union Law, Erasmus School of Law, Rotterdam, The Netherlands
e-mail: raulus@law.eur.nl

F.A.N.J. Goudappel and E.M.H. Hirsch Ballin (eds.), *Democracy and Rule of Law in the European Union*, DOI 10.1007/978-94-6265-066-4_3

from the scope of the Union policies and action: this is the Union's role in protecting rule of law and democracy in the Member States.

According to Article 2 TEU, EU is based on the values of protection of rule of law and democracy; however, it has traditionally had very limited ways of dealing with the protection of the rule of law,[1] and very limited means to supervise the Member States if they breach it. Often it has been described following Williams as an irony,[2] how in order to become a Union Member State, an applicant State is rigorously monitored and advised on protection of rule of law,[3] or how human rights and democracy are often relevant for the Union external policies,[4] whereas the Union is in effect not capable of doing much with regard to its own Member States.

The EU has its own fundamental rights system and institutional framework. The Treaty of Lisbon made the EU Charter of Fundamental Rights binding on the Union.[5] Traditionally the Union has not had adequate mechanisms for monitoring rule of law, and it has rather relied on the Council of Europe (CoE). This has recently been remedied to some extent by the setting of the Copenhagen criteria when the Commission is assessing the acceding Member States, and the establishment of the Union Fundamental Rights Agency (FRA).[6] However, the Charter binds and the FRA can monitor only matters falling within the scope of the Union action, including the Member States only when they act in the scope of Union law.

With regard to the rule of law protection and the Member States, where there is no connection with the Union policies, Article 7 TEU procedure is available. However, as will be argued, it is almost impossible to initiate. The Hungarian legal developments, the French Roma policies, or the Romanian rule of law problems[7] provide good examples of how the Union reaction may remain quite feeble, even when a Member State is severely criticized in and by the Union. Therefore, for all

---

[1]Fundamentally, there is no common European understanding for rule of law, see Council conclusions on fundamental rights and rule of law and on the Commission 2012 report on the Application of the Charter of Fundamental Rights, 29 May 2013, 10 168/13, point 9. In this paper the substantive approach is adopted, whereby "the rule of law is inseparable from democracy, respect for fundamental rights and equal treatment", and the content of rule of law is equally important as the form. Therefore, matters relating to the protection of fundamental rights as well as democratic values fall within the scope of the paper.

[2]Williams 2004.

[3]European Parliament Resolution of 3 July 2013 on the situation of fundamental rights: standards and practices in Hungary, P7_TA(2013)0315, see point 73, the Parliament calls this as the "Copenhagen dilemma".

[4]See for instance Wetzel 2011, Introduction, pp. 12–13.

[5]Article 6 TEU.

[6]Reg. 168/2007 establishing a European Agency for Fundamental Rights, OJ 2007/L53/1-14 and FRA website, http://fra.europa.eu/en. Accessed 4 March 2015.

[7]Commissioner Reding, EU and Rule of Law—What Next? European Commission, 4 September 2013, SPEECH/13/677, and for Romania, Report from the Commission to the European Parliament and the Council on the progress in Romania under the Cooperation and Verification Mechanism, COM(2013)47final.

practical purposes, where there is no connection with the Union policies, the Union is unable to intervene, and the Member States' own constitutional systems for protecting rule of law and democracy apply, with the oversight from the CoE. These situations have also been noted now by the Union Institutions and some Member States, and they have begun to demand for new solutions for the Union to get involved in protecting of rule of law *vis-à-vis* its Member States.

This contribution examines further the problematic application of Article 7 TEU action and the new proposals to strengthen the Union action in these areas. Hungarian legal developments are used in the analysis of the difficulties posed for the Union action. However, while it seems obvious that the Union should have a role in this area, as there are expectations that the Union is able to intervene or act if the values under Article 2 TEU are breached by the Member States, the proposals still raise difficult questions about the nature of the Union action. If monitoring is developed, how to provide for adequate enforcement? How to protect the Union institutional framework and the Union's own rule of law? Is another Treaty amendment needed?

2 The Scope of Union Action in Protection of Rule of Law and Article 7 TEU

The TEU limits very clearly the EU competences in protection of rule of law with respect to the Member States. Even though the Charter of Fundamental Rights became binding at the entry into force of the Treaty of Lisbon, it has been made clear in the Charter itself how it is to be applied solely within the scope of Union law,[8] and it does not apply to situations where there is no connection with other Union policies.[9] Furthermore, Article 6 TEU does not allow any extension for the Union com-

[8]Article 51 Charter. This raises somewhat complicated questions, when are issues falling within the scope of Union law. The Member States are acting in the scope of Union law even if a Member States tries to use a derogation from Union law, Case C-260/89 ERT [1991] ECR I-2925, or if a Member State is given a discretion under Union law provision, see Joined Cases C-411/10 and C-493/10 NS, *ME and Others*, judgment of the Court 21 December 2011. Finally, in the Case C-617/10, *Åklagaren v. Åkerberg*, judgment of the Court 26 February 2013, the Court seemed to decide that in the matters falling within the scope of Union law, Union standards of protection are applied, and where the Member State has the competence, the national provisions are applied, see paras 21 and 22, even though the application seems to go wider whereby if there is a connection to the implementation of the Union policies seems to suffice, para 28, in particular.

[9]For instance, there have been several referrals from the national courts to the ECJ asking whether the Charter applies independently, and in each case the ECJ has decided that it does not have jurisdiction. See for instance Orders in the following cases: Case C-466/11, *Gennaro Currà* et al. *v. Bundesrepublic Deutschland* (from Italia), Joined Cases C-483-484/11, *Andrei Boncea* et al. *v. Statul român* (from Romania), Case C-128/12 *Sindicato dos Bancários do Norte* et al. *v. BPN* (from Portugal), Case C-312/12, *Agim Ajdini v. Belgian State* (from Belgium), and Case C-14/13, *Cholakova* (from Bulgaria).

petences under the Charter or the accession to the ECHR. Thus, the Charter, even though binding, does not create an independent legal basis for EU action.[10]

Article 7 TEU provides the only means for the EU to sanction Member States for breaches in protection of rule of law and democracy outside the scope of Union law. There are considerable hurdles for the Union to become involved.[11] First as to substantive application, action may only be based where there is a clear risk of a serious breach of rule of law, democracy, or protection of fundamental rights. Second, there are procedural hurdles, whereby action may be initiated only if four-fifths of the Member States agree there is such a clear risk of a serious breach. Finally, with regard to punishment, at the first instance, only warning is available, and if the Council considers that the situation deserves more serious reaction, then a State's membership rights may be suspended.

Article 7 TEU been dubbed as the "nuclear option,"[12] and with good reason. Article 7 TEU does not allow intervention in objective terms, but it lays down a process for intervening when and if a situation arises that can be described as politically unbearable for all other Member States. As the next example of the Hungarian legal developments shows, if there is no political agreement on the part of the Member States, the Union response to the situation remains very limited.

3 Hungary and the Union Response

While there are several examples on the problematic or complicated relationship between the protection of rule of law of the Member States and the Union, here only the Hungarian situation is more closely discussed. The Hungarian situation is perhaps the gravest, and the most deeply system changing in nature, with a wide spread of proposals and legislative acts having impact on freedom of the press, independence of the judiciary, electoral reform, rights of minorities, and freedom of religion.[13] The Hungarian Government's rule of law undermining proposals has been criticized both inside the Union[14] and outside the Union in the CoE.[15] The

[10] Editorial comments 2012, p. 878, describes it thus: "As is well known, EU fundamental rights do not produce their own conditions of applicability. They do not stand alone, but rely on trigger factors stemming from other EU law provisions."

[11] See in particular Williams 2006, pp. 12–13.

[12] See for instance Commissioner Reding, Safeguarding the rule of law and solving the "Copenhagen dilemma": Towards a new EU mechanism, European Commission press release, 22 April 2013, SPEECH/13/348.

[13] For an overview of the Hungarian situation, see European Parliament resolution of 3 July 2013.

[14] For the EP, ibid. For the Commission, see for instance statement by the Commissioner Reding for the European Parliament, Hungary and the Rule of Law, 17 April 2013, Commission Press Release, SPEECH13/324.

[15] Through for instance the Venice Commission or the Human Rights Commissioner. Very recently, the Parliamentary Assembly of the Council of Europe voted for not place Hungary under special monitoring, though, see Politics.hu, 25 June 2013. The Venice Commission and the Human Rights Commissioner still continue to oversee developments in Hungary.

bottom line is the question of how far can a Union Member State government, which has a considerable majority in the parliament, freely change the rules of governance, the power balance of institutions, or change the rules on the basis of which society is governed.

The limitations with regard to the Union power to intervene have been visible since the Fidesz Government took over in 2010 and started with the legislative agenda. In the first round with the Hungarian Government in 2010, the Commission was able to bring proceedings only against specific proposals affecting data protection authority, retirement age of judges, and the independence of the central bank.[16] With regard to the more controversial rule of law issues, such as press freedom, only the EP could act by adopting resolutions,[17] or the Commission by persuasion. Article 7 TEU proceedings were flagged by the European Parliament and the Commission; however, there has been no proposal to bring these proceedings because of reports from some Member States of how their parliaments support Hungary.[18]

Therefore, even in cases of clear, serious, and persistent problems with rule of law Article 7 TEU does not provide for a solution. Yet, the Union is clearly perceived as an actor here. Both the EP and the Commission have been vocal in their criticism, creating expectations for the Union intervention. Furthermore, it is not simply the Institutions' criticism of the situation, but also deeper considerations according to which the Union should be able to intervene in protection of rule of law that seem to underlie the expectations for the Union action. There seems to be substance to Article 2 TEU according to which the Union is based on respect of rule of law, which seems to have failed by the inability to take action.[19]

4 Way Forward with Article 7 TEU

There are several proposals on how to strengthen the Union's role in this area. The EP, when investigating the Hungary situation, has adopted resolutions expressing the need for change and detailing some possible ways forward with the future action.[20] Furthermore, the governments of Germany, the Netherlands, Finland, and Sweden have sent an open letter to the Commission President Barroso with their

---

[16]European Commission, Press release, 17 January 2012, IP/12/24.

[17]From earlier see for example European Parliament Resolution of 16 February 2012 on the recent political developments in Hungary, P7_TA(2012)0053.

[18]Reported by Politics.hu, Government asks Parliament to officially thank Poland, Lithuania for support during "attacks against Hungary", 14 February 2012. Similar point has been made with reference to the French treatment of Roma, Dawson and Muir 2011, at p. 757.

[19]Von Bogdandy et al. 2012, at pp. 500–501.

[20]See in particular European Parliament Resolution of 16 February 2012, and European Parliament Resolution of 3 July 2013.

ideas and proposals.[21] Finally, Commissioner Reding has replied to the EP and Member States and at the same time made known the Commission's position and solutions.[22]

None of the proposals go so far as to give the Union a role in individual breaches and all concentrate on allowing the Union to intervene where there are serious infringements by the Member States. Therefore, the substantive scope of Article 7 TEU may remain, and there will be no change in the nature of the Union action in that respect. With this respect, the proposals have identified the importance of developing two aspects of the Union policies in this context: monitoring and enforcement.

4.1 Monitoring

The issue of monitoring is picked up by the EP and the Commission. The Union has traditionally simply not lacked power in the protection of rule of law, but also it has not had mechanisms for monitoring of the rule of law in the Member States. There have been some developments in strengthening the monitoring the rule of law issues.

The Commission has recently launched the Justice Scoreboard[23] for the purposes of providing data on the Member States justice systems, in particular the "quality, independence and efficiency" of the justice systems. This ambitious project provides data with respect to the functioning of the justice systems, and through that will be both informative as well as provide new means to the Union monitoring rule of law in areas which are connected with the Union policies and their enforcement.

Furthermore, for an expert assessment and review of fundamental rights, the FRA was established in 2007. The FRA has started to monitor and review the Member State actions and policies in particular in relation to nondiscrimination,[24] access to justice, asylum, migration and border management issues, and data protection and privacy; in other words areas where there are EU policies. The

[21]Letter to the Commission President Barroso, from the Governments of Finland, Germany, The Netherlands and Sweden, 6 March 2013.

[22]Commissioner Reding, EU and the Rule of Law—What Next?, http://europa.eu/rapid/press-release_SPEECH-13-677_nl.htm. Accessed 20 December 2014.

[23]The EU Justice Scoreboard, A tool to promote effective justice and growth, Communication from the Commission to the European Parliament, the Council, the Economic and Social Committee and the Social Committee, COM(2013)160final.

[24]Out of the ten themes that the FRA is specifically involved with, five relate directly to discrimination: Gender, LGTB, people with disabilities, racisms and related intolerances and Roma, see http://fra.europa.eu/en/themes. Accessed 30 September 2013.

jurisdiction of the FRA is, indeed, currently limited with regard to the Member States, and it can review Member States' policies only if there is a connection with Union law.[25]

Although the FRA's jurisdiction is the same as the Union's scope on fundamental rights, the FRA has taken a more proactive approach. For instance, in relation to nondiscrimination, even though most of the Union directives apply only in the context of access to employment or access to employment,[26] the FRA has reviewed not only discrimination at work, but also more generally, outside the scope of the Union directives and, for instance, has completed research of the LGBT discrimination also in the economic as well as social context.[27] These reports have been influential especially in the EP debates on the discrimination in the Member States, and the EP has been able to put pressure using them on the Member States, which have less liberal views on equality.[28]

Yet, the FRA does not have the power to review generally protection of rule of law by the Member States. The EP has proposed that the FRA should be given authority to do this, even where there is no connection with the Union policies,[29] and Commissioner Reding has echoed this.[30] This is a supportable notion, since it is the only body that has the knowledge and expertise in monitoring of fundamental rights and rule of law protection. The Commission does not have the adequate resources[31] for this task. Furthermore, for more all-encompassing assessment, in areas which are politically very sensitive and where there is no link to be made to the Union policies, it would be ideal to have FRA rather than the Commission involved. Even though the Commission is independent from the Member States, it is a player both in the enforcement and the Union legislative processes. Therefore, its other functions may be impeded if it alone were to make concrete assessments of the rule of law protection by the Member States.

[25]FRA Reg. 168/2007, Article 3.

[26]See for instance Directive 2000/78/EC establishing a general framework for equal treatment in employment and occupation which applies to discrimination on grounds of religion or belief, disability, age or sexual orientation, OJ 2000/L303/16-22; or Directive 2006/54/EC on the implementation of equal opportunities of men and women in matters of employment or occupation, OJ 2006/L204/23-35.

[27]See http://fra.europa.eu/en/theme/lgbt. Accessed 30 September 2013.

[28]See for instance, European Parliament, Press release, MEPs urge Lithuanians to reject anti-gay law, 19 January 2011.

[29]European Parliament Resolution of 12 December 2012, points 44–47. In addition, the EP has proposed for establishment of a "Copenhagen Commission" or "commission of wise men" to monitor the protection of the rule of law, European Parliament Res. 3 July 2013, point 79.

[30]Commissioner Reding, above n. 7.

[31]Ibid., the Commissioner Reding quite directly stated that the Commission DG Justice is not yet anything similar to the US Department of Justice, "The Commission has a young and small DG Justice, just 4 years old and with barely 250 officials, most of them kept very busy with implementing the legislative agenda laid down in the Stockholm Programme…".

4.2 New Process Including Enforcement Powers for the Union in Protection of Rule of Law

While the EP proposals do not contain any concrete suggestions as to the enforcement, in this respect the proposal from the governments of Germany, the Netherlands, Finland, and Sweden goes further. They proposed that the Commission should have a stronger role as a guardian of the Treaties, having monitoring powers, powers to ask for a structural dialogue with the Member State, bring the issue at the Council, or conclude bilateral agreements between it and the Member State. This is not yet very effective. If the Member State is of the opinion that its actions do not breach rule of law or democratic principles, it would be unlikely to comply with such mechanisms and agree to amend its ways. However, as an ultimate measure, the governments are proposing that the Commission should be allowed to suspend Union funding. The Council has taken a note of this proposal[32] and has instructed the Commission to proceed with public debate on how to improve the situation.[33]

The power to suspend distribution of the Union funds is an interesting proposal; this way the enforcement by the Union would be given a wholly different approach, as well as a potentially effective tool, to strengthen the protection of the rule of law in the framework of the Union funding policies. A Member State could stand to lose a considerable amount of money in the end.[34] Furthermore, it comes at a time when there are examples of decisions to suspend Union funds within the framework of the Union Cohesion Funds. The Commission has reportedly taken decisions to refuse the distribution of cohesion funds for the Czech Republic, because the State had not taken adequate action against the rampant corruption in the State and at local levels.[35] Furthermore, the Union shortly froze Hungarian funds, first because of the budget deficit,[36] then it also threatened further suspen-

[32]General Affairs Council, Press Release of the 3235th Council meeting, 8577/13, PRESSE 153 PR CO 21, 22 April 2013, p. 8.

[33]Council conclusions on fundamental rights and rule of law and on the Commission 2012 Report on the Application of the Charter of Fundamental Rights of the European Union, point 9 in particular.

[34]See for example Commission Press Release, Commission proposes to suspend 495 million Euro of Cohesion Fund for Hungary for 2013 for failure to address excessive deficit, IP/12/161, 22 February 2012.

[35]Centre for Eastern Studies, Czech problems with European funds. http://www.osw.waw.pl/en/publikacje/ceweekly/2012-03-21/czech-problems-european-funds. Accessed 20 September 2013.

[36]Council Implementing Decision 2012/156/EU of 13 March 2012, later the Hungarian funds were released by the Council after Hungary had satisfied the Council that it was still tackling the deficit, Council Press Release, Hungary: Council lifts Cohesion Funds suspension, 22 June 2012, PRESSE 278, 11 648/12. Reportedly, the Hungary has been threatened again with another suspension, EU policy website of the Hungarian Government, Enikő Győri: discussions on the suspension of EU funding to resume again in September, 27 August 2013. eu.kormany.hu. Accessed 4 March 2015.

sions allegedly because of graft allegations[37] and other irregularities in Hungarian accounts.[38]

However, the proposal also raises some questions as to the procedure. Should it be the Council or the Commission that initiates and adopts the decisions? The present funding framework adopts both options, only depending on the topic. Under Regulation 1084/2006 on Cohesion Funds, the Council may adopt the decision to suspend funding if a Member State breaches the government deficit rules,[39] and under the general Regulation 1083/2006 on the Union funds, the Commission may suspend any funds in case there are problems with the management of the money.[40] The more likely choice in this field would be the Council, because it is not foreseeable that the Member States will surrender their decision-making powers with regard to the rule of law.

Yet, the threshold for initiating proceedings must then be made lower than in the present Article 7 TEU, otherwise there is still no improvement. Furthermore, seeing how difficult the application of Article 7 TEU currently is, and how divisive the topic is, it could be the Commission taking the initial decision. However, as this is a radical departure from the normal infringement proceeding, if the Commission were to be given this power, it needs to be asked whether it should be subjected to the opinion from the Court of Justice, or simply allowed that the Member State will ask the Court to review the Commission's decision, as is the case for instance with the state aid decisions. The involvement of the Court of Justice is the crucial final link in giving legitimacy for the new process. The Commission, while independent from the Member States, is not fully impartial like the Court. In this case the bottom line is that if the Court of Justice were not involved in the process, it might be damaging from the perspective of the Union's own rule of law.

The Commission has not at least initially endorsed the notion of the right to suspend funding. Commissioner Reding proposed rather the review of Article 7 TEU mechanism so that the Commission could have a more proactive role in bringing proceedings against a Member State, and lowering the thresholds in triggering the first part of the procedure.[41] Furthermore, she has envisaged that the Court of Justice should have a role also in decisions on substance, i.e., whether there has been breach. This is keeping within the framework of the Treaty, and bringing in the Court of Justice is recommendable for the legitimacy of the procedure; however, these kinds of changes would require another Treaty amendment, and therefore are not presently available.

---

[37]Reuters, Hungary grappling with suspension of vital EU funds, 12 August 2013 by Krisztina Than and Gergely Szakacs. reuters.com. Accessed 4 March 2015.

[38]Financial Times, 14 August 2013, Brussels suspends funding to Hungary over alleged irregularities, by Kester Eddy and James Fontanella-Khan. There is possibility for the Council to suspend the cohesion funds in the event of an excessive deficit by a Member State, Reg. (EC) No. 1084/2006 establishing a Cohesion Fund, OJ 2006/L210/79-81, Article 4.

[39]Article 4 of the Reg. 1084/2006.

[40]Article 92 of the Reg. 1083/2006.

[41]Commissioner Reding, see above n. 7.

However, there would be need for a Treaty amendment also where enforcement would be based on suspending the Union funding. As is well known, the Union has limited powers with regard to Romania and Bulgaria to suspend Union funds under the Cooperation and Verification Mechanism,[42] with respect to strengthening the role of judiciary or fight against corruption and organized crime. Importantly, this power is specifically based on the arrangements made at the accession of Bulgaria and Romania to the Union, on the Accession Treaty[43] and the Act of Accession.[44]

Finally, there might be even more fundamental limitation for setting enforcement mechanisms for the rule of law protection. Considering the limitations set out under Article 6 TEU, which prohibits the extension of the Union competences in the fundamental rights, and how Article 7 TEU has been specified under Treaties as the only mechanism available for enforcement of the rule of law, this signals that enforcement mechanism needs to be adopted through a Treaty amendment.

5 Conclusions

The limitations of the Union competences in the protection of rule of law in its Member States continue to create severe restrictions for the Union action. Despite the recent problematic cases, such as the Hungarian example explored here, the Union has been unable to act in any other ways than using diplomatic pressure on the rule of law breaches. This has its foundations in the Article 7 TEU procedure, which is simply not functional with its requirement of support from four-fifths of the Member States. The Hungarian situation shows this as well, how the procedure has not been even initiated, because it is known that it would be a failure.

It is now noted how the situation needs remedying. The Union is involved in creating further mechanisms for monitoring the protection of rule of law, and the Commission has been asked by the Council and the EP to come forward with new proposals. In addition, the EP and few Member States have already started to table ideas on how to proceed. Strengthening and developing two areas are particularly of importance: the monitoring and enforcement capabilities of the Union in protection of rule of law.

With regard to monitoring, especially using the FRA would be beneficial. This would be a step forward for creating common and independent standards for the Union action. Using the Commission in this respect would be less effective. The

[42]Commission Decision of 13/XXII/2006 establishing a mechanism for cooperation and verification of progress in Bulgaria to address specific benchmarks in the areas of judicial reform and the fight against corruption and organized crime, COM (2006)6570final, and with respect to Romania, Commission Decision of 13/XXII/2006, COM(2006)6596final.

[43]Article 4(3) of the Treaty concerning the accession of Bulgaria and Romania into the Union.

[44]Articles 37 and 38 of the Act of Accession of Bulgaria and Romania.

Commission does have the resources on top of the legislative and other enforcement work. Furthermore, it might have a negative impact on these other roles, when negotiating with the Member States if it were required to also assess and monitor the rule of law issues. Using, therefore, FRA in this context would be ideal.

With regard to enforcement, the proposal from the Member States to allow the Union to suspend distribution of funds is certainly interesting. However, it is still questionable how and to whom to give the power to decide on the freezing of distribution of funds. Furthermore, as this is a considerable departure from the present infringement mechanism, it needs to be critically thought whether there is a sufficient protection of the impartiality and the Union's own rule of law. If there is a view that this mechanism would be used more for some States, whereas not for others, this is not supportable. And, the only way to ensure the impartiality would be the involvement of the Court of Justice, preferably earlier than later in the proceedings. It could be so that the decision by the Council or the Commission is subjected to the opinion of the Court of Justice.

Ultimately, the inherent limitations set out in Articles 6 and 7 TEU for the Union action to intervene for protection of rule of law vis-à-vis its Member States continue to restrict the Union attempts to create enforcement procedure. In the end, therefore, if the Union is to have enforcement powers with regard to the Member States' breaches of rule of law, there is need for Treaty amendment. Not only needed, but the Treaty amendment would also be a show of wide political support of how the Union should have a role in protecting the rule of law. In that regard the need for a Treaty amendment in creating methods of enforcement should be considered as desirable and this part of the process is not to be by-passed.

Case law, legislations, and documents

Case law

Case C-260/89 *ERT* [1991] ECR I-2925

Case C-105/03 *Pupino* [2005] ECR I-5285

Joined Cases C-411/10 and C-493/10, *NS, ME and Others*, judgment of the Court 21 December 2011

Case C-617/10, *Åklagaren v. Åkerberg*, judgment of the Court 26 February 2013

Orders from the Court of Justice, where there was no jurisdiction

Case C-466/11, *Gennaro Curra et al. v. Bundesrepublik Deutschland*, Order of the Court 12 July 2012

Joined Cases C-483/11 and C-484/11, *Andrei Emilian Boncea, Filofteia Catrinel Boncea et al. v. Statul roman*, Order of the Court 14 December 2011

Case C-128/12, *Sindicato dos Bancários do Norte, Sindicato dos Bancários do Centro, Sindicato does Bancários do Sul e Ilhas, Luis Miguel Rodrigues Teixeira de Melo v. BPN*, Order of the Court 7 March 2013

Case C-312/12, *Agim Adjani v. Belgian State*, Order of the Court 21 February 2013

Case C-369/12, *Corpul National al Poltistilor v. Ministerul Administratiei si Internelor*, Order of the Court 15 November 2012
Case C-14/13, *Gena Ivanova Cholakova v. Osmo Rayonno Upravlienie pri Stolichna direktsia na vatreshnite raboti*, Order of the Court 6 June 2013
Case C-73/13, *T*, Order of the Court 8 May 2013
Case C-106/13, *Francesco Fierro and Fabiana Marmorale v. Edoardo Ronchi and Cosimo Scocozza*, Order of the Court 30 May 2013

Legislation
Directive 2000/78/EC establishing a general framework for equal treatment in employment and occupation, which applies to discrimination on grounds of religion or belief, disability, age or sexual orientation OJ 2000/L303/16-22
Directive 2006/54/EC on the implementation of equal opportunities of men and women in matters of employment and occupation, OJ 2006/L204/23-35
Regulation 168/2007 establishing a European Agency for Fundamental Rights OJ 2007/L53/1-14

Press Releases and Other Information from the Institutions

European Parliament
European Parliament, Press release, MEPs urge Lithuanians to reject anti-gay law, 19 January 2011
European Parliament Resolution of 16 February 2012 on the recent political developments in Hungary, P7_TA(2012)0053
European Parliament resolution of 12 December 2012 on the situation of fundamental rights in the European Union (2010-2011), P7_TA(2012)0500
European Parliament Resolution of 13 December 2012 on the review of the EU's human rights strategy, P7_TA(2012)0504
European Parliament, Intergroup on LGBT rights, Press release, Press conference: EU anti-discrimination law still stalled after five years, MEPs regret, 2 July 2013
European Parliament Resolution of 3 July 2013 on the situation of fundamental rights: standards and practices in Hungary (pursuant to the European Parliament Resolution of 16 February 2012), P7_TA(2013)0315

Council of ministers
Council of Ministers, General affairs, Press release, 22 April 2013, 8577/13
Council of the European Union, Council conclusions on fundamental rights and rule of law and on the Commission 2012 Report on the Application of the Charter of Fundamental Rights in the European Union, 29 May 2013, 10 168/13
Council of the European Union, General affairs, Press release, 25 June 2013, 11 443/13

Member States
Letter to the Commission President Barroso, from the Governments of Finland, Germany, the Netherlands, and Sweden, 6 March 2013

Commission

European Commission press release, European Commission launches accelerated infringement proceedings against Hungary over the independence of its central bank and data protection authorities as well as over measures affecting the judiciary, 17 January 2012, IP/12/24

Report from the Commission to the European Parliament and the Council on the progress in Romania under the Cooperation and Verification Mechanism, COM(2013)47final

The EU Justice Scoreboard, A tool to promote effective justice and growth, Communication from the Commission to the European Parliament, the Council, the Economic and Social Committee and the Social Committee, COM(2013)160final

Commissioner Reding, Safeguarding the rule of law and solving the "Copenhagen dilemma": Towards a new EU-mechanism, European Commission press release, 22 April 2013, SPEECH/13/348

Commission President Barroso, Reply to the Governments of Finland, Germany, the Netherlands and Sweden, 13 May 2013, BARROSO (2013) 308 871

Commissioner Reding, EU and the Rule of Law—What Next?, European Commission press release, 4 September 2013, SPEECH/13/677

References

Dawson M, Muir E (2011) Individual, institutional and collective vigilance in protecting fundamental rights in the EU: lessons from the Roma. Common Market Law Rev 48:751–775

Editorial comments (2012) Hungary's new constitutional order and 'European unity'. Common Market Law Rev 49:871–884

Von Bogdandy A, Kottman M, Antpöhler C, Dickschen J, Hentrei S, Smrkolj M (2012) Reverse Solange—protecting the essence of fundamental rights against member states. Common Market Law Rev 49:489–520

Wetzel JE (ed) (2011) The EU as a 'global player' in human rights? Routledge Research in Human Rights Law. Routledge, London

Williams A (2004) EU human rights policies: a study in irony. Oxford University Press Studies in European Law. Oxford University Press, Oxford

Williams A (2006) The indifferent gesture: Article 7 TEU, the Fundamental Rights Agency and the UK's invasion of Iraq. Eur Law Rev 31(1):3–27

The Rise and Rise of EU Citizenship

Fiona Murray

Abstract Any individual holding the nationality of an EU Member State is ascribed EU Citizenship. This was first determined in the 1992 Maastricht Treaty and further elaborated upon in the Lisbon Treaty and the EU Charter of Fundamental Rights. Since the adoption of the Lisbon Treaty, many developments in EU citizenship have taken place that enforce and clarify a citizen's rights. The 2010 First EU Citizen Report, published by the European Commission, identified a number of obstacles that EU citizens face with regard to their rights in everyday life. A set of concrete actions to deal with these obstacles are mentioned by the author. In May 2013 there was a second report to view the progress. The Commission then announced six areas to strengthen citizens' rights. At the same time, a report on the EU Charter of Fundamental Rights was published with a detailed overview of the implementation of these rights in the EU in 2012. Fundamental rights will further be enhanced with the EU's accession to the European Convention of Human Rights. The 2013 EU Citizen Report was intended to be used in the European Year of Citizens 2013, which consisted of a range of activities and events. This year was aimed to give EU citizens more insight into their rights and responsibilities and to prepare them for the 2014 elections. The author concludes by mentioning the broadening and deepening of EU citizenship over the past 20 years. This growth can be viewed both quantitatively in the amount of citizen's rights and qualitatively in the range of these rights.

CEU at Passerelle Public Affairs in Brussels and previously Director for Schumann Associates and Associate at White & Case.

F. Murray (✉)
Passerelle Public Affairs, Brussels, Belgium
e-mail: fiona@passerelle-pa.com

F.A.N.J. Goudappel and E.M.H. Hirsch Ballin (eds.), *Democracy and Rule of Law in the European Union*, DOI 10.1007/978-94-6265-066-4_4

Contents

1 Introduction

2013 was a year of 'significant birthdays'. It was the 100th anniversary of the Erasmus University of Rotterdam, the 20th anniversary of the Maastricht Treaty and thus of the concept of 'European Citizenship'. To mark the 20th birthday of EU citizenship and to give added impetus to EU Citizenship, the EU allocated 2013 as the European Year of Citizenship.

Briefly, EU citizenship' is ascribed to any individual holding the nationality of an EU country.[1] EU citizenship does not replace national citizenship. Instead, it confers upon all EU citizens an additional set of rights, guaranteed by the EU Treaties.

The concept of citizenship of the EU has brought a new 'political' element to what had been primarily an 'economic' integration. From its inception in 1993 to the present day, EU citizenship has continued to evolve. In May 2013 the European Commission published a second report on EU citizenship reviewing existing policy and legislation in this area and setting out a number of new initiatives to help EU citizens make better use of their rights. This chapter will look at the background to EU citizenship, how it emerged, became enshrined in EU law and how it has developed and grown to become an integral part of the rule of law and democracy in the EU today.

2 History

The concept of EU citizenship was first set down in the 1992 Maastricht Treaty. The Lisbon Treaty and the EU Charter of Fundamental Rights reinforces EU citizens' rights. The 1992 Maastricht Treaty established concept of 'citizenship of the Union' in Part Two of the Treaty. Article 8(1) provided that 'every person holding the nationality of a Member State shall be a citizen of the Union'. Articles 8a–e went on to specify certain of these rights including the right to move and reside freely within the territory of the Member States, the right to vote and to stand as

[1]See European Commission DG JUST website on EU Citizenship. http://ec.europa.eu/justice/citizen/index_en.htm. Accessed 28 October 2014.

a candidate at municipal elections in the Member State in which he resides, under the same conditions as nationals of that State, the right to petition the European Parliament and European Ombudsman.

The entry into force of the Lisbon Treaty strengthened the concept of EU citizenship in a number of ways. Article 9 of the TEU provides:

> In all its activities, the Union shall observe the principle of the equality of its citizens, who shall receive equal attention from its institutions, bodies, offices and agencies. Every national of a Member State shall be a citizen of the Union. Citizenship of the Union shall be additional to and not replace national citizenship.

In particular, Articles 20–24 of the TFEU strengthened the link between citizenship and non-discrimination and reinforced and clarified consular and diplomatic protection for unrepresented EU citizens. The Treaty further provided in Article 20(2) that the list of rights is not exhaustive. In addition, the right of EU citizens in third countries to enjoy protection by the consular and diplomatic authorities of all Member States is enshrined as a clear individual right in Article 20(2)(c) TFEU and elaborated in Article 23 TFEU, which also gives the Commission the power to initiate legislation in this field.

Moreover, other provisions of the Lisbon Treaty complement these specific rights in various ways. Article 11(4) TEU set out a new right, the Citizens' Initiative, which enables one million citizens to invite the Commission to bring forward legislative proposals. The citizens' perspective is reaffirmed in the new definition of members of the European Parliament *as* 'representatives of the Union's citizens' (Article 14(2) TEU) and not simply as 'representatives of the peoples of the States brought together in the Community' as was set out in Article 189 of the Treaty of the European Communities (TEC).

The rights inherent in EU citizenship are further enshrined in the Charter of Fundamental Rights of the EU—which entered into force in December 2009—specifically in Title V (Articles 39–46) on Citizens Rights. This legally binding Charter represents a major step forward in terms of the EU's political commitment toward fundamental rights. According to the Charter's Preamble, the Union 'places the individual at the heart of its activities, by establishing a citizenship of the Union and by creating an area of freedom, security and justice'.

The European Court of Justice has consistently supported the concept of EU citizenship. For example, in the *Grzelczyk* case, the ECJ said 'Union citizenship is destined to be the fundamental status of nationals of the Member States, enabling those who find themselves in the same situation to enjoy the same treatment in law irrespective of their nationality, subject to such exceptions as are expressly provided for'.[2] In particular, the ECJ has ruled that citizens are entitled to live in another Member State purely by virtue of being citizens of the EU, thereby recognizing EU citizenship as a source of the right of free movement.[3] More recently,

---

[2]Case C-184/99 *Grzelczyk* [2001] ECR I-6193, para 31.

[3]For example, Cases C-413/99 *Baumbast and R* [2002] ECR I-7091, para 84, and C-200/02, *Zhu and Chen* [2004] ECR I-9925, para 26.

the Court of Justice clarified that Article 20 TFEU precludes national measures which could deprive EU citizens of the genuine enjoyment of the substance of the rights conferred by their status as EU citizens.[4]

3 What Rights Are Guaranteed by EU Citizenship?

As already noted above, any person holding the nationality of an EU Member State automatically qualifies for EU citizenship. This is in addition to citizenship of their Member State.[5] In general, EU citizenship and the specific rights the concept embodies are guaranteed by the TFEU, specifically Part Two (Articles 18–25).[6] In addition to these specific rights guaranteed by the TFEU, EU citizens have other rights, e.g. the right to seek general information on the EU including citizens' rights and to get a response from any EU institution,[7] the right of access, under certain conditions, to the documents of the EU institutions (Commission, Parliament and Council), the right of access to the EU Civil Service, the right to

[4]Case C-34/09, *Ruiz Zambrano*, para 42.

[5]Article 20, Part Two TFEU.

[6]These rights include: Articles 18 and 19 TFEU: the right to non-discrimination on the grounds of nationality, or on other grounds eg sex, religion, race or age.
Article 20 TFEU: the right to move and reside freely within the territory of the Member States, the right to vote and to stand as candidates in elections to the European Parliament and in municipal elections in their Member State of residence, under the same conditions as nationals of that State; the right to enjoy, in the territory of a third country in which the Member State of which they are nationals is not represented, the protection of the diplomatic and consular authorities of any Member State on the same conditions as the nationals of that State; the right to petition the European Parliament, to apply to the European Ombudsman.
Article 21 TFEU: the right generally to move and reside freely within the territory of the EU Member States.
Article 22 TFEU: to EU citizen residing in a Member State of which he is not a national, the right to vote and to stand as a candidate at municipal elections in the Member State in which he resides, under the same conditions as nationals of that State; to every EU citizen residing in a Member State of which he is not a national, the right to vote and to stand as a candidate in elections to the European Parliament in the Member State in which he resides, under the same conditions as nationals of that State.
Article 23 TFEU: the right to be protected in a third country by the diplomatic and consular authorities of any EU Member State under the same conditions as nationals of that State.
Article 24 TFEU: the right to petition the European Parliament and to complain to EU Ombudsman.
Article 25 TFEU: clarifies that the list of EU citizens' rights is not limited to those specified in Part Two and that the EU may strengthen or add to these rights.

[7]Europe Direct Central Information Service. http://europa.eu/europedirect/index_en.htm. Accessed 4 March 2015.

non-discrimination based on nationality,[8] In addition, the Lisbon Treaty introduced the 'European Citizens Initiative' (ECI), which enables one million EU citizens from at least one quarter of the EU Member States to invite the European Commission to bring forward proposals for legal acts in areas where the Commission has the power to do so.[9]

The European Commission has created a special website with extensive information on EU citizens' rights.[10] The Charter of Fundamental Rights of the EU in Title V (Articles 39–46) dealing with 'Citizens' Rights' reinforces the rights of citizens guaranteed in the Lisbon Treaty, including the right to vote and stand as a candidate at the European Parliament elections (Article 39), the right of access to documents of the EU institutions (Article 42) and the right to petition the European Parliament (Article 44).

4 Recent Developments

Since the entry into force of the Lisbon Treaty, there have been a number of significant developments enforcing and clarifying the rights and scope of EU citizenship. In 2010, the European Commission published its First EU Citizenship Report.[11] The report identified a number of obstacles that EU citizens face when trying to make use of their rights in their day-to-day lives and set out a number of concrete actions towards eliminating these obstacles. In the report, the European Commission proposed some 25 measures to make peoples' lives easier when they exercise their EU rights to get married, buy a house or register a car in another EU country. The Commission subsequently delivered on these commitments.[12] In May 2013, the Commission adopted a Second EU Citizenship Report[13] to review pro-

[8]Part Two Treaty of the European Communities (TEC), Articles 18–25, Non-Discrimination and Citizenship of the Union, OJ C115/56, 9 May 2008.

[9]Article 24 TFEU. The rules and procedures governing the ECI are set out in Reg. (EU) No. 211/2011 of the European Parliament and Council of 16 February 2011 on the citizens' initiative, OJ L65/1, 11 March 2011. http://eur-lex.europa.eu/LexUriServ/LexUriServ.do?uri=OJ:L:2011:065:0001:0022:EN:PDF. Accessed 20 October 2014.

[10]Your Europe—citizens' portal. http://europa.eu/youreurope/citizens/index_en.htm. Accessed 20 October 2014.

[11]EU Citizenship Report 2010 Dismantling the obstacles to EU citizens' rights, COM(2010)603final, 27 October 2010. http://ec.europa.eu/justice/citizen/files/com_2010_603_en.pdf. Accessed 20 October 2014.

[12]EU Citizenship Report 2010. http://ec.europa.eu/justice/citizen/files/2010_citizenship_report_key_actions_en.pdf. Accessed 20 October 2014.

[13]EU Citizenship Report 2013. http://ec.europa.eu/justice/citizen/files/2013eucitizenshipreport_en.pdf. Accessed 20 October 2014.

gress as part of its contribution to the 2013 European Year of Citizenship. As part of its preparation for the report the Commission conducted a public consultation on EU citizenship in early May 2013 which confirmed the existence of a number of hurdles. Eurobarometer surveys on EU citizenship[14] and on electoral rights[15] and reports by other EU institutions, including the European Parliament,[16] all contributed to the Commission's Second Report.

In its report the Commission announced 12 new actions in six areas to strengthen citizens' rights: 'Removing obstacles for workers, students and trainees in the EU punishing citizens for having exercised their right to free movement'.

Parallel to the Second EU Citizenship report, the Commission also adopted its third annual report on the application of the EU Charter of Fundamental Rights[17] including citizens' rights such as the right to personal data protection, in May 2013. The report provides a detailed overview of how fundamental rights have been implemented in the EU during 2012. It highlights, for example, how the rights enshrined in the Charter are taken account of by the EU institutions when proposing and adopting EU legislation, while Member States are bound by the Charter only in cases where they implement EU policies and law. The report is structured into six chapters reflecting the six titles of the EU Charter of Fundamental Rights, including Citizens' Rights. Where the EU has competence to act, the Commission can propose EU legislation that gives effect to the rights and principles of the Charter. Examples of Commission proposals during 2012 include the proposed major reform of the EU's rules on the protection of personal data.

The European Court of Justice and national courts have also increasingly referred to the Charter in its decisions. For example, the number of decisions quoting the Charter in its reasoning almost doubled, from 43 in 2011 to 87 in 2012. Fundamental rights protection will be further enhanced with the EU's accession to the European Convention of Human Rights. Negotiations on the accession agreement have been finalized. Accession of the EU to the ECHR is intended to strengthen the protection of human rights in Europe by providing that the EU and its legal acts will ultimately submit to the European Court of Human Rights.

---

[14]Flash Eurobarometer 365—European Union citizenship—February 2013 (hereinafter 2013 Eurobarometer on EU citizenship).

[15]Flash Eurobarometer 364—Electoral Rights—March 2013 (hereinafter 2013 Eurobarometer on electoral rights). http://ec.europa.eu/public_opinion/flash/fl_364_en.pdf. Accessed 20 October 2014.

[16]EU citizenship joint European Parliament and Commission hearing of 19 February 2013 'Making the most of EU citizenship'. http://ec.europa.eu/justice/citizen/document/files/eu_hearing_report.pdf. Accessed 20 October 2014.

[17]2012 Report on the application of the EU Charter of Fundamental Rights. http://ec.europa.eu/justice/fundamental-rights/files/charter_report_2012_en.pdf. Accessed 20 October 2014.

5 The Way Ahead—2015 and Beyond

The 2013 EU Citizenship Report was intended to be used in the European Year of Citizens 2013[18] activities, together with the Citizens' Dialogues,[19] on the future of Europe. The latter were initiated by the Commission in the framework of the European Year of Citizens to continue to provide more information into citizens' concerns and suggestions for reform. The feedback from the dialogues is intended to contribute to a Commission Communication on the future of Europe.

As part of the 2013 European Year of Citizens the EU created and endorsed a whole range of activities and events. The main aims of these were to inform citizens of their rights and responsibilities as EU citizens, to bring the EU closer to the citizen, to show how the EU is supporting them, to encourage a broad debate on EU identity and to encourage mobility among young people. Dialogue was fostered at all levels and between all stakeholders including government, civil society and business at events and conferences around Europe and at grassroots level, by citizens and civil society organizations. This process of dialogue is intended to help the EU build a vision of how the EU should be for its citizens in 2020.

Both the Citizens Dialogues and European Year 2013 were intended to pave the way towards the European elections in 2014. The 2014 European elections were the first to be held under the Lisbon Treaty, which enhances the role of the EU citizen as a political actor in the EU. Specifically, the Lisbon Treaty stipulates that the next European Commission president will be chosen 'taking into account the results of the European elections'.[20] This is intended to strengthen both the say of the Parliament and of citizens in the selection of European Commission leadership. The Treaty also strengthens the powers of the European Parliament, consolidating its role as co-legislator and giving it additional responsibility.

In order to realize this development, in March 2013, the European Commission adopted a Recommendation[21] in which it called on national political parties to nominate a candidate for European Commission President in the next European elections and urged them to show their European political party affiliation. The Recommendation was intended to better inform voters about the issues at stake in the May 2014 EP elections, encourage a EU-wide debate and ultimately improve voter turnout, which has fallen significantly in previous EP elections.

---

[18]http://europa.eu/citizens-2013/. Accessed 20 October 2014.

[19]http://ec.europa.eu/debate-future-europe/index_en.htm. Accessed 20 October 2014.

[20]Article 17(7), Treaty on European Union, C83/26, 30 March 2010.

[21]Commission Recommendation of 12 March 2013 on enhancing the democratic and efficient conduct of the elections to the European Parliament, C(2013)1303final. http://ec.europa.eu/justice/citizen/document/files/c_2013_1303_en.pdf. Accessed 4 March 2015.

6 Conclusions

In just 20 years from its inception under the Maastricht Treaty, the concept of EU Citizenship has broadened and deepened. This growth is reflected not only quantitatively in the scope of rights accorded to EU citizens but also qualitatively in the range of those rights, such as the political role given to EU citizens under the Lisbon Treaty mentioned previously to select their EU leaders.

Speaking in September 2013 on the future of the rule of law to the EU, European Commission Vice President, responsible for justice, Viviane Reding commented that the EU is not just an internal market or economic and monetary union but 'also offers its citizens a European area of freedom, security and justice'. The completion of the latter, she continued, depends on the confidence of citizens as well as national authorities, 'This confidence will only be given and maintained if we can be sure that the rule of law is observed fully in all Member States. The need of this confidence is thus a further reason why the rule of law is of such great importance for the European Union'.[22] Later the same month European Commission President Barroso in his state of the union address recalled that 'safeguarding its values, such as the rule of law, is what the European Union was made to do'.[23] He mentioned that the Commission would come forward with a Communication on the rule of law in the near future. The reference by Commission President and Vice President to citizens in the context of the future rule of law debate in Europe illustrates not only the intrinsic part played by EU citizenship in the context of the rule of law. It also shows that the rise and rise of EU citizenship looks set to continue.

Case law, legislations and documents

Case law

Case C-184/99 *Grzelczyk* [2001] ECR I-6193, para 31
Case C-413/99 *Baumbast and R* [2002] ECR I-7091, para 84
Case C-200/02, *Zhu and Chen* [2004] ECR I-9925, para 26.
Case C-34/09, *Ruiz Zambrano*, para 42

Legislation

Treaty on the European Communities
Treaty on the European Union
Treaty on the Functioning of the European Union
Regulation (EU) No. 211/2011 of the European Parliament and Council of 16 February 2011 on the citizens' initiative, OJ L65/1, 11 March 2011

[22]'The EU and the Rule of Law—What next?', 4 September 2013. http://europa.eu/rapid/press-release_SPEECH-13-677_en.htm. Accessed 4 March 2015.

[23]State of the Union Address, 11 September 2013, Commission President Barroso. http://europa.eu/rapid/press-release_SPEECH-13-684_en.htm. Accessed 4 March 2015.

Reports

EU Citizenship Report 2010: Dismantling the obstacles to EU citizens' rights, COM(2010)603final, 27 October 2010
EU Citizenship Report 2010: 25 Key Actions to improve Citizens' Lives
2012 Report on the application of the EU Charter of Fundamental Rights
EU Citizenship Report 2013: EU Citizens: Your Rights, Your Future
Commission Recommendation of 12 March 2013 on enhancing the democratic and efficient conduct of the elections to the European Parliament, C(2013) 1303 final.

The Role of National Courts in the Process of Legal Integration in the European Union: Retrospective and Prospective

Urszula Jaremba

Abstract The functioning of national courts as decentralized EU courts has been and will likely remain one of the most constitutive, complex, and intriguing aspects of the process of integration in the European Union. The fact that the law of the European Union can directly affect interests of individuals in the EU, and may be invoked and relied upon by them before national courts, which are in turn obliged to protect the rights individuals derive from EU law, have tremendous implications for the functioning of national judiciaries, and can hardly be overstated. It is the aim of this contribution to briefly look at the development of the role national courts play in the process of legal integration within the EU and, consequently, provide several reflections on the preconditions which seem necessary for the proper fulfillment of the tasks that national judges are assigned by the law of the European Union.

Contents

U. Jaremba (✉)
EU Law, Utrecht University, Utrecht, The Netherlands
e-mail: u.jaremba@law.uu.nl

F.A.N.J. Goudappel and E.M.H. Hirsch Ballin (eds.), *Democracy and Rule of Law in the European Union*, DOI 10.1007/978-94-6265-066-4_5

1 Introduction

The functioning of national courts as decentralized EU courts has been and will likely remain one of the most constitutive, complex, and intriguing aspects of the process of integration in the European Union.[1] The fact that the law of the European Union can directly affect interests of individuals in the EU,[2] and may be invoked and relied upon by them before national courts, which are in turn obliged to protect those rights, have tremendous implications for the functioning of national judiciaries, and can hardly be overstated. As observed already two decades ago by Lord Slynn of Hadley: 'A judge sitting in a national court now has a dual function. His first task is to decide cases on the basis of domestic law. He must find the facts, apply the rule of domestic law, and give judgment in favor of one or other of the parties. At the same time, the national judge must, where relevant, apply European European law.'[3] In order to fully understand the immensity of the role of the national judge in applying and enforcing EU law that Lord Slynn of Hadley so briefly reflected upon, it is necessary to look into the process of legal development that has taken place within the Communities, later the European Union, since the 1960s of the last century. Even though much has been said and written, by both legal and political science scholars, about the role national judges play in the process of legal integration in the EU, the topic never seems to be exhausted.[4] It is the aim of this contribution to briefly look at the development of the role of national courts in the process of legal integration within the EU and, consequently, provide several reflections on the preconditions which seem necessary to the proper fulfillment of the tasks that national judges are assigned by the law of the European Union. Although this may seem like a somewhat ambitious aim, the analysis will have a somewhat sketchy character and a purely pragmatic

---

[1]This contribution is predominantly based on the doctoral thesis by the author, Jaremba 2012, defended on the 5th of October 2012, forthcoming in Nijhoff Studies in EU Law (2015).

[2]See Case 26-62 *NV Algemene Transport en Expeditie Onderneming van Gend & Loos v. Netherlands Inland Revenue Administration* [1963] ECR 1: '(...) The conclusion to be drawn from this is that the Community constitutes a new legal order of international law for the benefit of which the states have limited their sovereign rights, albeit within limited fields, and the subjects of which comprise not only Member states but also their nationals. Independently of the legislation of Member States, European law therefore not only imposes obligations on individuals but is also intended to confer upon them rights which become part of their legal heritage.'

[3]See Lord Slynn of Hadley 1993, p. 18.

[4]Just to mention several contributions: Miasik 2008; Kühn 2005; Bobek 2006; F. Mayer, The European Constitution and the courts. Adjudicating European constitutional law in a multilevel system. 9 Jean Monnet Working Paper, 2003; Prechal et al. 2005; Stone Sweet 2000; Jarvis 1998; Sciarra 2001; Weiler 1993; O. Pollicino, New emerging judicial dynamics of the relationship between national and the European courts after the enlargement of Europe. 14 Jean Monnet Working Paper, 2008; M. Cartabia, Taking dialogue seriously. The renewed need for a judicial dialogue at the time of constitutional activism in the European Union. 12 Jean Monnet Working Paper, 2007; Kilpatrick 1998; Chalmers 1997.

take, and will look into the practical obstacles which may jeopardize the proper functioning of national courts as decentralized EU courts at present and in the future.

This contribution consists of three parts. First, it will be looked into the judicial architecture in the EU and the role national judges are assigned to by the law of the Union. In this context, the problem of pivotal principles of EU law, such as supremacy, direct effect, and harmonious interpretation, will be sketched. Also the issue of the preliminary ruling procedure will be addressed. Subsequently, the obstacles which may hinder the proper fulfillment of the role EU law places to national judges will be briefly discussed. Finally, several conclusions will be drawn.

2 The Role of National Courts in the Process of Legal Integration Within the Union: Retrospective

2.1 Judicial Architecture in the EU

EU Treaties create a system of judicial protection at the level of the European Union, but they do not establish separate EU courts in each Member State which could protect the rights individuals derive from the law of the Union. From the Treaties it follows that individuals can gain direct access to the supranational Court of Justice of the European Union (hereinafter the ECJ or the Court of Justice) only in order to challenge illegal actions undertaken by the Union.[5] As a consequence of this judicial architecture, all disputes which involve EU-law-related problems that arise between individuals and public authorities of the Member States or between two or more individuals are heard in national courts and tribunals. National courts are obliged to protect the rights that individuals derive from EU law and, at the same time, are expected to ensure the effectiveness of EU law and its uniform application across the Union. By and large, all national courts are decentralized EU courts and, consequently, all national judges are EU judges. As plausibly observed by Martinico, national courts play 'a fundamental role in the multilevel system.'[6] The above should be seen in the framework of the increasing influence of EU law on national laws. This process of affecting national laws by various sources of EU law implies that more and more laws, rules, and provisions that national courts apply in their daily work does in fact origin from the law of the Union.[7] To put it very basically, EU law is practically everywhere,

[5]See Articles 263, 265, 277 and 340 of the Treaty on the Functioning of the European Union (TFEU).

[6]From Martinico 2011, p. 84.

[7]On the process of Europeanisation of national public and constitutional laws see for instance Prechal et al. 2005; on the process of Europeanisation of national private laws see for instance Twigg-Flesner 2008; Keirse 2011; Hesselink 2011. For a general overview of the Europeanisation process see Jaremba 2012.

since it has encroached and influenced national laws in nearly every field of law. It has crept into the sphere of not only public but also private relations, including parties such as undertakings, consumers, employees, and employers. In situations in which the rights of those parties are breached, or the legal obligations are not met, a dispute will very likely be heard and decided by a national judge, be it administrative, commercial, labor, or family law judge. As mentioned above, this constitutive role placed on national courts cannot be found in the EU Treaties which are almost silent on this issue.[8] It is the ECJ that has played a pivotal role in establishing the tasks of national courts regarding the application of EU law. This jurisprudential development started in the 1960s and will be briefly sketched below.

2.2 *Direct Effect, Supremacy, and Harmonious Interpretation*

In 1962, judges in the Dutch Administrative Tribunal (*Tariefcommissie*) adjudicating in final jurisdiction were dealing with a dispute between a postal and transportation company named Van Gend en Loos and the Dutch customs authorities. Van Gend en Loos imported urea-formaldehyde from West Germany to the Netherlands which was charged with a tariff on the import. The company paid the tariff but objected to this decision of the Dutch customs authorities and claimed a return of the customs paid. In order to support its claim it submitted that the tariff was incompatible with EC law, and more precisely with Article 12 of the Treaty of Rome, what is now Article 30 TFEU.[9] Having problems with interpretation of the mentioned Treaty article, the Dutch judges decided to resort to a relatively new and unknown legal instrument, that is to say, to the possibility of referring a preliminary question to the Court of Justice under Article 177 of Treaty Establishing the European Economic Community, what is now Article 267 TFEU. In its preliminary question the national court asked the ECJ whether the concerned Treaty article could directly confer rights on the nationals of a Member State and whether those rights could be enforced in national courts.[10] The referring Dutch court

[8]Only Article 267 TFEU directly refers to national courts. However, several Treaty articles refer to national courts or concern national courts in an indirect way, for instance Article 4(3) TEU which enshrines the principle of royal cooperation and Article 19 TEU in which it can be read that 'Member States shall provide remedies sufficient to ensure effective legal protection in the fields covered by Union law.'

[9]Article 30 TFEU prohibits any custom duties on imports and exports and any charges having equivalent effect. This prohibition also applies to custom duties of a fiscal nature.

[10]Case 26-62, above n. 2. The first of referred questions was as follows: 'whether Article 12 of the ECC Treaty has direct application within the territory of a Member States, in other words, whether nationals of such a state can, on the basis of the article in question, lay claim to individual rights which the courts must protect'.

could by no means have an idea that this rather straightforward (but at the same time very complex) question would become one of the most fundamental and landmark issues in the legal development of integration process within the European Union. The answer provided by the ECJ, in which it was held that the concerned article is indeed capable of 'creating individual rights which national courts must protect' was of utmost importance. From this moment, those are the national courts of the Member States which are involved in the system of judicial protection of the rights individuals derive from EC/EU law and which are obliged to protect those rights against unlawful actions of their own states. Put bluntly, the decision of the Dutch administrative court to resort to the ECJ with her legal question concerning EC law, and the groundbreaking answer provided by the Court of Justice to this question changed the legal reality in national courts of the Member States for ever.

However, the above is not intended to imply that just one single judgment of the ECJ was sufficient to change the course of legal developments in the Union. It quickly occurred that the *Van Gend en Loos* case was just the first one in a set of ECJ's decisions that increasingly involved national courts in the process of EU integration, and by means of which the ECJ changed the nature of judicial work. In course of time the ECJ pronounced various decisions in which the obligations of national courts with regard to the application of EU law were broadened and enhanced. Just one year after *Van Gend en Loos*, the ECJ decided that not only can EU law be invoked and relied upon by individuals in national courts, it also takes precedence over national law in case of collision between both.[11] The general argument underlying this decision was that the European Union creates its own legal system, which constitutes an integral part of legal systems of Member States, and the efficacy of it would be undermined if national law could take precedence over the law of the Union.[12] The principle of supremacy, also called primacy, became a frequent matter addressed by the Court of Justice ever since. In several judgments, the ECJ gradually gives a practical shape to the principle. For instance, in the *Simmenthal* case, the ECJ arrived at the conclusion that national courts which deal with a situation of collision between national and EU law are obliged to set aside those conflicting national provisions and apply the relevant EU law provisions instead.[13] In the following years, the Court of Justice pronounced dozens of important decisions in which the principles of supremacy and direct effect, and the legal obligations of national courts which are attached to both principles were defined and elaborated upon.[14]

[11]See Case 6/64, *Flaminio Costa v. E.N.E.L* [1964] ECR 585, the part on the submission that the Court was obliged to apply the national law.

[12]See ibid.

[13]See Case 106/77, *Amministrazione delle Finanze dello Stato v. Simmenthal SpA* [1978] ECR 585, paras 14, 16, 21, and 24. See also C-159/91, *Criminal proceedings against Jean-Claude Levy* [1993] ECR I-4287, para 9; C-347/96, *Solred SA v. Administración General del Estado* [1998] ECR I-937, para 30.

[14]For a broad overview of the jurisprudential development in that regard see Jaremba 2012.

From the extensive line of jurisprudence of the Court follows, however, that different rules apply to different sources of EU law. In that context, it was for instance held by the ECJ that specific Treaty provisions can be invoked by individuals against their Member States and other individuals[15] but provisions of directives which are invoked in horizontal situations (that is to say between two individuals) are not capable of producing direct effect.[16] The latter implies that in specific situations the concerned individual might not be capable of enforcing her rights that stem from EU law provisions, and that the national court hearing the dispute is not obliged to directly apply those EU provisions to the case at hand. To partly remedy this evident gap in the system of judicial protection, the Court of Justice established another principle, namely the principle of harmonious interpretation,[17] interchangeably called indirect effect, consistent or conforming interpretation. Basically speaking, the principle of harmonious interpretation expects national courts to interpret national law in conformity with EU law, "insofar as it is given discretion to do so under national law,'[18] whereby it broadens the obligations assigned to national courts by EU law even further. Without going too much into the details of the principle, it should be observed that conforming interpretation carries several practical implications for national courts. First, national judges are obliged to interpret the provisions of national law in light of the EU legislation in question, and they are expected to give effect to it by means of interpretation. Provisions of national law must be given such a meaning that it will conform to EU law and achieve an outcome consistent with its objective. From a more technical point of view, it does not matter whether the specific national law predates or postdates the concerned EU legislation,[19] and it is necessary that the national judge looks into the entire body of national law and interprets it in a manner to achieve the prescribed results. Finally, the obligation to construe national law in conformity with a directive is limited by the notion of *contra legem*

[15]See for instance Case C-415/95, *Union royale belge des sociétés de football association and others v. Bosman and others* [1995] ECR 4291, where the ECJ ruled that Article 45 TFEU (ex Article 39 EC) has a horizontal direct effect, or Case C-281/98, *Roman Angonese v. Cassa di Risparmio di Bolzano SpA* [2000] ECR 4139, where the Court held that Article 54 TFEU (ex Article 48 EC) applies also to private parties. See also a recent Case C-171/11 *Fra.bo SpA v. Deutsche Vereinigung des Gas- und Wasserfaches eV (DVGW) – Technisch-Wissenschaftlicher Vereinin* [2012] ECR 00000, in which the ECJ decided to give horizontal direct effect to Article 34 TFEU on the free movement of goods in specific situations.

[16]See Case 152/84, *M. H. Marshall v. Southampton and South-West Hampshire Area Health Authority* [1986] ECR 723, para 48.

[17]See judgment in Case 14/83, *Sabine von Colson and Elisabeth Kamann v. Land Nordrhein-Westfalen* [1984] ECR 1891, para 26.

[18]Case 14/83, *Von Colson*, para 28. In the C-397/01 to C-403/01, *Bernhard Pfeiffer* et al. *v. Deutsches Rotes Kreuz, kreisverband Waldshut eV* [2004] ECR I-8835, the Court of Justice uses the term 'to as far as possible extent', see para 113.

[19]See Joined Cases C-397/01 to C-403/01, *Bernhard Pfeiffer*, para 115.

interpretation,[20] by general principles of law such as legal certainty and non-retroactivity, and by the prohibition of imposing criminal liability.[21] The principle of harmonious interpretation together with the principles of direct effect and supremacy constitute three fundamental rules that explain the role of national courts *vis-à-vis* EU law. From the above discussion it follows that national courts are endowed with a very fundamental task which boils down to, on the one hand, enabling individuals to invoke and rely on EU law and, on the other hand, requiring them to apply and enforce EU law and protect individuals' rights flowing from it in order to ensure the *effet utile* of EU law. However, the story of the participation of national courts in the process of legal integration in the Union would be incomplete without the preliminary ruling procedure which will be sketched below.

3 The Preliminary Ruling Procedure

In fact, the principles discussed above would have never been established if national courts had not resorted to the procedure of preliminary question which is enshrined in Article 267 TFEU.[22] Those national courts had decided to refer to the ECJ their legal questions regarding interpretation of EU law that had arisen with regard to cases pending before them. It follows from Article 267 TFEU that the ECJ has jurisdiction to give preliminary rulings concerning the interpretation and validity of the Treaties, and on the validity and interpretation of acts of the EU institutions, bodies, offices, or agencies.[23] When a question concerning the aforementioned areas arises before any national court or tribunal, a judge may request the ECJ to give a ruling on it if she considers it necessary to give a judgment. If such a question is raised before a court or tribunal of last instance, that court or

[20]See Case C-212/04, *Konstantions Adeneler and others v. Ellinikos Organisamos Galaktos* (ELOG) [2006], para 110.

[21]See for instance Case C-101/01, *Bodil Lindqvist* [2003] ECR I-12971, para 24, and Case C-305/05, *Ordre des barreaux francophones et germanophone and Others* [2007] ECR I-5305, para 28.

[22]Previously Article 234 EC Treaty. The Treaty of Lisbon slightly reformed the preliminary ruling procedure. As a result of the disappearance of the pillars, the ECJ acquired jurisdiction to give preliminary rulings also in the area of freedom, security and justice. Regarding police and judicial cooperation in criminal matters, the jurisdiction of the Court has become binding and no longer subject to a declaration by each Member State. Regarding the issue of visas, asylum and immigration, any national court or tribunal (not only the highest courts) has now the competence to request preliminary rulings.

[23]Any EU measure, also a non-binding measure, may be subject to review by the ECJ; see Case C-322/88, *Salvatore Grimaldi v. Fonds des maladies professionnelles* [1989] ECR 4407, para 8.

tribunal is then obliged to bring the case to the ECJ.[24] The preliminary ruling has gradually proved to be one of the most fundamental mechanisms for building and elaborating the legal order of the European Union.

Namely, the national judges who decided to resort to the ECJ with their EU-law-related problems gave the Court of Justice the possibility to define and develop the Union's system further by means of giving specific interpretation to the general and often open-ended provisions of Union's law. To put it simply, national courts have been propelling the process of legal integration within the Union by providing the Court with legal questions concerning EU law.[25] In Rheinmühlen-Düsseldorf, the ECJ held that the procedure of preliminary ruling is cardinal for the 'preservation of the Community character of the law established by the Treaty. It aims at ensuring the coherence of European law across all the Member States.'[26] Elsewhere, the Court observed that the participation of national courts in the procedure is 'an index both of judicial cooperation between the Court of Justice and the national courts of the Member States and of the integration of European law into national law.'[27]

It should be emphasized that the procedure of preliminary ruling can be put in motion exclusively by the national judge, and it is also left to the national judge to apply the interpretation provided by the ECJ to the factual case pending before her.[28] This is why the willingness of national judges to involve in the process of dialogue with the ECJ, and their cooperation with the Court of Justice have been crucial for the further development of the Union's legal framework and the legal integration within the Union. Hence, the willingness of national judges to use the procedure is a *sine qua non* for the evolution of a European legal system.[29] As observed elsewhere '(…) under today's circumstances, national and European judges should collaborate and communicate more with one another, showing that they are co-actors in European law.'[30] This is why the involvement of national

---

[24]The term of the last instance court should be understood as including the highest courts, and all the courts against the decisions of which there exist no further remedy. See Case 6/64, *Costa v. ENEL*, the part on the application of Article 177; see also Case C-99/00, *Criminal proceedings against Lyckeskog* [2002] ECR I-4839.

[25]See Craig and De Búrca 2011, pp. 442–443.

[26]Case 166-73, *Rheinmühlen-Düsseldorf v. Einfuhr- und Vorratsstelle für Getreide und Futtermittel* [1974] ECR 33, para 2.

[27]From ECJ 1973, pp. 16–17. Stone Sweet formulates it as follows: 'As the ECJ's doctrines of direct effect and supremacy gradually took hold, Article 234 EC emerged as a kind of central nervous system for the enforcement of EC law and the coordination of the EC and the national legal order.' See Stone Sweet 2007, p. 924.

[28]See for instance Case 17/81, *Pabst and Richarz KG v. Hauptzollamt Oldenburg* [1982] ECR 1331, para 12.

[29]From Chalmers 1997, p. 174.

[30]From Hirsch Ballin 2005, p. 19.

courts in the process of dialogue with the ECJ has gained enormous academic attention, and has been broadly discussed by legal and political science scholars ever since.[31]

4 National Courts in the EU: Prospective

From the above it clearly follows that national courts have been playing an essential role in the process of legal integration within the European Union. With the entry into force of the EU Charter of Fundamental Rights as EU primary law, the role of national courts has become even more prominent. It namely occurs that national courts should also protect the rights stemming from the Charter when Member States implement EU law.[32] One of the anticipated implications of the Charter is the increasing number of requests for a preliminary ruling by national courts received by the Court of Justice.[33]

The discussion above addresses only the most fundamental tasks of national judges in the context of EU law,[34] but it supports the observation by Weiler that 'when European law is spoken through the mouths of the national judiciary it will also have the teeth that can be found in such a mouth and will usually enjoy whatever enforcement value that national law will have on that occasion.'[35] Without, first, the input of national judges and, then, their willingness to cooperate and fulfill their EU-law-related tasks, the European Union might be a different organization from what it is now. The increasingly broadening scope of the tasks and obligations which national courts are expected to fulfill in relation to EU law implies that the application thereof and consequently its effectiveness and uniformity are very much dependent on national courts. However, the system of obligations which are placed on national courts soon proved to be troublesome, for it required that national courts execute tasks that they would normally not exercise

[31]Those authors provide various and often competing theories aimed at explaining the problem of the determinants of national judges' behavior in the process of legal integration within the European Union. To name just a few contributions: Alter 2001; Dehousse 1998; Jarvis 1998; Micklitz 2005; Slaughter, Stone Sweet, Weiler (eds) 1997; Volcansek 1986; Tridimas and Tridimas 2004; Wind 2010.

[32]See orders in case C-339/10 Asparuhov Estov and Others [2010] ECR I-0000, para 13; and Case C-457/09 Chartry [2011] ECR I-0000, para 25. It should however be stressed that the Charter is intended to complement the existing system of protection of fundamental rights, it does aim at replacing it.

[33]See European Commission 2013, p. 7. As observed in the document: "The community of law, on which the Union is based, relies on national courts. Only if national judges fully exercise their powers, can the rights that Union law grants to citizens be effectively guaranteed", see p. 8.

[34]There are also other tasks and obligations which are placed on national courts by means of EU law which follow from for instance the principle of state liability, the obligation to apply EU law *ex officio*, or the principle of effectiveness.

[35]See Weiler 1993, p. 422.

under national law, or that would in fact extend far beyond their constitutional competences, and were not necessarily in accordance with the local legal traditions.[36] National developments clearly show that the relationship between the ECJ and national judges, and between the judges and EU law is not per se smooth and bright.[37]

The reasons for this problem are multifarious. It seems that in order for the respective tasks and obligations to be adequately fulfilled by national courts several preconditions must be met. The first one relates to the Member States' legal frameworks. It is essential that the national constitutional, institutional, and procedural legal frameworks create an environment that simply allows national courts to fulfill the tasks which are placed on them by EU law. All Member States should therefore undertake all possible steps to eliminate the existing constitutional and procedural obstacles at the national level that impede the fulfillment of the EU-law-related tasks.

Secondly, the national judges must be adequately prepared to decide on EU law matters. This implies that they must be properly educated in the field of the law of the European Union, be it institutional, procedural, or material EU law. The national judge will not resort to EU law and apply it if she is not familiar with it, or even worse, not aware that specific EU law regulates the matter at question. The national judge will be skeptical about turning to the ECJ if she does not know the ins and outs of the preliminary ruling procedure and the existing jurisprudence of the ECJ regarding the concerned EU law matter. One should agree that without a certain amount of confidence in the field of EU law and its application, the national judge will likely remain somewhat hesitant to resort and apply EU law to the cases at hand, or will even try opposing it. It is therefore necessary to undertake even more steps that will provide national judges with relevant EU law knowledge and skills. This in turn will actively involve them in the structure of judicial protection system in the European Union. It is on the national and European policy makers to enhance their activities aimed at providing national courts with relevant EU law knowledge, be it at the university level or during judicial vocational training.[38]

Thirdly, the judicial environment and the 'operational context'[39] in which national judges function play an immense role. It can be observed that most judges have a common goal, i.e., to be as efficient as possible and decide the cases

---

[36]See Lasser 2009, p. 248. See for instance Case C-213/89, The *Queen v. Secretary of State for Transport, ex parte: Factortame Ltd and others* [1990] ECR I-2433 in which there was no competence for English courts to grant interim relief to the applicants. In accordance with the claim of the applicant, such a situation was in breach of EU law. The Court decided that any national rule that may impede the full effect of Union law must be set aside by the national court.

[37]To name just a few contributions: Alter 2001; Dehousse 1998; Jarvis 1998; Micklitz 2005; Slaughter et al. 1997; Volcansek 1986; Tridimas and Tridimas 2004; Wind 2010.

[38]On the problem of education in the area of EU law see Jaremba 2012 and Coughlan et al. 2011.

[39]The term 'operational context' is borrowed from Bell 2006, p. 30.

without any undue delay.[40] This implies that judges may tend to rely on heuristics and may tend to resort to the law which they are most knowledgeable of, and which is directly at their disposal, that is to say, national law. The daily backlog of cases, accompanied by the notorious lack of time may therefore effectively hamper the engagement of national judges with EU law, since overwhelmed judges can simply have not enough time at their disposal to deepen the EU-law-related matter, and/or resort to the preliminary ruling procedure and wait for the answer of the ECJ to their question.[41] Finally, the Court of Justice needs to more closely examine the uniformity and coherence of its own jurisprudence and it should be more open to the fact that local legal cultures may establish boundaries which the judges are not supposed to exceed. Also, chances that the national judge resorts to the ECJ and the Court's judgments are followed, and enforced by national courts will be higher if its case law is communicated in a clear language to the national courts, and is transparent and concise.[42] Put differently, the process of cooperation between national courts and the ECJ can only proceed in a positive manner if it is based on mutual openness, respect, responsiveness, and collaboration.

5 Conclusions

The involvement of national judges in the process of legal integration in the Union is one of the most outstanding features of the legal order of the EU. Undoubtedly, the European Union expects much from the national judge. It gives her new tasks and responsibilities but it also endows her with new competences. However, the fact that all national judges in all Member States eagerly participate in the process of legal integration in the European Union, eagerly apply EU law and turn to the Court of Justice with their problems concerning interpretation of EU law, and eagerly resort to the sources of EU law in their daily practice can by no means be taken for granted.

Some judges are not properly educated in the matters of EU law and its application which render the fulfillment of the discussed tasks impossible. They may also be unfamiliar with specific methods of legal interpretation, such as teleological or systemic interpretation, the use of which is encouraged by the Court of Justice but which overstep the locally accepted boundaries of judicial discretion. Some are hindered by such prosaic reasons as lack of access to EU law sources or

[40]See Jaremba 2012.

[41]Ibid.

[42]See M. Bobek, 'Of feasibility and silent elephants: the legitimacy of the Court of Justice through the eyes of national courts'. http://papers.ssrn.com/sol3/papers.cfm?abstract_id=2129683. Accessed 3 December 2012, who suggests that the Court should avoid controversial judgments, and be predictable, feasible, and concise. Furthermore, the style of the case law should, in the opinion of the author, be more discursive, analytical, transparent, and conversational.

foreign language skills. Others are hampered by national constitutional, procedural, or institutional legal framework, or a simple lack of time. Some may also lack willingness to cooperate and engage with EU law, or trust in the ECJ. They may also lack courage to step out of the common line of proceeding and go beyond the mere application of the state rules. Hence, without sufficient commitment on the part of the Member States and the EU institutions to do everything in their power to facilitate the functioning of national courts as decentralized EU courts, and without *loyal cooperation*[43] on the part of national judges themselves, the full uniformity and effectiveness of EU law may remain somewhat elusive notions.

Case law, legislation, and documents

Case law

Case 26-62, *NV Algemene Transport en Expeditie Onderneming van Gend & Loos v. Netherlands Inland Revenue Administration* [1963]

Case 6/64, *Flaminio Costa v. E.N.E.L.* [1964] ECR 585

Case 166-73, *Rheinmühlen-Düsseldorf v. Einfuhr- und Vorratsstelle für Getreide und Futtermittel* [1974] ECR

Case 106/77, *Amministrazione delle Finanze dello Stato v. Simmenthal SpA* [1978] ECR 585, paras 14, 16, 21 and 24

Case 17/81, *Pabst and Richarz KG v. Hauptzollamt Oldenburg* [1982] ECR 1331

Case 14/83, *Sabine von Colson and Elisabeth Kamann v. Land Nordrhein-Westfalen* [1984] ECR 1891, para 26.

Case 152/84, *M. H. Marshall v. Southampton and South-West Hampshire Area Health Authority* [1986] ECR 723, para 48.

C-322/88, *Salvatore Grimaldi v. Fonds des maladies professionnelles* [1989] ECR 4407

C-213/89, *The Queen v. Secretary of State for Transport, ex parte: Factortame Ltd and others* [1990] ECR I-2433

C-159/91, *Criminal proceedings against Jean-Claude Levy* [1993] ECR I-4287, para 9

C-415/95, *Union royale belge des sociétés de football association and others v. Bosman and others* [1995] ECR 4291

C-347/96, *Solred SA v. Administración General del Estado* [1998] ECR I-937, para 30.

C-281/98, *Roman Angonese v. Cassa di Risparmio di Bolzano SpA* [2000] ECR 4139

C-99/00, *Criminal proceedings against Lyckeskog* [2002] ECR I-4839

[43]Article 4(3) TEU.

C-101/01, *Bodil Lindqvist* [2003] ECR I-12971, para 24
C-397/01 to C-403/01, *Bernhard Pfeiffer* et al. *v. Deutsches Rotes Kreuz, kreisverband Waldshut eV* [2004]
C-212/04, *Konstantions Adeneler and others v. Ellinikos Organisamos Galaktos* (ELOG) [2006], para 110
C-305/05, *Ordre des barreaux francophones et germanophone and Others* [2007] ECR I-5305, para 28
C-171/11, *Fra.bo SpA v Deutsche Vereinigung des Gas- und Wasserfaches eV (DVGW) - Technisch-Wissenschaftlicher Vereinin* [2012] ECR 00000

Legislation
Treaty on the Functioning of the European Union (TFEU)

Report
European Commission (2013) Report from the Commission to the European Parliament, the Council, the European Economic and Social Committee and the Committee of the Regions. 2012 Report on the Application of the EU Charter of Fundamental Rights. Brussels, 8 May 2013, COM(2013)271final.

References

Alter K (2001) Establishing the supremacy of European law. The making of an international rule of law in Europe. Oxford University Press, Oxford
Bell J (2006) Judiciaries within Europe: a comparative review. Cambridge University Press, New York
Bobek M (2006) A new legal order, or a non-existent one? Some (early) experiences in the application of EU law in central Europe. Croatian Yearb Eur Law Policy 2:265–298
Chalmers D (1997) Judicial preferences and the Community legal order. Mod Law Rev 50:163–199
Coughlan J, Opravil J, Heusel W (2011) Judicial training in the European Union member states. Study. European Parliament. Directorate General for Internal Policies, Brussels
Craig P, De Búrca G (2011) EU law. Text, cases, and materials, 5th edn. Oxford University Press, Oxford
Dehousse R (1998) The European Court of Justice. The politics of judicial integration. Macmillan Press, Houndmills—London
Hesselink MW (2011) A toolbox for European judges. ELJ 17(4):441–469
Hirsch Ballin EMH (2005) Reflections on co-actorship. In: Hirsch Ballin EMH, Senden LAJ (eds) Co-actorship in the development of European law-making. The quality of European legislation and its implementation and application in the national legal order. T.M.C. Asser Press, The Hague, pp 3–23
Jaremba U (2012) Polish civil judges as European Union law judges: knowledge, experiences and attitudes. Manuscript defended on October 5, 2012
Jarvis MA (1998) The application of EC law by national courts. The free movement of goods. Clarendon Press, Oxford
Keirse ALM (2011) Europe impact on contract law. A perspective on the interlinked contributions of legal scholars, legislators and courts to the Europeanisation of contract law. Utrecht Law Rev 7:34–51

Kilpatrick C (1998) Community or communities of courts in European integration? Sex equality dialogues between UK courts and the ECJ. Eur Law J 4:121–147
Kühn Z (2005) The application of European law in the new member states: several (early) predictions. Ger Law J 6:563–582
Lasser M.de S.-O.-l'E. (2009) Judicial Transformations, The Rights Revolution in the Courts of Europe, Oxford University Press, Oxford
Lord Slynn of Hadley (1993) European law and the national judge. Butterwort Lect 1991–92:18–33
Martinico G (2011) Born to be together: the constitutional complexity of the EU. Rev Const Stud 16:63–95
Miasik D (2008) Application of general principles of EC law by Polish courts—is the European Court of Justice receiving a positive feedback. In: Bernitz U, Nergelius J, Cardner C (eds) General principles of EC Law in a process of development. Kluwer Law International, Alphen aan den Rijn, pp 357–392
Micklitz H-W (2005) The politics of judicial co-operation in the EU. Sunday trading, equal treatment and good faith. Cambridge University Press, Cambridge
Prechal S, van Ooik RH, Jans JH, Mortelmans KJM (2005) 'Europeanisation' of the law: consequences for the Dutch judiciary. 1 Raad voor de Rechtspraak Research Memoranda
Sciarra S (2001) Labour law in the courts. National judges and the European Court of Justice. Hart Publishing, Oxford
Slaughter AM, Stone Sweet A, Weiler JHH (eds) (1997) European Court and national courts—doctrine and jurisprudence. Legal change in its social context. Hart Publishing, Oxford
Stone Sweet A (2000) Governing with judges. Constitutional politics in Europe. Oxford University Press, Oxford
Stone Sweet A (2007) The juridical coup d'état and the problem of authority. Ger Law J 8:916–928
Tridimas G, Tridimas T (2004) National courts and the European Court of Justice: a public choice analysis of the preliminary reference procedure. Int Rev Law Econ 24:125–145
Twigg-Flesner Ch (2008) The Europeanisation of contract law. Current controversies in law. Routledge-Cavendish, London
Volcansek ML (1986) Judicial politics in Europe. An impact analysis. Peter Lang, New York
Weiler JHH (1993) Journey to an unknown destination: a retrospective and prospective of the European Court of Justice in the arena of political integration. J Common Mark Stud 31:417–446
Wind M (2010) The nordics, the EU and the reluctance towards supranational judicial review. J Common Mark Stud 48:1039–1063

Towards a European Council of the Judiciary: Some Reflections on the Administration of the EU Courts

Marc van der Woude

Abstract The EU Charter provides that each person whose rights and freedoms have been violated has the right to an effective remedy. Courts and tribunals have to be independent and impartial, and their hearings fair, public and within reasonable time. In most Member States, this is guaranteed by the principle of the trias politica. One of the biggest problems at the European level is the workload of the Courts. In 1989 the Court of First Instance was created with certain competencies. In 2001, this became a General Court and the possibility for specialised courts was created. The three jurisdictions of the Court now exist: The Court of Justice, the General Court and the specialised courts. Furthermore, both the Court of Justice and the General Court have tried to address their huge workload, for example through internal organisational measures and through new rules of procedure. The ECJ is also faced with budgetary constraints so all resources must be shared over the jurisdictions. Since the Court of Justice requires most of the resources, this jurisdiction has a huge responsibility. According to the author, neutral decision making cannot always be guaranteed because of these constraints. As the ECJ is a large institution with many employees, it must keep administrative and jurisdictional powers strictly separate.

M. van der Woude (✉)
General Court of the European Union, Erasmus School of Law, Rotterdam, The Netherlands
e-mail: marc.van_der_woude@Curia.europa.eu

F.A.N.J. Goudappel and E.M.H. Hirsch Ballin (eds.), *Democracy and Rule of Law in the European Union*, DOI 10.1007/978-94-6265-066-4_6

Contents

1 Introduction

According to the preamble and Article 2 of the Treaty on the European Union (TEU), the rule of law is one of the values and principles upon which the Union was founded. The Charter on Fundamental Rights specifies the main elements of this foundation. It not only lists the various rights and freedoms which everyone in the Union shall enjoy, but also stipulates the basic conditions underlying how justice shall be rendered in the Union. Article 47 of the Charter thus provides that everyone whose rights and freedoms are violated has the right to an effective remedy. Such a remedy implies that the courts and tribunals that are supposed to safeguard these rights must not only be independent and impartial but must also ensure fair and public hearings within a reasonable time.

Fortunately, there are few who would disagree with the importance of rendering effective justice within a reasonable time period. Disagreement is more likely, however, when it comes to the practical implementation of this important principle. Courts do not render judgments spontaneously and for free. Just like any other public service, the judiciary needs to be organised and financed. In most Member States the organisation of the judiciary is regulated by the Constitution and/or formal laws enacted by Parliament. These formal rules are most often inspired by the principles of the trias politica developed Montesquieu. The judiciary is one of the three pillars upon which modern democracies rely.

The trias politica principles are also reflected in the Treaties which led to the current European Union, albeit in a complex manner. The European Council and the Council belongs in many respects both to the legislative and executive powers. The role of the Court of Justice of the European Union (ECJ) is easier to define. It unambiguously belongs to the judicial pillar of the European Union. It shall ensure, according to Article 19 of TEU, that in the interpretation and application of the Treaties the law is observed. This mission has not changed since 1952. However, the Union has evolved since the early days of the Coal and Steel Community. It has evolved into a complex legal system that intensively and continuously interacts with the legal orders of its Member States.

The ECJ itself has also changed since 1952. With the increased reach and intensity of European law, the ECJ has been adapted to the needs of its time on several occasions. With the European Single Act of 1986, the Member States created the possibility to alleviate the workload of the ECJ by setting up a Court of First Instance to which certain competencies could be transferred with the exception of the power to rule on preliminary rulings. This Court of First Instance was effectively created in 1989. The other major change in the Union's judicial organisation dates from 2001 when the Member States signed the Treaty of Nice. This Treaty which transformed the Court of First Instance into a General Court and instituted the possibility to set up specialised courts is still the basis of the judicial architecture of the Union.

Despite these important changes, the Member States never addressed the question as to how the ECJ should be organised in practice. Unlike the other Union institutions, the Treaties do not contain specific rules on the governance of the ECJ and the practical functioning of its three jurisdictions. In fact, the governance of the ECJ has barely changed since 1952. It is managed, as a matter of fact, by the general assembly of the Court of Justice which is the Union's supreme jurisdiction.

Although this governance system has served the institution well throughout the past 60 years, there are various reasons why it needs to be reconsidered. As will be discussed in this paper, there are medium- to long-term institutional reasons why managerial tasks have to be separated from judicial ones and why the judicial pillar of the Union has to be reinforced. But there are also more practical short-term reasons why the lack of clear governance rules becomes a cause of concern for the proper functioning of the ECJ. These reasons relate to the continuous increase in the workload of the General Court and budgetary constraints. The adage that more work has to be done with fewer means not only applies to national governments, but also to the European Union. And this naturally includes its judiciary. Under the latest budgetary rules, the European Union institutions have to make annual or triennial savings of 5 % on their costs.

Such constraints are particularly hard to ingest by a judicial organisation that is unable to control its workload. The influx of cases before the Court of Justice has increased from 503 in 2000 to 537 in 2006 and 632 in 2012. The General Court has experienced a similar increase: 398 in 2000, 432 in 2006 and 617 in 2012. Although the number of judges at the Court of Justice and the General Court has increased with the accession of new Member States in recent years, the output of judgments from the two Union courts has not kept pace with the increased input of cases, in particular as regards the General Court. This has led to a backlog of cases before this latter court and increased the duration of proceedings beyond acceptable limits. The Court of Justice recently found, for example, that a duration of nearly 60 years for a competition case was incompatible with the requirements of Article 47 of the Charter.[1]

In this difficult context, both the Court of Justice and the General Court are studying means to address their workload problem. Both courts have taken internal organisational measures to increase efficiency. Productivity and efficiency are also two of the objectives of the new rules of procedures of the Court of Justice which entered into force in autumn 2012. New rules for the General Court are currently being discussed between the latter and the Court of Justice pursuant to the fifth paragraph of Article 254 TFEU. Irrespective of the outcome of these efficiency enhancing measures, both courts consider that purely internal reforms will not suffice to address the workload problem and that more structural solutions are required. However, the General Court and the Court of Justice do not seem to agree on the precise nature of these structural reforms. The General Court considers that setting up a specialised tribunal for trademark cases, on the basis of Article 257 TFEU, is the most efficient solution to lighten its workload and to shorten the average duration of its proceedings. The Court of Justice rejected this option and has proposed, pursuant to Articles 254 and 281 TFEU, an increase in the number of judges of the General Court.[2] It should be noted that the Court of Justice presented this proposal on behalf of the ECJ.

The diverging views as to the proper functioning of the institution to which they belong, raises the question of the legitimacy of the powers of the Court of Justice to represent this institution. This paper will suggest solutions as to how these representational and governance problems can be overcome. It will plead in favour of the creation of a High Council of the European Judiciary that will bear the final responsibility for the governance of the ECJ. Such a body, whose potential powers are already allocated to a variety of different bodies, could ultimately develop into an authority which could combine the European and national judiciaries, and could act as a counterweight, by analogy to Montesquieu's trias politica, to the increasingly integrated executive and legislative powers that characterise today's decision-making organisms within the Union.

These explorative ideas and proposals will be developed as follows. The first section of this paper concerns the provisions of primary and secondary EU law that relate to the governance of the ECJ. The second section highlights the legal and practical difficulties resulting from the lack of clarity prevalent in the current system, which are exacerbated in times of budgetary constraints. The third section deals with the proposal for the creation of a High Council of the European Judiciary, which would not only regroup current administrative powers and activities, but would also have the final say in the management of the ECJ. The fourth and final section contains some concluding remarks.

---

[1] *Groupe Gascogne*, Case C-58/12, 23 November 2013.

[2] See for an overview of the discussions concerning this proposal: European Union Committee of House of Lords, 16th Report on the Workload of the Court of Justice 2013, http://www.parliament.uk.

2 The ECJ and Its Jurisdictions

2.1 The Treaties

Article 13 of Title III of the Treaty of the European Union specifies that its institutional framework consists of seven institutions. This Title subsequently lays down the main organisational provisions of these institutions. The level of detail differs per institution. For example, Title I does not contain provisions on the functioning of the European Central Bank and the Court of Auditors. Also, the institutional provision dealing with the ECJ (Article 19) does not contain any rules on the nomination of its president, unlike the provisions dealing with the European Parliament (Article 14), the European Council (Article 5), the Council (Article 16) and the Commission (Article 17).

The first paragraph of Article 19 states that the ECJ shall include three types of jurisdictions: the Court of Justice, the General Court and specialised courts. Its second paragraph briefly describes the professional qualifications that the judges of the Court of Justice and the General Court must possess as well as the appointment procedure by a common accord of the governments of the Member States. It also follows from this paragraph that the number of judges of these jurisdictions may differ. The Court of Justice shall consist of one judge per Member State, whereas the number of judges of the General Court is left more open as the provision states only that it shall include at least one judge per Member State. The third and last paragraphs of Article 19 also give a brief overview of the type of actions that can be brought before the ECJ.

Article 19 TEU thus makes a clear distinction between the institution, which is the ECJ, and the three types of jurisdictions which it encompasses, but it does not contain any rule on the governance or administration of the institution. The same holds true for the Treaty on the Functioning of the European Union. Here again, this Treaty contains detailed provisions on the governance and voting procedures of all other institutions, including the European Central Bank and the Court of Auditors, but remains silent as regards the governance of the ECJ.

Articles 251–253 TFEU relate to the functioning of the Court of Justice and deal with the composition of its chambers (Article 251), the role of its advocates general (Article 252) and the appointment procedures of its members and its president, who shall be elected by the judges for a period of three years (Article 253). All these provisions refer to the Statute of the ECJ for further details. In addition, Article 253 provides that the Court of Justice shall establish Rules of Procedure that require the approval of the Council.

Article 254 concerns the organisation of the General Court. Its provisions mirror those relating to the Court of Justice. The major differences relate to the number of judges that shall be determined by the Statute and the absence of permanent advocates general. In addition, the Rules of Procedure of the General Court must be established together with the Court of Justice before they are submitted for approval to the Council.

An organisational provision that is relevant for both the Court of Justice and the General Court can be found in Article 255 TFEU. It concerns the appointment procedure for the judges and advocate generals. Article 255 TFUE sets up an advisory panel that shall give an opinion on the suitability of the candidates proposed by the Member States. This so-called Article 255 Committee is composed of seven individuals chosen from among former members of the Court of Justice and the General Court, members of national supreme courts and lawyers of recognised expertise. One of its members shall be proposed by the European Parliament. The Committee shall act on the initiative of the President of the Court of Justice.

Article 257 TFEU deals with the third category of jurisdictions that compose the ECJ. It allows the European Parliament and the Council to adopt regulations setting up, at the request of the Commission or the Court of Justice, specialised courts to be attached to the General Court. These courts are competent to rule in first instance on certain specific areas of law. Their decisions are subject to right of appeal on points of law before the General Court. The specialised courts shall establish their rules of procedure in agreement with the Court of Justice and shall require the approval of the Council. Until now, only one specialised jurisdiction exists. It is the court which is competent to judge in EU staff cases.

Finally, special mention should be made of Article 281 TFEU. As specified above, the organisational provisions of the TFEU refer to the Statute for further details, which is laid down in a separate protocol attached to the Treaty. Article 281 TFEU provides that the major part of this Statute can be amended by the European Parliament and the Council at the request of the Court of Justice or on proposal by the Commission.

It follows from this overview that, within the ECJ, the Court of Justice has certain rights reserved relating to the proper functioning of the institution. First, it has the right to request opinions of the Article 255 Committee as regards candidates for membership of both the Court of Justice and the General Court. Second, it has a say in the rules of procedure of the General Court and the specialised courts. Third, it has the right to request the European Parliament and the Council to set up specialised courts and/or to amend the Statute. However, the Treaty on the Functioning of the EU does not define the presidency of ECJ. Nor does it explain how the three types of jurisdictions are supposed to cooperate to reach a common view on the functioning of their institution and on the allocation of the resources available.

2.2 The Statute and the Rules of Procedure

A study of the Statute does not give greater insight into these governance issues. On the contrary, it further blurs the picture as to the functioning of the ECJ and its services. Indeed, none of its five titles deals with the issue of the presidency and governance of the ECJ. The first title of the Statute deals with the appointment and impartiality conditions of judges and advocates general of all three jurisdictions. The second and third titles concern, respectively, the organisation of, and the procedure before, the Court of Justice. The fourth title relates to the General Court. The fifth and final title contains some final provisions. The provisions on the specialised courts are contained in an Annex to which title IV refers. Until now, the Civil Service Tribunal is the only specialised court which has been established.

Nonetheless, Title I of the Statute offers some guidance on the respective roles which the three jurisdictions are expected to play within their common institution. According to Title I, the Court of Justice bears the final responsibility for deciding on the aptitude of the judges of all three courts. The Courts of Justice also decide on issues relating to their immunity, additional professional occupations, as well as on the resignation and dismissal of the members of all three jurisdictions (Articles 2–8 of the Statute).

The other titles are less clear, however. Article 12 of Title II of the Statute provides that officials and other servants shall be attached to the Court of Justice to enable it to function and that these individuals shall be answerable to the Registrar of the Court of Justice under the authority of its President. This wording suggests that the Court of Justice draws on human resources employed by the institution, which places personnel within the Court of Justice according to its needs. This wording seems to contrast with Article 52 of Title IV which states that the Presidents of the Court of Justice and the General Court shall determine the conditions under which the staff attached to the Court of Justice shall render services to the General Court. In other words, the General Court does not have any human resources and cannot address itself to the institution, but must rely on whatever capacity the Court of Justice is willing to grant. At the same time, Article 52 also specifies that certain officials shall report to the Registrar of the General Court under the authority of the President of this Court. So it is unclear whether the Court of Justice and General Court each have their own staff, or whether the staff are in fact employed by the ECJ and then put at the disposal of both jurisdictions or whether the staff are under the control of the Court of Justice and attached to it as well as the General Court.

The situation is even less clear when reading the Annex on specialised courts. Article 6 states that the Civil Service Tribunal shall be supported by the departments of the Court of Justice and those of the General Court. The President of the Court of Justice, or "in appropriate cases" the President of the General Court, shall determine with the President of the Civil Service Tribunal the conditions under which staff attached to the Court of Justice or the General Court shall render services to the Civil Service Tribunal. This formula is hard to reconcile with the interpretation of Article 52, according to which the General Court does not have its own resources or departments. Moreover, Article 6 of the Annex indicates that the Civil Service Tribunal, like the General Court, does have its own staff. Indeed, it states, just as Article 52 does for the General Court, that certain officials shall be answerable to the Registrar of the Civil Service Tribunal under the authority of the President of that Tribunal.

The Statute does not provide an unequivocal answer to the question of the relationship between the staff of the ECJ and the staff attached to each of the three jurisdictions and/or the relationship between the staff attached to the Court of Justice and the personnel that falls under the authority of the Presidents of the General Court and the Civil Service Tribunal. Even if Title I of the Statute confirms the leading role of the Court of Justice on the issue of deciding upon the suitability of the members of the ECJ to fulfil their judicial tasks, the Statute does not provide any clear guidance on the governance of the institution as a whole and the personnel that it employs. Nor does it contain any provision on the budgetary authority of the ECJ.

The new Rules of Procedure, which the Court of Justice established on the basis of Article 253 TFEU, and, in particular Article 9 thereof, further add to the confusion. This provision concerns the responsibilities of the President of the Court of Justice. The third paragraph deals with the relationship between the Court and its services. According to the English version of this provision, the "President shall ensure the proper functioning of the services of the Court". This corresponds to the text of Article 12 of the Statute: staff shall be allocated to the Court to enable its proper functioning. However, the versions of the Rules of Procedure in the other languages of the Union do not correspond to the English version. They state that the President of the Court is in charge of the services of the institution. They have the merit of being clear—the Court of Justice is in charge of the ECJ and its services—but go beyond the text of the Statute which remains silent on the precise relationship between the Court and the institution.

2.3 Conclusions

It follows from this overview that the governance of the ECJ is not clearly regulated by EU law. The Treaties make a distinction between the institution and its three jurisdictions but do not explain how this institution is supposed to function and, in particular, how its resources are supposed to be shared. The Statute contains some equivocal provisions on this issue, suggesting, on the one hand, that all resources are attached to the Court of Justice, and, on the other hand, that the other two jurisdictions have their own resources. With the exception of the English version, the recently adopted Rules of Procedure of the Court of Justice rely on the first of these two options.

By contrast, it is clear that the Treaties and the Statute confer on the Court of Justice a leading role as regards assessing the aptitude of the members of the ECJ to fulfil their judicial duties (Article 255 TFEU and Title I of the Statute), presenting legislative proposals regarding the reform of all three jurisdictions (Articles 257 and 281 TFEU) and adopting new rules of procedure. It is equally clear that neither the Treaties nor the Statute contain provisions on the Presidency and administration of the ECJ.

3 The Lack of Clarity and the Ensuing Difficulties

The lack of clarity as regards the governance of the ECJ causes a number of practical and legal problems.

3.1 Access to Resources

The first category of problems is relatively basic. The Court of Justice de facto controls all the resources of the institution and its budget. As a matter of fact, the ECJ and the Court of Justice are considered as one and the same entity. This has consequences for the other two jurisdictions. For example, the research and documentation department almost exclusively works for the Court of Justice. This can be explained to some extent by the fact that that the other jurisdictions do not have the same needs as the Court of Justice as regards in-depth research of national law issues. Similarly, decisions as regards priority access to the translation services are taken by the Court of Justice. More generally, when administrative decisions have to be made, such as IT-related choices, the Court of Justice has the final say. It should be emphasised that the choices which fit the Court of Justice do not necessarily fit the other two jurisdictions. Their judicial functions differ and these differences also affect their administrative needs. For example, many cases brought before the General Court are voluminous and involve many parties that raise all sorts of diverging confidentiality claims. Processing these types of case requires other administrative tools and skills than those required for the treatment of preliminary reference procedures.

Generally speaking, the Court of Justice has been conscious of its responsibility for the proper functioning of the administration as a whole. It occasionally involves the other two jurisdictions in its decision making. In the vast majority of cases, the internal consultation procedures lead to acceptable solutions. However, the tensions arising out of conflicting interests may increase in times of budget cuts. The reduction of expenditure affects the institution as a whole, but there is no institutional guarantee that they equally affect all three jurisdictions. There is no independent arbiter to balance their individual needs. It can therefore not be excluded that the proper functioning of one of the jurisdictions will be jeopardised. If deadlines can no longer be met or answers to parties cannot be given on time, the judicial machinery cannot deliver the type of justice that Article 47 of the Charter requires.

3.2 Conflicting Interests

The requirements of Article 47 of the Charter are also important when assessing the second type of problems to which the absence of clear governance rules gives rise. These problems concern the conflicts between, on the one hand, the interests of the institution as an administrative body, and, on the other hand, its duty to render justice impartially. These tensions may affect various areas of law, such as staff cases involving officials of the ECJ, public procurement procedures organised by the ECJ, contracts concluded by the institution, disciplinary measures involving judges of the three jurisdictions and requests for access to the ECJ's administrative documents. In all these situations, the Court of Justice may be called upon to rule on the legality of its own administrative behaviour.

Even if the Court of Justice manages to find practical solutions to work around these issues, for example by appointing judges to preside over cases who were not personally involved in the decision making at the centre of the dispute, the institutional problem remains that the Court of Justice is party and judge in its own case. The question as to whether this situation complies with Article 6 ECHR will become particularly compelling once the EU has joined the European Convention on Human Rights. This accession will imply that the Court of Justice will no longer have the final say as regards its impartiality on issues concerning the conduct of the ECJ. In matters falling within the ambit of Article 6, that power will no longer lie in Luxembourg, but in Strasbourg. It should also be noted that the impartiality requirements, as interpreted by the case law of the European Court on Human Rights are relatively high: any appearance of bias or legitimate doubts as to the independence of judges should be avoided.[3]

3.3 Representation

The question as to the independence of the EU courts also arises when the Court of Justice exercises its powers to represent the institution before the legislator. First, one could argue that this issue affects all three jurisdictions when the Court of Justice seeks the Council's approval for their rules of procedure. This right of approval, laid down in Articles 253 and 254 TFEU, implies that one of the parties (the Council), which regularly acts as a defendant in proceedings before the Court of Justice and the General Court, decides on the rules under which it will be judged. Although rules of procedure are limited in scope, some may consider that such a right conflicts with the principle of equality of arms between the parties.

The second issue concerns the power of the Court of Justice to propose changes to the Statute pursuant to Article 281 TFEU. Although the Court of Justice presents these proposals in the interest of the ECJ, views as to what these interests are may differ among the three jurisdictions. The reaction to the recent proposal concerning the increase of the number of judges at the General Court offers an example of such diverging views. In addition, the discussion concerning this proposal did not only concern the backlog of cases at the General Court, but also had a jurisdictional dimension. Indeed, the option put forward by the General Court in favour of a specialised trade mark court implies, according to Article 257 TFEU, that the Court of Justice loses its power to rule on appeal in trademark cases. Here again, institutional and jurisdictional issues are sometimes hard to separate.

---

[3]See for example, *Procola v. Luxembourg*, Case 14570/89, 28 September 1995: "That doubt in itself, however slight its justification, is sufficient vitiate the impartiality of the tribunal in question" (ground 45).

3.4 Conclusion

None of the issues described above give rise to immediate concern as to the proper functioning of the ECJ under the system as it has existed since 1952. The Court of Justice has until now managed rather well to compensate for the structural deficiencies resulting from the lack of clear governance rules of the ECJ. Even so, these structural issues do need to be addressed for various reasons. As mentioned above, in times of budgetary constraints, there is a need for an independent arbiter that ensures in a neutral and transparent manner that funds and resources are effectively allocated there where they are most needed. More fundamentally, the accession of the EU to the ECHR and compliance with Article 6 thereof would be better served if the governance of the ECJ were separated from its jurisdictions. In other words, the governance system set up in 1952 must be modernised so as to meet today's needs and requirements.

4 Towards a High Council of the European Judiciary

4.1 Not a Unique Problem …

The governance problem faced by the ECJ is not unique. Throughout Europe, states have sought to organise their judiciary in a more independent manner.[4] Although the concerns underlying these reforms mostly related to the strained relationship between the executive power and the judiciary, European States have acknowledged the need for judges to be able to work in an independent, impartial and efficient manner. Various initiatives have been developed at the level of the Council of Europe to that effect. Particular reference should be made to Recommendation CM/Rec.(2010)12 of the Committee of Ministers of 17 November 2010 and the Magna Carta of Judges adopted on the same date by the Consultative Council of European Judges. These texts underline the importance not only of their organisational independence, but also of their financial one. Similarly, hierarchical judicial organisation should not undermine the independence of individual judges.[5] One of the safeguards proposed by these texts concerns the creation of Councils for the Judiciary, composed of "judges chosen by their peers from all levels of the judiciary and with respect for pluralism inside the judiciary".

In the USA, similar measures have already been put into place since the 1920s. The Judicial Conference of United States is the policy maker for the administration of US Courts.[6] It is chaired by the Chief Justice of the Supreme Court and

---

[4] Wim Voermans and Pim Albers, Report for the European Commission for the Efficiency of Justice, Council of Europe, March 2003.

[5] Rule 22 of the Recommendation.

[6] http://www.uscourts.gov/FederalCourts/JudicialConference.aspx. Accessed 20 December 2014.

consists of 26 members, including the chief judge of each court of appeals, one district court judge from each regional circuit and the chief judge of the Court of International Trade. It operates through special committees, dealing with issues such as budget management, rules of procedure and court administration.

A more recent example of independent court management is offered by the draft agreement and draft statute on the Unified Patent Court. These statutory texts also provide for clear governance rules that separate administrative and budgetary issues from jurisdictional ones. These managerial issues are dealt with by a presidium that acts under the auspices of various committees. This presidium would be composed of the President of the Court of Appeal, who would act as chairperson, the President of the Court of First Instance, two judges of the Court of Appeal elected from among their number, three judges of the Court of First Instance who would be full-time judges of the Court elected from among their number, and the Registrar as a non-voting member.

It is submitted below that these various models could serve as an example to modernise the functioning of the EU courts.

4.2 … But a Unique Opportunity

Obviously, changing the governance rules of the EU Courts requires amending the Treaties and the Statute. The last two Treaty revisions have shown that the European public is not very keen on new European Union adventures. However, the EU integration or disintegration process is in continuous movement and its legal instruments need to be continually revised to match the economic and political realities of the Union. Whatever road the EU will take, the EU Treaties have to be revised in the medium or long term.

Upon a future revision, the rules on the functioning of the European judiciary should be modernised. This modernisation exercise should in my view not be confined to the relatively modest problem of the governance of the ECJ described above. On the contrary, the reform of the ECJ should be placed in the wider context of reinforcing the European judiciary as a whole by giving it additional weight as a judicial pillar countervailing the powers of the European executive and legislature. These latter two powers are increasingly integrated. The myriad of councils, groups, committees and expert forums combined with the decentralised system of application of EU law by national administrations make it nearly impossible to define where the powers of the national administration stop and those of the EU one begin. Even if the divide between national parliaments and the EU one is clearer, the two increasingly interact, as illustrated by the first protocol on the role of national parliaments in the Union.

By contrast, the European judiciary is relatively disintegrated. Even if the mechanism of Article 267 TFEU allows national courts to interact with the Court of Justice, the preliminary reference procedure is a one-way street in the sense that national courts ask questions to the Court of Justice, but do not allow the latter to refer issues to its national counterparts. Nor do national and EU courts share a common platform to discuss the functioning of the preliminary reference mechanism. The idea that the national judge is also an EU judge is an abstract one developed in legal writings, but has not been fully implemented in practical terms.[7] Where national courts are confronted with issues involving the legality of EU measures, the Court of Justice seems relatively reluctant to confer these courts an important role.[8]

In order to strengthen cohesion between Europe's magistrates, it could be envisaged to involve the national judiciary in the administration of the ECJ so as to make this institution their own court and to create a common body of the European judiciary. In line with the recommendations of the Council of Europe, the next Treaty revision may offer the opportunity to set up a High Council of the European Judiciary in which the ECJ is included.

4.3 Yet Another Institutional Body?

One may object to this idea that the EU already has too many institutions, organisations, agencies, councils and committees and that there must very compelling reasons to create yet another body. This objection is relatively easy to rebut. The High Council of the European Judiciary does not have to lead to additional public activities and expenditure. On the contrary, this High Council could regroup existing tasks and activities in a more structured and efficient manner and develop new activities that should lead to more informed decision making by the EU legislator.

Most of these existing tasks have already been referred to above. They concern the role of the 255 Committee, the adoption of the rules of procedure of the three EU jurisdictions (Articles 253, 254 and 257 TFEU), the management of the ECJ (Article 19 TEU) as well as its external ECJ representation (Article 281 TFEU). New tasks would essentially concern the representation of the EU Judiciary and an advisory role as regards judicial impact assessment (see below). As regards the first of these two activities, the High Council of the European Judiciary would formally take over the role which is already played informally by, on the one hand, ACA-Europe, which stands for the Association of Councils of State and Supreme Administrative Jurisdictions of the European Union, and on the other hand, the Network of the Presidents of the Supreme Judicial Courts of the European Union.[9]

---

[7]See for example Rosas 2012.

[8]Judgments of the Court of Justice of 22 October 1987, Case C-314/85, *Foto Frost* and 22 October 2002, Case C-9400, *Roquette Frères*.

[9]ACA-Europe. http://www.aca-europe.eu/index.php/en/. Accessed 4 March 2015. and the Network http://www.network-presidents.eu. Accessed 20 December 2014.

By contrast, judicial impact assessment is an activity that does not exist today at Union-level. This activity relates to advice to the EU legislator on the impact that new legislative measures may have on the judiciary and the additional costs which these activities entail for the judiciary and hence for the European tax-payer.[10] The absence of such opinions can lead to situations which the legislator not only did not envisage but also ones which he may have considered undesirable and or which would have led him to adopt other decisions. A typical example of a legislative measure that was adopted without a proper impact assessment is the Community trademark regulation. Litigation under this regulation now accounts for nearly 40 % of incoming cases at the General Court. This massive inflow prompted this court to propose a specialised trademark court within the meaning of Article 257 TFEU. Had the legislator been informed of this clog-up effect, he may have opted for another system of judicial review in trademark cases.[11] In other words, judicial impact assessment may have saved unnecessary legal costs.

It follows that a High Council of the European Judiciary should merely regroup existing activities and that any activity, such as judicial impact assessment, must be geared towards well-informed and more efficient decision making. Moreover, my proposal does not necessarily require the setting up of new bodies. From an administrative point of view, the secretariat of the High Council of the European Judiciary could replace the administration of the Article 255 Committee, which includes members of the supreme courts, the EU-sponsored secretariat of ACA-Europe in Brussels and the Paris office of the Network. It could be located in the offices of the ECJ in Luxembourg.

This leads to me to the role which the High Council of the European Judiciary should fulfil as regards the governance of this institution.

4.4 The ECJ as the Court of All European Judges

As explained in Sect. 2 above, there are various practical and legal reasons why the administration of the ECJ should be separated from its jurisdictions. It was also submitted, in the above Sects. 3.1–3.3, that the review of the governance of the ECJ could be embedded in a wider project aimed at reinforcing the coherence among the European Judiciary through the creation of a High Council of the European Judiciary. I will first develop some tentative ideas and suggestions for the internal governance of the ECJ and then explain those concerning the role of the High Council.

With respect to the functioning of the ECJ, the idea is to confer the responsibility of the management of the ECJ to an independent and neutral presidium. This

[10] See for example the judicial impact assessment opinions by the Raad voor de Rechtspraak in the Netherlands: 'wetgevings en beleidsadvisering' on www.rechtspraak.nl. Accessed 4 March 2015.

[11] See Van der Woude 2012.

independency does not imply, however, that the three jurisdictions composing the ECJ should not play a role in the management of their institution. On the contrary, Rule 41 of Recommendation CM(2010)12 encourages judges to be involved in court management. These objectives can be achieved by giving all members of the three jurisdictions, including its advocate generals, the right to elect a candidate for the presidency of the ECJ. Preferably this candidate should be an existing or former member of the Court of Justice, as it is the Union's highest jurisdiction. This candidate would become the President of the ECJ with the approval of the majority of the High Council of the European Judiciary (see below). If so, this person would have to resign as a judge so as to be dedicated solely to the management of the ECJ. He or she would be seconded by a Secretary General appointed by the High Council. These elected individuals, together with the Presidents of the three jurisdictions, would form the Presidium of the ECJ.

The President of the ECJ, assisted by the other members of the Presidium, would thus represent the institution in all administrative and legislative matters, such as the procedures foreseen for the adoption of the rules of procedure (Articles 253, 254 and 257 TFEU), the setting up of new specialised courts (Article 257 TFEU) and amendments to the Statute of the ECJ (Article 281 TFEU). It is submitted that this independent and neutral management will ensure an allocation of the ECJ's increasingly scarce resources in the interest of the institution as a whole and not on the basis of the views of one of its jurisdictions. This neutrality also applies to any legislative proposal regarding the reform of the institution. Last but not least, independent management in administrative decision making implies that the body taking these decisions is no longer the same as the jurisdiction that is supposed to rule on their legality.

The High Council of the European Judiciary, that will appoint the President and Secretary General of the ECJ along the lines set out above, would be composed of representatives of the supreme administrative and civil courts of the Member States and would, in addition to these nomination tasks, be in charge of the following tasks. First, the High Council would fulfil the role currently played by the Article 255 Committee as regards the suitability of the candidates which the Member States propose as EU judges. Second, it would approve the rules of procedure of the three jurisdictions. This implies that these rules would no longer be adopted by the Council which is one of the parties regularly appearing before the ECJ.

Apart from taking over these tasks which are identified in the Treaties itself, the High Council could contribute to better and more informed decision making by giving opinions on the judicial impact of important legislative proposals which may lead to increased litigation, as well as on Treaty amendments likely to have effects for the judiciary. Also, the High Council would be a platform for assessing the proper functioning of the preliminary reference procedure and for appointing national 'liaison judges' in EU-related matters. In the same vein, the High Council would facilitate the exchange of information between the EU courts as regards jurisprudential developments and any other element of common interest. This could imply that the High Council becomes a member of the European Network of

Councils for the Judiciary and maintains close ties with the European Judicial Network, as set up by Council Decision 2008/976/JHA of 16 December 2008.[12]

Finally, the High Council of the European Judiciary should be the voice of the EU judiciary as an integrated third pillar that, irrespective of the divide between national and EU powers, speaks up at each occasion where the rule of law is threatened in the Union. Recent events in some Member States illustrate that such occurrences are not purely hypothetical.

5 Concluding Remarks

The ECJ has played since 1952 an important role in guaranteeing the rule of law in the European Communities and Union. It has protected the legal foundations of the internal market and the rights of EU citizens. With the widening powers allocated to Union institutions and the development of EU law, the ECJ has had to be adapted on various occasions to meet its increasing workload. New courts have grown under the ECJ's institutional framework since 1989, but its institutional structure has remained the same since 1952.

One of the ECJ's new courts now faces major difficulties in dealing with cases within a reasonable time period. In addition, times of budgetary constraints require the three jurisdictions of the ECJ to do more with less. These constraints also imply that resources should be shared amongst the three jurisdictions. This calls for neutral decision making which the present governance structure does not necessarily guarantee. Workload and budgetary problems are not the main reason why the 1952 management structure needs to be revised, however. As a large institution employing over two thousand officials the ECJ is itself involved in legal issues. In order to avoid any doubt as regards the neutrality of the ECJ in dealing with these issues, administrative and jurisdictional powers should be separated, especially after the accession of the EU to the ECHR.

Addressing these governance questions is not an urgent matter. The ECJ institutional structure can be modernised on the occasion of a future Treaty revision. But when this occasion occurs, the Member States should seize the opportunity to further integrate the European and national judicatures by seeking inspiration from other judicial models, such as the federal judicial conference in the USA. The ECJ could be embedded in a High Council of the European Judiciary which would appoint its President and Secretary General, give opinions on the suitability of the judges proposed by Member States and approve the rules of procedures of the three jurisdictions. It is submitted that this High Council does not entail any additional costs as it will mostly take over existing functions from various formal and informal organisations. It could also give opinions which will lead to better informed decision making by the EU legislator. The integration of the EU

[12]European Network for Councils of the Judiciary. www.encj.eu. Accessed 4 March 2015.

and national judiciaries into a judicial pillar would also contribute to recalibrate the system of checks and balances within the EU, where an already integrated European and national executive power plays a predominant role.

Case law

C-314/85, 22 October 1987, Court of Justice, *Foto Frost*
C-14570/89, 28 September 1995, Court of Justice, *Procola v. Luxembourg*
C-94/00, 22 October 2002, Court of Justice, *Roquette Frères*
C-58/12, 23 November 2013, Court of Justice, *Groupe Gascogne*

References

Rosas A (2012) The national judge as EU judge: opinion 1/09. In: Cardonnel P, Rosas A, Wahl N (eds) Constitutionalising the EU judicial system: essays in honour of Pernilla Lindh. Hart Publishing, London, pp 105–122

Van der Woude M (2012) Judicial Reform and Reasonable Delay. J Eur Compet Law Pract 3(2):123–125

How to Define the European Union?

Christiaan Timmermans

Abstract Academics disagree about how to define the EU as a form of cooperation between sovereign States. The identity of the Union has considerably changed, an evolution characterized by two opposing trends: diminishing ambitions with regard to the ultimate goal, a federal vocation now being explicitly excluded by Article 4(2) TEU; the justiciability of this Article starts to be confirmed by the case law of the ECJ. At the same time, the supranational element has been remarkably reinforced. One of the EU characteristics is its direct and intensive relationship with the citizens of the Member States. A Union of States and Citizens could be a possible definition but remains of only modest informative value. A more precise definition almost impossible, also because of the meandering evolution of the integration process as again illustrated by the EU and Member States' responses to solve the euro crisis.

Contents

Former Judge at the European Court of Justice, Luxembourg.

C. Timmermans (✉)
The Hague, The Netherlands
e-mail: chrtim@me.com

F.A.N.J. Goudappel and E.M.H. Hirsch Ballin (eds.), *Democracy and Rule of Law in the European Union*, DOI 10.1007/978-94-6265-066-4_7

1 Introductory Remarks

How to define the form of cooperation between sovereign states as established by the *European Communities, now, since the Treaty of Lisbon, the European Union, taking also* into account the ultimate goal of that cooperation? And what is that ultimate goal? These questions have occupied generations of European law specialists and political scientists. Many answers have been suggested. To quote a few: a prefederal construct, *Zweckverbände funktionneller Integration* (Hans Peter Ipsen),[1] *ein Staatenverbund von souveräne Staaten* (German *Bundesverfassungsgericht*),[2] a Constitutional Order of States (Alan Dashwood),[3] an organization of shared or pooled competences,[4] a Union of States and peoples, a Democratic polity of States and citizens.[5] Indeed, academics have not been able to agree on a definition or a qualification that could be generally accepted. There seems to exist a fairly general acceptance that the Union is to be distinguished from the "normal" international organization because of its institutional structure (European Parliament, European Commission, Court of Justice), the scope of its legislative and administrative powers, the characteristics of its system of legal protection and judicial review. The definition probably most often referred to is not a definition at all, because of being entirely neutral and nondescript: an organization *sui generis*.

What is in a name, one could say and has been said. Well, it covers an identity. What is the Union's identity?

1.1 The Search for an Appropriate Denomination

This identity has changed considerably over the past 60 years. The evolution in that respect is marked by two somewhat opposing trends. The first trend is one of ever diminishing ambitions with regard to the ultimate goal of the Union.

Did the Schuman Declaration of 1952 still refer to a European Federation "*(réaliser) les premières assises concrètes d'une federation européenne indispensable à la préservation de la paix*", this found only a faint echo in the ECSC Treaty insofar as it qualified the High Authority as of a supranational nature. However, that qualification was removed by a subsequent Treaty amendment, never to reappear.[6] The EEC and Euratom Treaties of 1957 carefully avoided indicating the end terms of the integration process. Moreover, the subsequent evolution of that process made the federal perspective even more dim. It is true that the Customs Union

[1]Ipsen 1972, p. 182.

[2]BVerfG 30 June 2009, 2 BvE 2/08 (*Lissabon*).

[3]Arnull et al. 2011, p. vii.

[4]Weiler 1982, p. 267.

[5]Hoeksma 2011.

[6]Article 9 ECSC amended by Article 9 of the 1965 Merger Treaty.

was achieved ahead of schedule but there was the 1965/66 crisis which was basically triggered by a debate on maintaining national sovereignty. It took 20 years, with the Single European Act of 1986, for the Council to be able to proceed to qualified majority voting, when allowed by the treaties, instead of systematically looking for consensus.

During the negotiation process leading up to the Maastricht Treaty of 1992 attempts were made to define the ultimate goal with a reference to the federal vocation, *la vocation fédérale* of the EU. That discussion was short-lived: the F-word was replaced by the misty, compromise formula of the fifth objective of the Union as being "to maintain in full the *acquis communautaire* and build on it" (Article B of the Treaty on the EU). However, that same provision announced the convocation of a new intergovernmental conference for another attempt to do better. What became of that was the Treaty of Amsterdam of 1997, which basically maintained that formula. So did the Treaty of Nice of 2000.

The debate on the ultimate goal flared up again when Joschka Fischer in his famous speech at the Humbold University in 2000 opened the discussion on a Constitution for Europe. The Constitution without explicitly defining the ultimate goal of integration went some way in bringing the Union closer to a federal construct by codifying the principle of primacy of Union law. Personally, I see a basic difference in having that principle enshrined in the Treaty and formally approved through Member States' ratification procedures, that is, by national Parliaments and/or referenda, and the Lisbon Treaty. The Lisbon Treaty confirms the status quo by referring in a Declaration to the case law of the ECJ as explained in a note of the Council's legal service.[7]

The Constitution has failed. The Lisbon Treaty now has deprived the Union of the constitutional symbols, the flag, the anthem and Europe day, Saint Schuman as it is usually referred to from within the institutions. (In practice nothing has changed, the symbols continue to be used.) However, in a way the Lisbon Treaty is more in line with the tradition of European integration: step by step, functionalist, no solemn proclamations of precise, ultimate goals but a rather pragmatic mix of the supranational and the intergovernmental.

However, with regard to the definition of the ultimate goal the Lisbon treaty brings one, important innovation (so did the Constitution) and that is the much more detailed obligation imposed on the Union by Article 4(2) TEU to respect Member States' national identities. It seems to me that this obligation as it has now been defined excludes any federal vocation of the Union, at least *de lege lata*. I shall come back to that. And finally, it is also noteworthy that the earlier mentioned, fifth objective of the Union (maintain and build upon the *acquis communautaire*), traces of which could still be found in the Constitution, has now completely disappeared from the Treaty texts.

Consequently, we may conclude from this short historical survey that the subsequent texts reveal a retrograde evolution as to the indication of the ultimate goal of

[7]Declaration No. 17 concerning primacy.

the integration process: from a reference to a federal vocation in the early days to the explicit exclusion of such a vocation at present.

At the same time, and that is the second trend characterizing past evolution, one observes a remarkable reinforcement of the supranational nature of the Union over the past 60 years. This sounds like a paradox: a federal vocation being finally excluded, at the same time the supranational element ever more increased. Well, the first might be the consequence of the second. When using the term supranational I refer to the development of the Union into an organization with autonomous authority *vis à vis* Member States because of disposing of its own regulatory and administrative powers and being equipped with the necessary instruments to enforce respect of what has actually been decided. To discern this accrual of the supranational element it is sufficient to compare the Treaty of Lisbon with the original EEC Treaty. To mention some elements:

A European parliament, directly elected, with real co-legislative powers in most policy fields and budgetary powers. It is certainly true that the Parliament has problems with its democratic legitimacy but this is not because of a lack of competences.

The Council (of Ministers) may at present in many more cases than previously decide with qualified majority, even on matters of criminal law and police cooperation.

The European Commission now has a right of initiative also on these matters.

An exclusive competence for the EU on monetary policy with regard to the euro (Article 3(1)(b) TFEU).

And then finally the Court of Justice. When considering the supranational element, obviously also the position of the Court should be taken into account. The Court in qualifying Union law as being generated by and forming part of an autonomous legal order, has been able to allow ever more generously the subjects of that order, including natural and legal persons, to invoke Union law and rights derived there from in the national courts, rights enforceable also against opposing national law irrespective of its status (principles of primacy of Union law and direct effect). The Court moreover has patiently and steadfastly construed the Union's legal system and reinforced its requirements as to legal protection and respect for the rule of law, including respect of fundamental rights and general principles of law, all this to the direct benefit of the citizen.

The Court indeed has given shape to the legal identity of the Union. The treaty of Lisbon has still enlarged the jurisdiction of the Court, notably in the field of the Common Foreign and Security Policy and criminal law.

It can hardly be contested that the supranational element has been strengthened over the years, lastly also by the Treaty of Lisbon. But this does not at all imply that we are more and more dominated by a new, foreign superpower called Brussels. 'Brussels', also implies we the citizens, our Ministers and civil servants controlled by our national parliaments, and the Members of the European Parliament we have elected.

Moreover, Member States continue to be the *Herren der Verträge*. And the intergovernmental elements in the decision-making procedures have not disappeared, on the contrary, they may even have increased. That concerns more particularly the ever more important role of the European Council, the institution bringing together Heads of state or Government together with its President and the President of the European Commission, originally not foreseen at all by the Treaties but now firmly embedded in the Treaties as the highest political authority of the Union (Article 15 TEU). Characteristic for the Union as an organization is precisely the unique combination of intergovernmental and supranational elements. That also seriously complicates finding an adequate definition.

But there exists still another factor complicating the issue. That concerns the increasingly important position of the citizens in the Union's legal system. There has always existed a direct relationship between the Union and the citizens of the Member States. Union law directly grants them rights and imposes obligations upon them. To enforce those rights and obligations they can address the national courts. Internal market rules, consumer, environmental, immigration, transport rules, still many more examples could be given. Since the Treaty of Maastricht Member States have made serious efforts to bring the Union closer to the citizen, for instance by introducing Union citizenship, by adopting an EU Charter of fundamental rights and finally transforming it into a mandatory instrument, by inserting into the EU Treaty an entirely new title (II) on democratic principles and providing for a citizens' initiative as a new mechanism of direct democracy within the Union (Article 11(4) TEU). The Charter proclaims in its preamble: "It (the Union) places the individual at the heart of its activities, by establishing the citizenship of the Union and by creating an area of freedom, security and justice." And indeed the Court has declared this citizenship to be destined being the fundamental status of nationals of the Member States and fleshed out the rights to be derived therefrom.[8] From more recent case law it follows that these rights can even be invoked in situations which at first sight seem to be purely internal to a Member State. That they were nevertheless considered to come within the scope of Union law was due to the fact that the Union citizens in question risked to lose in law or in fact that status.[9]

To some extent all this is not really new. Jean Monnet, the co-designer of the Schuman declaration already said: "*Nous ne coalisons pas des États, nous unissons des hommes*". I fear, however, that for most EU citizens these will be hollow phrases; worse even, the average European citizen might be totally ignorant of all this. He cannot be reproached for that. Who tells him? Habermas rightly observes in his *Zur Verfassung Europas*:

> Angesichts des unerhörten Gewichts der Probleme wäre zu erwarten, dass die Politiker endlich–ohne Wenn und Aber– die europäische Karten auf den Tisch legten und die Bevölkerung offensiv über das Verhältnis von kurzfristigen Kosten und wahrem Nutzen, also über die historische Bedeutung des europäischen Projektes aufklärten. (…) Vor diesem Schritt zucken alle beteiligten Regierungen (…) zurück. Viele biedern sich stattdessen an einen Populismus an.[10]

---

[8] Case C-184/99, *Grzelczyk* (2001) ECR I-6193, para 31.

[9] Case C-135/08, *Rottman* (2010) ECR I-1449, Case C-34/09, *Zambrano* (2011) ECR I-1177.

[10] Habermas 2011, p. 79.

Ultimately, I would think, this is also a responsibility of our educational system, at secondary school level. Courses on civics, general education about democracy, and the functioning of the State should also add a European dimension.[11]

We may conclude that the Union as to its institutional structuring and functioning is characterized by a mixture of intergovernmental and supranational elements. Moreover, it has a direct relationship with the citizens of the Member States. How to define it? As a "Staatenverbund" according to the German Bundesverfassungsgericht,[12] this qualification in itself is perhaps not incorrect but fairly incomplete. As lawyers we should look at the texts in the first place. Do the present treaties contain any useful elements to contribute to our discussion on how to define the Union? Yes, I think so. Let me mention four points:

It follows clearly from Article 1(1) TEU that the EU is first of all a Union of States ("the High Contracting Parties establish among themselves a EUROPEAN UNION").

The second paragraph of that same article, moreover, allows to add to that qualification a reference to the peoples, so a Union of States and Peoples ("an ever closer union among the peoples of Europe"). Personally, I would have no difficulty whatsoever to follow Hoeksma's suggestion to replace peoples by citizens.[13] Indeed, a quick look at the opening articles of the EU treaty suffices to ascertain that the citizens are direct addressees and thus subjects of the Union (fundamental rights; Title II on democratic principles: principle of equality of citizens, citizenship of the Union, principle of representative democracy, the new instrument of the citizens' initiative, etc.).

A third, interesting point within this context of how to qualify the Union is that the Lisbon Treaty obviously does not represent the end of the integration process. The ultimate goal has neither been reached nor defined. This clearly follows also from Article 1 TEU ("a new stage in the process of creating an ever closer union among the peoples of Europe").

Finally, and that is my fourth point, whatever that ultimate goal may be, it cannot be, as the Treaty now stands, a Union of a federal nature. That brings us back to Article 4(2) TEU. Did the corresponding article in the Maastricht Treaty only generally refer to the national identities of Member States, which the Union had to respect; that identity has now been defined by a reference to Member States' "fundamental structures, political and constitutional". Moreover, according to this article the Union shall respect the essential functions of the State, including ensuring its territorial integrity, maintaining law and order and safeguarding national security. This enumeration of state functions which by the way is not exhaustive, together with the reference to the fundamental constitutional and political structures indirectly defines the hard core of national sovereignty, which the Union may not affect. Thus, in a way, the notion of national sovereignty, which may be invoked to oppose a Union action, has been unionized.

[11] See Grimonprez 2014.

[12] See above n. 2.

[13] See above n. 5.

Is it justiciable? I would think so. The definition is not exhaustive, I admit. Of course, it would be hard to imagine that the ECJ would determine what the fundamental constitutional structures of a Member State are. Nevertheless, the provision clearly conveys the message that Member States' discretion to define their fundamental structures and State functions, which should be considered untouchable for Union action, is not unfettered. Moreover, the Article imposes an obligation on the Union and its institutions, an obligation of Union law, which the Court by its very mission to ensure respect of that law must abide by and enforce. Indeed, contrary to the situation under the Maastricht Treaty (and likewise under Amsterdam and Nice), the Court now has full jurisdiction with regard to the opening Articles (Title I) of the EU Treaty.

In the past the Court has been generous in allowing Member States to uphold national, also constitutional specificities and granting them a large margin of appreciation in that respect.[14] Already in the *Van Duyn* case, the Court acknowledged "that the specific circumstances which may justify recourse to the concept of public policy may vary from one country to another and from one era to another. The competent national authorities must therefore be allowed a margin of discretion within the limits imposed by the Treaty".[15] More recent case law further develops this consideration by stating that the need for, and proportionality of, a national measure protecting a legitimate public interest but restricting a fundamental freedom, are not excluded merely because one Member State has chosen a system of protection different from that adopted by another State.[16]

At the same time, the Court has consistently claimed the possibility to police the dividing line, an outer limit where the exercise of this margin of appreciation is considered to trespass on basic principles, such as those of non-discrimination and proportionality, or otherwise considered contrary to Union law. The most recent case law seems to indicate that the Court will follow a similar approach with regard to Article 4(2) TEU. Invoking that article is not automatically accepted but made subject to further scrutiny albeit cautiously and until now mostly indirectly.[17]

[14]See for instance Cases 41/74, *Van Duyn* (1974) ECR 1337, 379/87, *Groener* (1989) ECR 3967, C-36/02, *Omega Spielhallen* (2004) ECR I-9609.

[15]*Van Duyn*, above n. 14, para 18.

[16]*Omega Spielhallen*, above n. 14, para 38 with further references.

[17]See Cases C-208/09, *Ilonka Sayn-Wittgenstein* (2010) ECR I-3693, C-391/09, *Runevic-Vardyn* (2011) ECR I-3787, C-202/11 *Las* judgment of 16 April 2013 not yet published. Most explicit in that regard is *Runevic-Vardyn*. This judgment is also interesting because the Court does not consider the obligation under Article 4(2) TEU as of an absolute nature but as the expression of a specific interest that may have to be balanced with other interests like that of protecting a fundamental right. For a contrary view about who should have the final say about the interpretation of Article 4(2) TEU, see Von Bogdandy and Schill 2011, p. 1417. Cp. also the annotation of the *Sayn-Wittgenstein* judgment by Besselink 2012.

These few textual elements derived from the EU Treaty could be considered as rather supporting a definition of the Union as a Union of States and citizens. Moreover, they warrant the conclusion that there is still room for further progress of the integration process, albeit the road to a federal union has now been blocked. Of course there exists yet another reason for that impediment: that is the position of the German Constitutional Court. The *Bundesverfassungsgericht* may finally have approved the Lisbon Treaty but its reasoning leaves little room for a substantial further transfer of competences to the Union. And the influence of this Court on the negotiating position of the German government is important and understandably so. The past and present negotiations on the solution of the sovereign debt and banking crises give ample evidence of that. Whether we like it or not, there are occasions on which the Karlsruhe Court has a place at the table of the European Council.

2 Concluding Remarks

However, to define the Union as a Union of States and citizens does not seem to bring us much further. This definition does not really reveal the characteristics of the Union. One of its merits might be that at least it draws attention to the position and the role of the citizen in the EU legal system. But it remains indeed an almost impossible challenge to find a satisfactory definition of a Union that reflects a work in progress, an integration process that develops haltingly with stops and go and without a clear ultimate goal. This has always been a characteristic of what has now become the European Union. Further progress to more integration has only been made if and in so far this really appeared necessary and the advantages were obvious to all or the large majority. The German language has a forceful expression for such a situation: *Sachzwang*. Grand designs with regard to institutional restructuring have repeatedly failed.

The present financial, banking, and euro crises give a good illustration. Because of the pressure built up by these crises much has been achieved:[18] more discipline in the banking sector on the road to a Banking Union, a much stricter regime to keep national budgets and financial households under control, the fiscal compact, further steps to equip the Monetary Union with an effective financial crisis mechanism, more particularly the European Stability Mechanism (ESM) and its predecessor the European Financial Stability Facility. Much of this would have been considered impossible only a few years ago. The *Sachzwang* works, even if decision making is often excruciatingly slow and it must still be awaited whether the results will be sufficient.

What causes anxiety is that a number of these new instruments (Fiscal Compact, ESM) have not been based on the existing treaties. They are not part

[18]See, also for further references, Amtenbrink 2011, p. 429; Adamski 2012, p. 1319; Borger and Cuyvers 2012, p. 370; de Gregorio Merino 2012, p. 1613.

of Union law and do not benefit from the guarantees attached to Union law. This would have been possible but Member States pressured by Germany have preferred to create these instruments by concluding new, classic international treaties outside the EU framework but conferring at the same time some responsibilities to the European Commission and the Court (not the European parliament). A hybrid, institutionally tortuous construct. But this approach could at the same time be considered illustrative for the meandering evolution of the integration process.

Case law and legislation

Case law

European Court of Justice, 4 December 1974, 41/74, *Van Duyn* ECR 1337

European Court of Justice, 28 November 1989, 379/87, *Groener v. Minister for Education* ECR 3967

European Court of Justice, 20 September 2001, C-184/99, *Grzelczyk* ECR I-6193

European Court of Justice, 14 October 2004, C-36/02, *Omega Spielhallen* ECR I-9609

Bundesverfassungsgericht, 30 June 2009, 2 BvE 2/08, *Lissabon*

European Court of Justice, 2 March 2010, C-135/08, *Rottman* ECR I-1449

European Court of Justice, 22 December 2010, C-208/09, *Ilonka Sayn-Wittgenstein* ECR I-3693

European Court of Justice, 8 March 2011, C-34/09, *Zambrano* ECR I-1177

European Court of Justice, 16 April 2013, C-391/09, *Runevic-Vardyn* ECR I-3787

Legislation

European Court of Justice, Declaration No. 17, concerning privacy

References

Adamski D (2012) National power games and structural failures in the European macroeconomic governance. CMLRev 49:1319–1364

Amtenbrink F (2011) Naar een effectievere economische governance in de Europese Unie? SEW 2011:429–443

Arnull A et al (eds) (2011) A constitutional order of states? Essays in EU law in honour of Alan Dashwood. Oxford

Besselink L (2012) Annotation case C-208/09 Ilona Sayn-Wittgenstein. CMLRev 49(2):671–695

Borger V, Cuyvers A (2012) Het verdrag inzake stabiliteit, coördinatie en bestuur in de economische en monetaire unie: de juridische en constitutionele complicaties van de eurocrisis. Tijdschrift voor Europees en Economisch Recht 60(10):370–390

De Gregorio Merino A (2012) Legal developments in the economic and monetary union during the debt crisis: the mechanisms of financial assistance. CMLRev 49(5):1613–16451613

Grimonprez K (2014) The European dimension in citizenship education: unused potential of article 165 TFEU. EL Rev 39(1):3–26

Habermas J (2011) Zur Verfassung Europas. Ein Essay. Berlin

Hoeksma J (2011) The EU as a democratic polity in international law. In: Hoeksma J, Schoenmaker D (eds) A polity called EU, essays on the exercise of sovereignty in the EU and the euro area. Wolf Legal Publishers, Tilburg

Ipsen HP (1972) Europäisches Gemeinschaftsrecht. Hamburg
Von Bogdandy A, Schill S (2011) Overcoming absolute primacy: respect for national identity under the Lisbon treaty. CMLRev 48(5):1417–1453
Weiler J (1982) The community system: the dual character of supranationalism

Part II
Procedures

Negotiations in the Ordinary Legislative Procedure: The Perspective of the European Parliament

Anita Bultena

Abstract The ordinary legislative procedure of the EU consists of a process where the European Council proposes legislation and the European Parliament and the Council adopt it together. This codecision procedure was created by the Maastricht Treaty and balances three European interests: The European Parliament must protect the interests of the citizens; the Council must protect those of the Member States and the Commission must promote the general European Interest. The ordinary legislative procedure consists of three readings. First, the Commission submits a proposal to the EP and the Council. The plenary will then adopt or reject the proposal, with or without amendments. If the proposal cannot be adopted at the first reading, a second reading follows. The EP receives the Council's position and must make a decision within 3 months after that. If the proposal is still not adopted, a Conciliation Committee is composed, that has the task of reaching an agreement based on the positions of the EP and the Council. In the past years, a trend can be seen where more and more proposals are concluded in the first reading. This shows the flexibility of the codecision procedure and the willingness between institutions to cooperate. The author concludes by stating that the European Parliament has become a real actor within this ordinary legislative procedure. She, however, warns about the potential lack of transparency that can take place within these trilogue discussions between the EP, EC and the Council. The European Parliament has taken new procedural measures to address this issue.

Administrator, Committee on Civil Liberties, Justice and Home Affairs, European Parliament, Brussels.

A. Bultena (✉)
Committee on Civil Liberties, Justice and Home Affairs, European Parliament,
Brussels, Belgium
e-mail: anje.bultena@europarl.europa.eu

F.A.N.J. Goudappel and E.M.H. Hirsch Ballin (eds.), *Democracy and Rule of Law in the European Union*, DOI 10.1007/978-94-6265-066-4_8

Contents

1 Introduction

In view of democracy and the rule of law in the European Union, I thought it would be good to write about the European Parliament and its role as a negotiator in the ordinary legislative procedure, which in practice is still often referred to by its former name 'codecision' since this volume focuses on democracy. The ordinary legislative procedure and its dynamics remain a fascinating theme even after 20 years of application. Under the EEC Treaty of 1957, the Parliament was only consulted on proposals and its opinions could just be put aside. Thanks to different Treaty amendments, it now has become a full co-legislator with the Council. The interinstitutional negotiations in ordinary legislative procedure take place through so-called 'trilogue negotiations', which are not mentioned in the Treaty. These trilogues have become an important element in today's decision-making process. Having had the privilege of attending many of these negotiations, at different stages of the procedure (from first reading until conciliation), I gradually came to better understand the dynamics of this process. In this contribution, I would like to share some of my impressions.[1]

Under the ordinary legislative procedure, the European Parliament and the Council together adopt legislation proposed by the European Commission. It was the Maastricht Treaty which some 20 years ago[2] introduced the codecision procedure, which gave the European Parliament substantial influence on the

[1]The author wants to thank Steven Noë for his valuable comments. The views expressed, however, are strictly personal and solely the responsibility of the author and they do not necessarily reflect the view of the institution.

[2]On 5 November 2013, under the auspices of the vice-presidents for conciliation, Gianni Pittella, Aledo Vidal Quadrats and Georgio Papastamkos a conference on 20 years of codecision took place in the Parliament. A number of imminent speakers will comment on the codecision procedure (past, present and future).

decision-making process.[3] The ordinary legislative procedure involves balancing three legitimate interests at European level: it is the European Parliament's task to defend the citizens' interest, it is the Council's task to defend the interests of the Member States, and it is the European Commission's task to promote the general European interest. Negotiations are necessary to balance these interests and to reach agreement.[4] Codecision at its introduction mainly concerned the area of the internal market, including the free movement of persons. It also included some 'new areas' as environment and consumer protection, covering some fifteen Treaty articles in total. Its object was to address the wish of the European Parliament to participate in the decision-making process on an equal footing with the Council. Subsequent Treaty amendments (the Treaty of Amsterdam created 24 new provisions and the Nice Treaty created an extra 11) extended the scope of the codecision procedure, but the most substantial progress was made with the entry into force of the Lisbon Treaty in 1999. The European Parliament is now genuinely a co-legislator with the Council: 'The European Parliament shall, jointly with the Council, exercise legislative and budgetary functions (…).'[5]

Since the entry into force of the Lisbon Treaty, the ordinary legislative procedure applies to 85 areas of activities. The new competences are found in the area of freedom, security and justice, international trade, as well as in agriculture and fisheries. Under the ordinary legislative procedure, the Commission submits its proposal in parallel to the European Parliament and to the Council. Both institutions sign the final legislative act that is co-produced by the two parties. The ordinary legislative procedure may consist of up to three 'readings' and can be closed at each of these three stages. The Lisbon Treaty has not changed the former codecision procedure considerably. The European Parliament and the Council still adopt legislation together, the Council acting mostly by qualified majority, on a proposal from the Commission. One new post-Lisbon element is that it is not only the Commission that can propose legislative proposals. In specific cases legislation can also be adopted on the initiative of a group of Member States, on a recommendation from the European Central Bank, or at the request of the European Court of Justice. Another new element is the right for national parliaments to send the Presidents of the European Parliament, the Council, and the Commission a 'reasoned opinion' on draft legislative acts, indicating whether they comply with the principle of subsidiarity. Furthermore, the Treaty now states that the European Parliament adopts at first and second reading a 'position', as the Council does, and not just an 'opinion' (Article 294, para 3, TFEU).

This contribution starts in Sect. 2 by discussing the ordinary legislative procedure in theory, as set out in Article 294 of the TFEU. Section 3 discusses how the ordinary legislative procedure works in practice, highlighting the important

---

[3]Kapteyn-VerLoren van Themaat 1995, p. 268.

[4]See Huber, *forthcoming*.

[5]Article 14 of the Treaty on the European Union.

role of interinstitutional negotiations and early agreement. Then, Sect. 4 focuses on trilogue negotiations. Section 5 outlines some thoughts about transparency and democratic legitimacy of the procedure as applied in practice, and is followed by the conclusions (Sect. 6).

2 The Ordinary Legislative Procedure in Theory

The ordinary legislative procedure consists of the joint adoption by the European Parliament and the Council of a regulation, directive or decision on a proposal from the Commission (Article 289, para 1 TFEU). It is to be distinguished from the special legislative procedure, under which legislation is adopted by the European Parliament with the participation of the Council, or—more often—by the Council with the participation of the European Parliament (Article 289, para 2 TFEU). The ordinary legislative procedure may consist of up to three 'readings'.

2.1 First Reading

Nearly all legislation is adopted upon a proposal by the Commission. According to the Treaty, the Commission *'shall submit a proposal to the European Parliament and the Council'* (Article 294, para 2 TFEU). Within the European Parliament, a Commission proposal is referred to the 'responsible committee'. It depends on the subject matter which committee is responsible.[6] The responsible committee appoints a 'rapporteur' from a specific political group, whose main task is to lead the proposal through the different stages of the procedure. The rapporteur may propose amendments to the Commission proposal, which will be laid down in a 'draft report'. Members from other political groups may also propose amendments and these amendments will be put to the vote together, firstly at committee level (the outcome is a 'report') and then in the plenary. The plenary will then adopt the position of the European Parliament, rejecting or approving, with or without

[6]There are 22 standing committees that prepare the work of the plenary: Foreign Affairs (AFET), Subcommittee on Human Rights (DROI), Subcommittee on Security and Defence (SEDE), Development (DEVE), International Trade (INTA), Budgets (BUDG), Budgetary Control (CONT), Economic and Monetary Affairs (ECON), Employment and Social Affairs (EMPL), Environment, Public Health and Food Safety (ENVI), Industry, Research and Energy (ITRE), Internal Market and Consumer Protection (IMCO), Transport and Tourism (TRAN), Regional Development (REGI), Agriculture and Rural Development (AGRI), Fisheries (PECH), Culture and Education (CULT), Legal Affairs (JURI), Civil Liberties, Justice and Home Affairs (LIBE) Constitutional Affairs (AFCO), Women's Rights and Gender Equality (FEMM), Petitions (PETI) and one special committee Organised Crime, Corruption and Money Laundering (CRIM).

amendments, the Commission's proposal. During the first reading there are no time limits within which the European Parliament should adopt its position. It is possible, although rare that the Parliament rejects the Commission proposal at first reading.[7] Once the European Parliament has adopted its position at first reading, it shall communicate it to the Council (para 3). If the Council approves the European Parliament's position, i.e. if it accepts all amendments made by the European Parliament or agrees with the original proposal in case the European Parliament did not amend it, the act will be adopted in the wording which corresponds to the position of the European Parliament (Article 294, para 4, TFEU). If the Council is unable to fully accept the outcome of the European Parliament's first reading, it will adopt a 'Council position' and communicate that to the European Parliament (Article 294, para 5, TFEU). Both the Council and the Commission must inform the European Parliament fully of the reasons which led them to adopt their respective positions (Article 294, para 6, TFEU). During the first reading, the Commission may alter its proposal with a view to facilitating agreement (Article 293, para 2, TFEU).

2.2 *Second Reading*

If it proves impossible to adopt the act at first reading, a second reading follows. Within a period of 3 months after receiving the Council's position at first reading, the European Parliament must approve, reject or amend the Council's position. This period of 3 months can be extended by 1 month at the initiative of the European Parliament or the Council (Article 294, para 14, TFEU). If the European Parliament approves the Council position (this is called 'endorsement') or has not taken a decision, the act concerned shall be deemed to have been adopted in the wording which corresponds to the position of the Council (Article 295, para 7(a) TFEU). A simple majority of the members present during the vote in the plenary is sufficient to approve the Council's position. The European Parliament can also reject the Council's position; in this case the proposed act shall be deemed not to have been adopted. A rejection requires an 'absolute majority', that is a majority of the component members of the European Parliament (Article 294, para 7(b), TFEU).[8] Finally, the European Parliament can propose, by absolute majority, amendments to the Council's position. The amended text is forwarded to the Council and to the Commission, which shall deliver an opinion on those amendments (Article 294, para 7(c) TFEU). The Council then has a further 3 months (or four if there is an extension) to conclude the second reading. If the Council approves the amendments of the European Parliament, the act in question is adopted. If the Council does not approve all the amendments, its President will

[7]Rule 56 of Parliament's Rules of Procedure. See also Craig and de Burca 2011, p. 126.

[8]Currently (2015) this would be 384 votes in favour (out of total of 766 Members).

convene, in agreement with the President of the European Parliament, a meeting of the Conciliation Committee (Article 294, para 8 TFEU). The Council acts by a qualified majority, but it must act unanimously on the amendments on which the Commission has delivered a negative opinion (Article 294, para 9 TFEU).

2.3 Conciliation and Third Reading

The Conciliation Committee is composed of equal numbers of representatives of the Council and the European Parliament, and it has the task of reaching agreement on a joint text on the basis of the positions of the European Parliament and the Council at second reading. The Commission takes part in the proceedings of the Conciliation Committee but it can no longer formally influence the decision-making process.[9] If the Conciliation Committee does not approve a joint text, within six (or eight) weeks of being convened, the proposed act shall be deemed not to have been adopted. If the Conciliation Committee does approve the joint text, the European Parliament and the Council have a period of six (or eight) weeks to adopt the act. The European Parliament acts by a majority of the votes cast (simple majority) and the Council by qualified majority. If they fail to do so, the proposed act shall be deemed not to have been adopted.

3 The Ordinary Legislative Procedure in Practice: Negotiations and Early Agreements

The description of the ordinary legislative procedure above is not sufficient to fully understand how things work in practice. The Treaty does not mention what has become very important in practice: i.e. negotiations between the European Parliament, the Council, and the Commission. Reading Article 294 TFEU may give the impression that the Council only starts its work once it has received the position of the European Parliament. In reality, however, the Council also starts working when it receives a Commission proposal, and one of the Council's 'working parties'—composed of national officials, colleagues from the Council's general secretariat and highly specialised—will review the proposal in parallel with

[9]The task of the Conciliation Committee is not coming to an agreement on the amendments proposed by the European Parliament, but of reaching agreement on a joint text, that is a draft of the legislative proposal agreed in the conciliation meeting. It must be adopted at third reading by both Parliament and Council. Thus, provisions that have not been amended in second reading are not necessarily excluded from the discussions. See Case C-344/04, *Iata and ELFAA* [2006] ECR I-443, paras 57–59.

the responsible parliamentary committee.[10] Once the European Parliament has adopted a report and the Council working group has examined the proposal for the first time, interinstitutional negotiations may start (see Sect. 6), with a view to reaching a first reading agreement. If this proves possible, the European Parliament recommends to the parliamentary committee/plenary to endorse the compromise package as agreed with the Council, and the Council commits itself to approve this position.[11] The chair of COREPER shall forward details of the substance of the agreement by a letter to the chair of the relevant committee. The letter indicates the willingness of the Council to accept the outcome should it be confirmed by the vote in plenary.[12]

In the course of the first reading negotiations on the Regulation on macro-financial assistance to third countries—an international trade file—an interesting question came up. After several quite intensive rounds of trilogue negotiations, at a point where the European Parliament and the Council were about to strike a deal, the Commission decided to withdraw its proposal. The withdrawal was announced in a letter which only refers to Article 293 para 2 TFEU as its basis, without any further specifications. In informal meetings held afterwards it became clear that the withdrawal had to do with 'institutional' reasons related to the Commission's right of initiative. This exceptional event had quite an impact politically on the interinstitutional relations and questions were raised whether the Commission had the right to do this at this specific moment (it withdrew the proposal on the day the compromise would be sealed in trilogue). In my opinion, as the file was in first reading, the Commission could withdraw its proposal as one could argue that a withdrawal should be seen as the corollary of the right of initiative. However, Article 293, para 2, TFEU to which the Commission referred in its letter, does not provide for a withdrawal explicitly. As a withdrawal for institutional reasons is exceptional and here its timing was also quite unfortunate it would in my opinion have been appropriate, also in view of Article 296 TFEU and the (general) principle of loyal cooperation as set out in Article 4, para 3 TEU, that the Commission would have motivated its decision properly and formally.

It is only if no agreement can be found that the European Parliament will adopt a position that has not been previously agreed with the Council. In this situation, it can be safely excluded that the proposed act will be adopted at first reading. The negotiations will continue normally and if they prove successful, the result may be

---

[10]See http://www.consilium.europa.eu/council/council-configurations/list-of-council-preparatory-bodies?lang=en for a list of the Council's working parties (there are around 150 committees). Accessed 20 December 2014. Meetings of these Working parties are not open to EP Members or officials, the Commission, however, participates.

[11]An interesting case was what recently happened in the course of the negotiations on the car CO2 emission limits. An agreement between the Parliament and the Council was reached before summer, but in a highly unusual move, Germany reportedly blocked a Council vote to agree on the deal (because of concerns about the impact of the new rules on its car manufacturers).

[12]See para 14 of the Joint Declaration on the practical arrangements for the codecision procedure of 13 June 2007, OJ C 145 of 30 June 2007, p. 1.

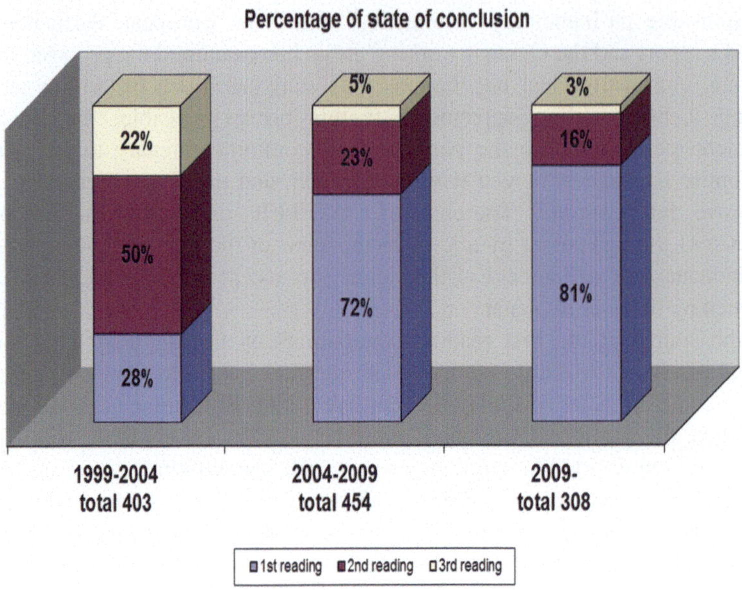

Fig. 1 Percentage of state of conclusion

a so-called 'early second reading agreement' where Council's position has been negotiated together with the European Parliament. In such a case a letter will be sent by the chair of the relevant parliamentary committee to the chair of COREPER. The chair shall indicate in this letter his recommendation to the plenary to accept the Council Position without amendments.[13] The advantage of negotiations in an (early) second reading for the European Parliament is that the Parliament's position is based on the plenary vote which provides for a broad mandate. If no agreement can be found, the Council will either adopt a Council position not agreed with the European Parliament, or it will not act at all (Fig. 1).

In recent years, more and more files tend to be concluded at an early stage of the procedure. So far in the current 7th legislature (2009-2014), 81 % of the files (308) have been concluded at first reading and 16 % at second reading, 10 % were 'proper' second readings and 6 % were so-called 'early second readings'. Only 3 % of the files went to conciliation. Thus, 87 % of the files were concluded at an early stage of the procedure. In comparison, during the 6th legislature (2004–2009), 72 % of the files (454) were first reading agreements, 23 % of the files second reading agreements, and 5 % went to conciliation. During the fifth legislature (1999–2004), 28 % of the files (403) were first reading agreements, 50 % second reading agreement, and 22 % went to conciliation.

[13]Joint Declaration on practical arrangements for the codecision procedure of 13 June 2007, para 18.

The question arises as to how this trend towards first reading agreements can be explained. One possible answer may be that there is an increasing familiarity with the ordinary legislative procedure—and in particular with the possibility of concluding negotiations in first reading following a simple majority vote in European Parliament by all institutions involved. Sometimes, it is also feared that files with controversial issues may be blocked in the Council. Also, there are more and better contacts between the institutions whose representatives start talking to each other earlier in the procedure. Furthermore, there is the agenda-setting at the highest level for politically sensitive issues. Finally, the Council Presidencies seem eager to reach agreements during their Presidencies and seem to favour first reading negotiations, for which the arrangements are more flexible than arrangements in later stages of the procedure (e.g. in the first reading there are no time limits). The European Parliament tends to try and use this eagerness and the internal debating in the Council to get better results in the negotiations. In addition, the Commission often pushes for an early adoption because it will be able to demonstrate efficiency and perhaps hopes that its proposal will be adopted with as few changes as possible.

4 Trilogue Negotiations[14]

The negotiations between the European Parliament, the Council, and the Commission take place in so-called 'trilogue meetings'. The practical role of these meetings is acknowledged in the 'Joint Declaration on the practical arrangements for the co-decision procedure' adopted by the three institutions,[15] which provides for practical guidelines on the different stages of the ordinary legislative procedure.[16] It reminds in its para 1 that the: 'current practice involving talks between the Council Presidency, the Commission and the chair of the relevant committees and or rapporteurs of the European Parliament has proven its worth. In para 2 the institutions confirm 'that this practice (…) "must continue to be encouraged" (…) with a view of making more effective use of the codecision procedure as established by the EC Treaty'. Paragraph 4 states: 'the institutions shall cooperate in good faith throughout the procedure with a view to reconciling their positions as far as possible and thereby clearing the way, where appropriate, for the adoption of the act concerned at an early stage of the procedure'.

[14]An interesting and short film can be found on the Website of the European Parliament at EuroparlTV: 'How it works: trilogue'. http://europarltv.europa.eu/en/player.aspx?pid=772450bd-0a08-4555-8946-a18d00ef94b2. Accessed 22 December 2014.

[15]OJ C 148, 28 May 1999, p. 1 (updated in 2007).

[16]Joint Declaration of the European Parliament, the Council and the Commission on the practical arrangements for the codecision procedure, OJ C 145 of 30 June 2007, p. 1.

Paragraph 7 of the Joint Declaration states that: 'the cooperation between the institutions in the context of codecision often takes the form of tripartite meetings ('trilogues'). Such trilogues are usually conducted in an informal framework. They may be held at all stages of the procedure and at different levels of representation depending on the nature of the expected discussion (…)'.[17]

These trilogues have become a crucial element in the interinstitutional cooperation. The importance is also underlined in the Joint Declaration '… This trilogue system has demonstrated its vitality and flexibility in increasing significantly the possibilities for agreement at first and second reading stages as well as contributing to the preparation of the work of the Conciliation Committee'.[18] The Rules of Procedure of the European Parliament provide for explicit rules on these trilogue negotiations, e.g. with regard to the mandate for the negotiations, the composition of the negotiating team and how and when to provide feedback to the committee (see Sect. 6).

In a trilogue, the Council Presidency, the Commission and the European Parliament, negotiate a possible compromise text.[19] The Commission shall facilitate such contacts and shall exercise its right of initiative in a constructive manner with a view to reconciling the positions of the European Parliament and the Council (…).[20] The number of participants varies but generally the institutions try to limit the number. Most of the trilogues take place inside the European Parliament and are so far not open to the public. Many of them are conducted in English as well as are the documents used in the trilogue. This may sometimes be problematic in particular if the main negotiator(s) (mostly on the European Parliament side) do not feel comfortable working in that language. Interpretation facilities are available although nowadays with the number of codecision files under negotiations (around 124 files in first or second reading[21]) it has become more and more of a problem. Normally the Council Presidency and the European Parliament will set the agenda of a trilogue together. The representation of the institution varies (and may also change during the negotiation process). The Council will normally be represented by the chair of the working party, generally an experienced civil servant. The Commission will be represented by the relevant officials (mostly at head of unit level) and European Parliament will be represented by politicians (the rapporteur, chair or vice-chair and shadow rapporteurs[22]). The three delegations will be supported by staff. The Council negotiating team consists of desk officer(s) from the General Secretariat of the Council, the

[17]Para 8 of the Joint Declaration.

[18]Para 7 of the Joint Declaration.

[19]However in the area of external relations we see that besides the Presidency and the Commission the European External Action Service will be participating in the trilogue meetings due to the specific division of competences in that area of cooperation.

[20]Joint Declaration para 13.

[21]Figure based on situation mid-August 2013.

[22]Shadow rapporteurs are appointed by political groups to follow the work of the rapporteur.

legal service, the codecision unit, as well as lawyer linguists. The Commission negotiating team consists of colleagues from the relevant Directorate General, the legal service and the General Secretariat. The European Parliament team will be supported by the administrator(s) responsible for the file, staff from the different political groups, a colleague from the codecision unit, the legal service, as well as lawyer-linguists. It is a setting which provides for efficient decision-making but which fits uneasily with a parliamentary style of open public debate.[23]

The difference in representation between the institutions (politicians vs. officials) may sometimes be problematic as these actors do not necessarily speak the same language. Generally, one can say that Parliament's negotiators will be focused more on the political elements of a file, while the Council and Commission would tend to look more to the technical elements. This was also what happened in the negotiations on the revision of the rules regarding novel foods.[24] The European Parliament aimed to achieve a ban on food derived from cloned animals, including food derived from the descendants of clones. It supported its request for a ban on the basis of ethical, animal welfare and public opinion arguments. Council and Commission opposed the European Parliament's arguments stating that such food is safe to consume. They also focused on practical difficulties of traceability as well as on trade relations as the requests of European Parliament would lead to a 'trade war'. The European Parliament reacted to such arguments by stating that possible trade implications (although far from sure to happen) should not be an obstacle if the overwhelming majority of citizens simply opposes cloning for food. In a last attempt to find a compromise the European Parliament suggested moving from a ban of the food from the descendants of cloned animals to a labelling scheme covering at least the first generation after the cloned animal. It was thought that with a label such food will not be bought and therefore it would not be done as there would be no commercial interest. Council opposed this, with the exception of fresh bovine meat, on grounds of feasibility of labelling.

The statements made by the representatives of the three institutions after failure of the negotiations clearly show the controversy. The Hungarian Minister of rural development, said on behalf of the Presidency: 'The EP chose to go down the road of political grandstanding instead and tried to push the Council to accept a misleading, unfeasible "solution" that in practice would have required drawing a family tree for each slice of cheese or salami.' Similarly Commissioner Dalli commented: 'I remain convinced that the only way to guarantee a good deal for EU consumers and food business operators is to deliver a proposal that is based on common sense and one that is both practicable and enforceable including on the issue of labelling.' The European Parliament's main negotiators commented:

> It is deeply frustrating that Council would not listen to public opinion and support urgently needed measures to protect consumer and animal welfare interests. The European

---

[23]See Huber and Shackleton 2013, p. 1045.

[24]See Huber, *forthcoming*, pp. 18 and 19.

> Parliament had overwhelmingly called for a ban on food from cloned animals and their descendants (…). We made a huge effort to compromise but we were not willing to betray consumers on their right to know whether food comes from animals bred using clones. Since European public opinion is overwhelmingly against cloning for food, (…) a commitment to label all food products from cloned offspring is a bare minimum. Council would only assure its support to label one type of product: fresh beef.

This example clearly is one in which the three institutions did not reach a common understanding.

It is more and more a trend that the Ambassador (or his/her deputy) from COREPER is brought into the negotiations as from a certain stage. Also the Commission brings in senior management or the competent Commissioner at some point in the negotiations. Bringing in the political level may sometimes be helpful in bringing a file forward, as between these actors there generally will be a more common understanding. The Council Presidency's negotiation team works as a sort of filter. Its key negotiator will have to go back to the Council (and/or to the working party or Coreper) to report what has happened in the trilogue and get a mandate (or updated mandate) therefrom. There is a certain unbalance between the Commission and the Council's teams, on the one hand, and the European Parliament's team on the other hand in the amount of information available. The meetings of the Council working party (and/or COREPER), in which the mandate of the Council's negotiating team will be established or updated, are not open to European Parliament's team, but the Commission is participating. On the other hand the parliament's committee meetings are open to Council's and Commission's representatives.

It sometimes happens that a Presidency shows a certain 'fatigue' when going through the text for the first time with the EP team. Although it is understandable—often the Presidency already faced intensive discussions on the same issues in the Council Working Party—this may give EP Members the impression that some things are already pre-cooked between the Commission and the Council Presidency especially, when it is not always so clear to what extend the European Parliament's amendments were discussed within this frame. Also, it sometimes is unclear whether a position taken by a Council Presidency indeed is a position that represents the (majority opinion) of the Council, or whether it is rather a Presidency proposal ('testing'). After the trilogue, the European Parliament's negotiating team will have to provide feedback to the parliamentary committee.

5 Transparency and Democratic Legitimacy of Trilogue Negotiations? Rule 70 and 70a and the Code of Conduct

The trend of having more agreements at an earlier stage of the procedure not only demonstrates the flexibility of the codecision procedure itself, but also shows the trust and willingness between the institutions to cooperate. At the same time transparency and accountability are very important in conducting these negotiations.

This is of course particularly salient in the EU context given the wide-ranging nature of its legislative and executive powers.[25] Article 10, para 3, TEU states that '(…) Decisions shall be taken as openly and closely as possible to the citizen'. Transparency and participation can also be seen as a means of applying the principle of democracy more fundamentally.[26] With specific regard to trilogue negotiations, criticism is sometimes voiced because of a potential lack of transparency.[27] Rule 70 of European Parliament's Rules of Procedure and the European Parliament's Code of Conduct for negotiating in the context of codecision procedures (approved by the Conference of Presidents in September 2008) try to address these legitimate concerns and are useful tools in addressing them.

The Code of Conduct gave rules for the decision of the parliamentary committee to enter into negotiations, the composition of the negotiating team and its mandate, and the consideration by the committee of any agreement reached. In addition, it entailed provisions on the documents used in trilogues and on the administrative assistance to be provided for the negotiating team.

On 6 May 2009 the plenary adopted a revision of the Rules of Procedure to incorporate the Code of Conduct, which is annexed to the Rules. Rule 70 (Interinstitutional negotiations in legislative procedures) provided that 'negotiations with the other institutions aimed at reaching an agreement in the course of a legislative procedure shall be conducted having regard to the Code of conduct'. The second paragraph of Rule 70, however, stipulated that before entering into negotiations 'the committee should, in principle, take a decision by a majority of its members and adopt a mandate, orientations and priorities'.

In March 2011, the Conference of Presidents held an exchange of views on the negotiations on first-reading agreements under the ordinary legislative procedure, against the background of the trend of more agreements at an early stage of the procedures. Consequently, the accountability and transparency of these agreements as well as the question as to how these negotiations are conducted have become more important. It therefore tasked the Committee on Constitutional Affairs (AFCO) to review Rule 70 of Parliament's Rules of Procedure in order to make the procedures relating to the conduct of negotiations on first-reading agreements more effective, more transparent and more inclusive through the inclusion of the key elements of the 'Code of Conduct' for negotiating in the context of the ordinary legislative procedures' in the binding part of the Rules of Procedure, and in particular those parts on:

- the decision of the committee concerned to enter into negotiations;
- the decision for the composition and mandate of the negotiating team;
- the regular report-back to the committee concerned on the progress; and

[25] See Curtin 2011, p. 71.

[26] See Curtin 2011, p. 72.

[27] See Corbett et al. 2011, p. 244.

- outcome of the negotiations, including any agreement reached;
- the re-consultation of the committee on the text agreed before the vote in plenary.[28]

The AFCO report was adopted by the plenary in November 2012 and the revised Rules 70 and 70a entered into force in December 2012. These rules apply to all negotiations on first, 'early second' and second reading agreements. One of the main elements is that the committee should, on a case-by-case basis, take a formal decision (a vote) whether to open negotiations. In most of the cases this means that the committee will adopt a report as well as a decision on whether or not to open negotiations. The decision shall also determine the mandate and the composition of the negotiating team.[29] After that negotiations can start immediately. The European Parliament's negotiating team shall be led by the rapporteur and presided over by the chair of the committee responsible (or by a vice-chair). It shall comprise at least the shadow rapporteurs from each political group. The document generally used is a so-called 'four-column document', with the respective positions of the institutions. Each institution designates its own participants to the trilogue meetings. A record of progress is kept by updating the four-column document. After each trilogue the negotiating team shall report back to the following meeting of the committee responsible. If the negotiations lead to a compromise the committee responsible shall be informed without delay. The committee will consider the text and vote on it. If adopted the text is submitted to the plenary.

A first evaluation of the experiences with the new Rules 70 and 70a was made at an internal workshop on 28 June 2013 in the European Parliament, the rules having been in place for 6 months. One can say that the committees quickly adapted to the systematic use of new Rule 70. The procedure of Rule 70a, the so-called 'exceptional' procedure[30] was used only for a few cases. The new Rule 70 formalises good practices by making the provisions on the reporting back to the committee and the re-consultation of the committee on a text agreed before the plenary vote mandatory. It has enhanced transparency.

---

[28]The report of Enrique Guerrero Salom on amendment of Rule 70 of Parliament's Rules of Procedure on interinstitutional negotiations in legislative procedures A-7-0281/2012 of 25 September 2012.

[29]Rule 70a describes the so-called 'exceptional procedure, in which under certain conditions negotiations can take place prior to the adoption of a report in committee. Negotiations cannot start immediately but are subject to control by the Conference of Presidents and of the plenary.

[30]The procedure on the adoption of a decision to open interinstitutional negotiations prior to the adoption of a report in committee, whereby the decision has to pass by the Conference of Presidents and the plenary.

6 Conclusions

After 20 years, one can say the European Parliament has become a real actor in the ordinary legislative procedure. Over the years the system evolved and it has become the normal procedure for legislating with the Council. From a practical perspective, although Article 294 TFEU does not mention trilogue negotiations, they have become a very important element in establishing legislation. Nowadays the awareness of the potential lack of transparency of these trilogue negotiations has grown. The European Parliament adopted new procedural rules to address these potential problems. There is in these trilogue negotiations a certain inequality with respect to the information available. It could therefore be considered to open up the Working party (and perhaps sometimes even COREPER) meetings to EP officials when legislation is discussed. With regard to so-called 'early' agreements, which are a trend that will perhaps be difficult to change, I think that decisions to open negotiations should not be taken more or less automatically but case by case. The new rules may also contribute to this and provide the possibility of some reflection. Sometimes it may be appropriate to continue discussions in second reading or even conciliation. For some files first reading conclusion may not be the appropriate option.

Case law, legislation and documents

Case law

European Court of Justice, *IATA and ELFAA v. Department of Transport, Preliminary Ruling*, C-344/04 200

Legislation

Treaty on the European Union

European Parliament's Rules of Procedure

Joint Declaration on the practical arrangements for the codecision procedure of 13 June 2007, OJ C 145 of 30 June 2007

Joint Declaration of the European Parliament, the Council and the Commission on the practical arrangements for the codecision procedure

Documents

Enrique Guerrero Salom, report on the amendment of Rule 70 of Parliament's Rules of Procedure on interinstitutional negotiations in legislative procedures A-7-0281/2012 of 25 September 2012

Official Journal of the European Communities, C 148, 28 May 1999

Official Journal of the European Communities, C 145, 30 June 2007

References

Corbett R, Jacobs F, Shackleton M (2011) The European Parliament, 8th edn. John Harper Publishing, London

Craig P, de Búrca Gráinne (2011) EU law, texts, cases and materials. Oxford University Press, Oxford

Curtin D (2011) Open European Union government through pinhole glasses. In: Today's Multilayered Legal Order: Current issues and perspectives, liber amicorum in honour of Arjen W.H. Meij. Zutphen

Huber K (forthcoming) The European Parliament as negotiator, factors for its success, a comprehensive study on the role of the parliament in the negotiations

Huber K, Shackleton M (2013) Codecision: a practitioner's view from inside the parliament. J Europ Public Policy 20(7):1040 et seq

Kapteyn-VerLoren van Themaat PJG (1995) Inleiding tot het recht van de Europese Gemeenschappen na Maastricht

The European Union Development Policies Are Based on European Values, Democracy, Respect for the Rule of Law and Human Rights

Cornelius James

Abstract The primary focus of this paper is not mainly the involvement of the European Union in the achievements of the Millennium Development Goals (MDG) of the United Nations, but the interrelationship between the EU's assistance for sustainable development to third countries by means of granting financial and technical support on the one hand and on the other hand for the said support the inclusion of general principles of EU law regarding the respect for Human rights, good governance, democracy, the rule of law and other similar key elements. In EU agreements with third countries (be it bilateral or regional) both financial and technical support goes hand in hand together with these international standards and principles in order to achieve sustainable development. For violation of these agreed international standards, the EU applies agreed sanctions or adopts measures to ensure the upholding of these principles. The suspension of financial and/or technical support can form part of these agreed measures. The application of these international standards are not only being applied to financial or technical support for sustainable development, but also to international trade agreements, which is currently becoming customary law in international trade agreements, the so-called "Human rights clauses".

Retired director of the St Maarten House in The Hague. Retired Director at the Cabinet for the Minister Plenipotentiary of St Maarten, The Hague.

C. James (✉)
St Maarten House, The Hague, The Netherlands
e-mail: cdja@ziggo.nl

F.A.N.J. Goudappel and E.M.H. Hirsch Ballin (eds.), *Democracy and Rule of Law in the European Union*, DOI 10.1007/978-94-6265-066-4_9

Contents

1 Introduction

The European Union is founded on a shared objective to promote peace and stability and to build a world based on respect for human rights, democracy and the rule of law. These principles underpin all aspects of the internal and external policies of the European Union. In the area of development cooperation, a human rights-based approach will be used to ensure that the EU strengthens its efforts to assist partner countries in implementing their international human rights obligations.[1] The United Nations Secretary-General Ban Ki-moon stated at The United Nations Millennium Campaign in 2002 that

> Eradicating extreme poverty continues to be one of the main challenges of our time, and is a major concern of the international community. Ending this scourge will require the combined efforts of all, governments, civil society organizations and the private sector, in the context of a stronger and more effective global partnership for development. The Millennium Development Goals set time bound targets, by which progress in reducing income poverty, hunger, disease, lack of adequate shelter and exclusion—while promoting gender equality, health, education and environmental sustainability—can be measured. They also embody basic human rights—the rights of each person on the planet to health,

[1]Council decision of the European Union, Luxembourg, 25 June 2012, 11855/12 regarding EU Strategic Framework and Action Plan on Human Rights and Democracy.

> education, shelter and security. The Goals are ambitious but feasible and, together with the comprehensive United Nations development agenda, set the course for the world's efforts to alleviate extreme poverty by 2015.[2]

Today the European Union is one of the biggest active and proactive players in the eradication of poverty and also the largest supporter of promoting on a world-wide level the respect for human rights, good governance, democracy and the rule of law. The EU develops policies for economic development in order to reduce hunger and preserve natural resources. The EU is the major donor of development aid to help countries make progress economically, politically and socially. On the other hand one might argue that it is not the quality of spending, or even the insufficient quantity, but the fact that other EU policies damage poor countries, because its policies are not always coherent with its own strategy for sustainable development. For example, EU policies on trade, agriculture and fisheries etcetera are not always in favour of the poor countries. The EU and its Member States commit to playing an active and constructive role in all ongoing processes and to support their convergence in order to achieve a single overarching post-2015 Development Framework and will work closely with the UN system to achieve the Millennium Development Goals.

The "United Nations Millennium Declaration", endorsed in 2000, and the accompanying Millennium Development Goals (MDGs), adopted in 2002, have been important instruments in streamlining and coordinating international development action. Since the targets were defined, significant progress has been achieved in almost all the MDGs but there are also numerous challenges that have not been addressed with the necessary commitment by the various stakeholders. New global realities and challenges have enormous implications on new development strategies.[3] Aid will remain an important instrument post-2015, but the number of recipients of traditional official development assistance (ODA) is likely to shrink, as more countries reach middle-income status. The emergence of new donors is not the only reason for traditional donors, like the EU, to think long and hard about partnerships with emerging economies. Partnerships are required to achieve shared goals in a wide range of policy spheres, from management of the global economy, through climate change, to the mitigation of risks like disease. Some partnerships will be based on shared values; others will be more instrumental.[4] Section 2 refers to the institution of the EU for designing and executing policies for EU external action. In Sect. 3 a description of the financial instruments and programmes will be outlined. Whereas in Sect. 4 reference will be made to the general rules of EU law, which are being mainstreamed into the development strategies of the EU with third countries: such as human rights, democracy, the rule of

[2]See UN Millennium Campaign on poverty, education, women's empowerment, maternal health and the environment. www.un.org/millenniumgoals/bkgd.shtml. Accessed 4 March 2015.

[3]See the study on the Millennium Development Goals and beyond 2015, for a strong EU engagement done by Directorate-General for External policies of the EU 2013 (Directorate B of the policy department).

[4]Report "EU development cooperation, where have we got to and what's next" re a conference for EU Change-makers held at ODI, London, on 24 & 25 June 2013. See nrs 4 and 5 of the report.

law and good governance. Section 5 will outline the bilateral and multilateral organisations dealing with EU cooperation on these principles of EU law. Section 6 will then be dealing with the human rights clause in international trade agreements. In the finalisation of this chapter some conclusions will be set out.

2 EU Directorate-General EuropeAid Responsible for EU Policy Development and Cooperation

This Directorate-General for EuropeAid and Cooperation is the responsible institution for designing European development policy and delivering aid throughout the world (hereafter: EuropeAid), which delivers aid through a set of financial instruments with a focus on ensuring the quality of EU aid and its effectiveness. In fact the EU has always been among international organisations before imbedding general rules of EU Law in its founding Treaties, such as the United Nations, in promoting human rights, democracy, good governance and the rule of law. As the Lisbon Treaty states, supporting developing countries' efforts to eradicate poverty is the primary objective of development policy and a priority for EU external action in support of EU's interests for a stable and prosperous world Development policy, which also helps address other global challenges and contributes to the EU-2020 Strategy. At EU level, the Lisbon Treaty has firmly anchored development policy within EU external action. The creation of the post of High Representative/Vice-President (HR/VP), assisted by the European External Action Service (EEAS), offers new opportunities for more effective development cooperation and a more joined-up policy-making. The EU has already done much to help reduce poverty in terms of the Millennium Development Goals and in particular to support the achievement of the post 2015-MDGs. Yet severe poverty persists in many parts of the world.[5]

3 Financial Instruments Design to Achieve Sustainable Development

For the period 2007–2013, the EU's action in the area of development was financed through two types of instruments:

(a) the implementation of the policy at national and regional levels was supported by geographical instruments, such as the European Development Fund (in the African, Caribbean and Pacific countries); the Development Co-operation Instrument (in Latin America, Asia and South Africa), and the European Neighbourhood & Partnership Instrument (in the neighbouring regions);

[5]See COM(2011)637final "increasing the impact of EU Development Policy: an Agenda for Change", para 1.

(b) the European Instrument for Democracy and Human Rights (EIDHR) which was launched in 2006 and has as its aim to provide support for the promotion of democracy and human rights in non-EU countries, grants aid where there are no development cooperation links and intervene without the agreement of the governments of third countries. Another characteristic of this instrument is that it works with, for and through civil society organisations. It can support groups or individuals within civil society defending democracy as well as intergovernmental organisations which implement the international mechanisms for the protection of human rights. Under EIDHR complements other tools which are used to implement EU policies for democracy and human rights. These range from political dialogue and diplomatic initiatives to various instruments for financial and technical cooperation, including the Development Co-operation Instrument and ENPI (European Neighbourhood & Partnership Instrument). The Development Co-operation Instrument (DCI) is also divided up into (1) geographic programmes; (2) thematic programmes; and others such as (3) programme of accompanying measures for the African, Caribbean and Pacific Countries (ACP).

3.1 Budget Support for Achieving Sustainable Development

Budget support is an important instrument in EU's comprehensive development policy towards partner countries. The Commission will ensure that EU budget support is consistent with the overarching principles and objectives of EU external action (Article 21 TEU) and development policy (Article 208 TFEU). This new approach should strengthen the contractual partnership on EU budget support between the EU and partner countries in order to build and consolidate democracies, pursue sustainable economic growth and eradicate poverty. The said approach must be based on mutual accountability and shared commitment to fundamental values of human rights, democracy and the rule of law. It should enable greater differentiation of budget support operations, allowing the EU to respond better to the political, economic and social context of the partner country. It will require close coordination between Commission services, the EEAS and Member States. In this context budget support to third countries can be referred to as "State Building Contracts" (to ensure vital state functions), where the EU is essential committed to apply the fundamental values of human rights, democracy and the rule of law when establishing any partnership or cooperation agreement between the EU and third countries.

In the case of the OCTs it is mentioned in the EU Commission's document regarding "the future approach to EU Budget support of 2011 (COM (2011) 638 final", under para 2.2.4, that "There budget support can have an important impact, given the strong level of accountability and commitment to addressing their structural vulnerability and climate change issues, including the decline of biological diversity and other environmental shocks. Budget support can offer an efficient way of addressing these crosscutting, long-term and structural challenges and threats". Delivering budget support in terms of State Building Contracts, require a global, coherent and coordinated response for which budget support can be instrumental. Together with other aid modalities (humanitarian aid, pooled funds, project aid, technical assistance, etc., it has to be accompanied by reinforced political and policy dialogue. Furthermore it is also mentioned in aforementioned EU document that the EU should work with Member States in particular towards a "single EU Good Governance and Development Contract"; it is notable that the EU should assess whether pre-conditions exist to entrust Good Governance and Development Contracts to a partner country, i.e. whether fundamental values of human rights, democracy and rule of law or a clear path towards international standards exist and whether such a Contract could clearly act as a driver to accelerate this movement. By non-compliance with these universal standards of general rules of international law a country cannot receive development assistance whether in terms of financial aid or in terms of technical assistance. In this context one can refer to the speech given by EU High Representative Catherine Ashton in Strasbourg on 11 September 2013[6] to the European Parliament on the current situation in Egypt:

> We believe in a constitution that will support democracy; we believe in the Rule of Law; we believe in Justice; And we believe in Respect for human rights and fundamental freedom. I want to say something about funding. We don't provide budget support. We do support socio-economic projects for the people, especially the most vulnerable, in health, school feeding programmes, poor neighbourhoods and programmes for women. I proposed to member states that we should continue with these programmes - we must continue to support the people. And I hope that I will have support in this house to continue to do that. We want this country to succeed. We want to support it. But to do so with the principles and values that we hold.

4 Human Rights, Democracy, Good Governance, the Rule of Law and Other Related General Principles of EU Law/International Law

4.1 Some General Observations

Poverty reduction cannot be achieved without a government (receiving funds and technical assistance) able to serve the public interest effectively by being accountable to its citizens and respecting the rule of law, democracy and good governance. According to the authors Barbara Brandtner and Allan Rosas,[7] "Since the early 1990s, human rights have gained increasing importance in the external policies of

[6]Press Release Strasbourg, 11 September 2013, A 454/13.

[7]See Brandtner and Rosas 1998, p. 1.

the European Union (EU) and, in particular the European Community (EC)". Within this context reference can also be made to the Lomé agreements, in which these general principles of EU law were part of said agreements before the existence of Lisbon Treaties. The aforementioned Article 21 of the Treaty on European Union has reaffirmed the EU's determination to promote human rights and democracy through all its external actions. The entry into legal force of the EU Charter of Fundamental Rights, and the prospect of the EU's acceptance of the jurisdiction of the European Court of Human Rights (ECHR) through its accession to the European Convention on Human Rights, underline the EU's commitment to human rights in all spheres including all key elements such as democracy and good governance etcetera. Within the frontiers of the EU and its Member States it is already committed to be an example in ensuring respect for human rights.

Outside the frontiers, the EU is promoting and speaking out on human rights and democracy, which is a joint responsibility of the EU and its Member States. From the outset reference can also be made to the Treaty of Amsterdam with respect to fundamental rights in which the European Union continues to develop the rule of law and respecting fundamental rights, as guaranteed by the ECHR and as they result from the constitutional traditions common to the Member States, as general principles of European law.[8] The EU will promote human rights in all areas of its external action without exception. In particular, it will also integrate the promotion of human rights into trade, investment, technology and telecommunications policies, Internet, energy, environmental, corporate social responsibility and development policy as well as into Common Security and Defence Policy and the external dimensions of employment and social policy and the area of freedom, security and justice, including counter-terrorism policy.

4.2 Human Rights Approach in the Area of Sustainable Development Corporation

The European Union believes that democracy and human rights are universal values that should be vigorously promoted around the world. They are integral to effective work on poverty alleviation and conflict prevention and resolution, in addition to being valuable bulwarks against terrorism. Having come into force on 1 January 2007, the European Instrument for Democracy and Human Rights (EIDHR) is the concrete expression of the EU's intention to integrate the promotion of democracy and human rights into all of its external policies. In the area of development cooperation, a human rights-based approach will be used to ensure that the EU strengthens its efforts to assist partner countries in implementing their international human rights obligations. The EU will encourage and contribute to

[8]The Amsterdam Treaty also introduced Article F1 (now Article 6 TEU), according to which the Union is founded on the principles of liberty, democracy, respect for human rights and the fundamental freedoms, and the rule of law, principles which are common to the Member States.

the implementation of the UN Guiding Principles on Business and Human Rights (The Human Rights Council endorsed the Guiding Principles in its Resolution 17/4 of 16 June 2011).[9]

The EU will place human rights at the centre of its relations with all third countries, including its strategic partners. However, when faced with violations of human rights, the EU will make use of the full range of instruments at its disposal, including sanctions or condemnation and will continue to speak out in the United Nations General Assembly, the UN Human Rights Council and the International Labour Organisation against human rights violations. The independence and effectiveness of the UN Office of the High Commissioner for Human Rights, as well as of the treaty monitoring bodies and UN Special Procedures, is essential. The EU underlines the leading role of the UN Human Rights Council in addressing urgent cases of human rights violations and will contribute vigorously to the effective functioning of the Council; the EU stands ready to cooperate with countries from all regions to this end.[10]

In the event of a breach, a range of measures can be considered, with the provision that their application should respect the principle of proportionality between the breach and the degree of reaction. These measures include: alteration of the contents of cooperation programmes or the channels used; reduction of cultural, scientific and technical cooperation programmes; postponement of a Joint Committee meeting; suspension of high-level bilateral contacts; postponement of new projects; refusal to follow up partner's initiatives; trade embargoes; suspension of arms sales, suspension of military cooperation and suspension of cooperation.

4.3 Good Governance Approach in the Area of Sustainable Development Corporation

With regard to the EU policy on the principle of "good governance" in its political, economic, social and environmental terms, this principle is also vital for achieving sustainable development.[11] EU support to governance should feature more prominently in all partnerships, notably through incentives for results-oriented reform and a focus on partners' commitments to human rights, democracy and the rule of law and to meeting their peoples' demands and needs. Support for governance

[9]This UN publication contains the "Guiding Principles on Business and Human Rights: Implementing the United Nations 'Protect, Respect and Remedy' Framework", which were developed by the Special Representative of the Secretary-General on the issue of human rights and transnational corporations and other business enterprises.

[10]See Press Release of the Council of the EU re "EU Strategic Framework and Action Plan on Human Rights and Democracy" dated 25 June 2012/11855/12 in which the plans on Human Rights and Democracy were outlined.

[11]COM(2011)638, re "The Future Approach to EU Budget Support to Third Countries".

may take the form of programmes or project-based interventions to support actors and processes at local, national and sectorial level. EU general budget support should be linked to the governance situation and political dialogue with the partner country, in coordination with the Member States.[12] The EU will continue to support democratisation, free and fair elections, the functioning of institutions, media freedom and access to internet, protection of minorities, the rule of law and judicial systems in partner countries, including the principle of good governance. The EU should help its partner countries tackle corruption through governance programmes that support advocacy, awareness-raising and reporting and increase the capacity of control and oversight bodies and the judiciary. The EU will scale up its support for governance reforms that promote the sustainable and transparent management of natural resources, including raw materials and maritime resources, and ecosystem services, with particular attention to the dependence of the poor. The fight against corruption is increasingly becoming part of the international and EU agenda for poverty reduction. In the Global Programme against Corruption run by the UN, corruption is defined as the abuse of power for private gain and includes the entire public and private sector.[13] Corruption undermines the government's credibility and the legitimacy of democracy.

4.4 EU Cooperating with Partners on a Bilateral and Multilateral Level

The EU will work with partner countries in identifying areas where EU geographic funding instruments can be used to support projects which bolster human rights, including the support for democracy and human rights in connection with education and training. The EU will also make its effort to best use the 'human rights clause' in political framework agreements with third countries. Since the early 1990s, the human rights clause has been systematically included in EU external agreements of a general nature.[14] According to the article written by Der-Chin Horng of the Institute of European and American Studies, Academia Sinica, it is mentioned that this clause is implemented by a suspension clause which provides for appropriate measures to be taken by the party which invoked the violation of human rights. The human rights clause is unique in the EU's bilateral agreements. This essential clause stipulates that respect for fundamental human rights and democratic principles as laid down in the Universal Declaration on Human Rights (UDHR) underpin the internal and external policies of the signatory parties and constitute an 'essential element' of the agreement.

---

[12]Above n. 11.

[13]Corruption is: "every transaction between actors from the private and public sectors through which collective utilities are illegally transformed into private gains".

[14]See Der-Chin Horng 2003.

The essential clause is enhanced by the additional clause that deals with non-execution of the agreement. Accordingly, in all new drafts negotiating directives for EU agreements with non-EU countries, the following clauses and content are included:

(1) the Preamble, general references to human rights and democratic values;
(2) an Article X defining the essential elements of the agreement;
(3) an Article Y on non-execution of the agreement; and
(4) an interpretation of the Article Y declaration.

A violation of human rights may allow the EU to terminate the agreement or suspend its operation in whole or in part. The human rights clause, based on cooperative aid and consultation, represents an important policy change in EU external relations. Since 1992, the EU has been conducting a more active strategy with a 'civilizing nature' in dealing with non-EU countries. Human rights considerations obviously give a new context to the EU's external agreements and enrich the EU's foreign policy. In the case of the Cotonou Partnership Agreement, 77 ACP countries and the EU agreed to set up consultation procedures linked to the respect for the key elements of the Partnership. Article 9 of Cotonou states that respect for human rights, democratic principles and the rule of law constitute its essential elements, and good governance, its fundamental element. Consultations under Article 96 aim at examining the situation with a view to finding a solution acceptable to both parties. If no solution is found, or in emergency cases, or if one party refuses the consultations, appropriate measures can be taken. Appropriate measures, which should be proportional to the violation of an essential element, are intended to give a clear signal to the government regarding the respect of the aforementioned Article 9 of the Cotonou Agreement.

5 EU Cooperating with Partners on a Bilateral and Multilateral Level

5.1 EU Bilateral Agreements for Sustainable Development

In the European Neighbourhood Policy countries, the EU has firmly committed itself to supporting a comprehensive agenda of locally-led political reform, with democracy and human rights at its centre, including through the policy of "more for more", where Human rights will remain at the heart of the EU's enlargement policy. Through its European Neighbourhood Policy (ENP), the EU works with its southern and eastern neighbours to achieve the closest possible political association and the greatest possible degree of economic integration. This goal builds on common interests and on values—democracy, the rule of law, respect for human rights, and social cohesion. Partner countries agree with the EU for an ENP action plan demonstrating their commitment to democracy, human rights, rule of law, good governance, market economy principles and sustainable development. The EU supports the achievement of these objectives by delivering financial support (grants worth €12 bn were given to ENP-related projects from 2007 to 2013); economic integration and access to EU markets (in 2011 trade between the EU and its ENP partners totalled €230 bn); Easier travel to the EU (3.2 m Schengen visas were issued to citizens, and in particular to students from ENP countries in 2012); Technical and policy support given to the civil society which plays an important role in bringing about deep and sustainable democracy in partner countries.[15] There are sixteen ENP countries in total: Algeria, Armenia, Azerbaijan, Belarus, Egypt, Georgia, Israel, Jordan, Lebanon, Libya, Moldova, Morocco, Palestine, Syria, Tunisia, and Ukraine. The European External Action Service and the European Commission publish yearly ENP progress reports. Whereas the Eastern Partnership regards the Euro-Mediterranean Partnership (EUROMED) (the Euro-Mediterranean Partnership, formerly known as the Barcelona Process) Black Sea Synergy (launched in Kiev in February 2008). Eastern Partnership Civil Society Forum and Eastern Partnership Integrated Border Management Panel.

5.2 EU Multilateral Cooperation Agreements for Sustainable Development

As already mentioned above, the EU cooperates with the United Nations General Assembly, the UN Human Rights Council and the International Labour Organisation as well as regional international organisations to promote these universal principles of law. With regard to the Universal Periodic Review (UPR) on Human Rights and Democracy, the EU and its Member States are committed to implement UPR recommendations which have been accepted, as well as recommendations of treaty monitoring bodies and UN Special Procedures, in bilateral relations with all third countries; the Member States are equally determined to ensure implementation of such recommendations within their own national frontiers. Within the Kingdom of the Netherlands all autonomous parts of the Kingdom are committed to execute and implement these periodic reviews. In forthcoming UPR rounds, the EU will pay close attention to the degree of implementation by third countries of UPR commitments which they have accepted and will endeavour to provide support for their implementation. The EU will continue its engagement with human rights work of the Council of Europe (the Commissioner for Human Rights of the Council of Europe who also pays special attention to the most vulnerable groups of people, such as children, the elderly and persons with disabilities).[16] and the OSCE (Organisation for Security and

[15]See EU External Action. http://eeas.europa.eu/enp/.

[16]More resolute commitment is also needed to promoting and protecting the human rights of women, minorities and migrants. New challenges, such as those arising from a rapidly evolving information society, require a balanced approach which protects human dignity, fundamental freedoms, and promotes mutual understanding.

Cooperation in Europe). Recently the representative for the OSCE stated in Vienna, 13 September 2013, that criminal prosecution of journalists in Bosnia and Herzegovina endangers the right to free expression, which was confirmed in case law that it has taken a criminal indictment by a group of journalists against other journalists in Bosnia and Herzegovina, which can lead to EU action for the violation of the partnership agreement.[17]

5.3 Regional and Other International Organisations Involved in the Promotion of Regional Human Rights

The EU will work in partnership with regional and other organisations such as the African Union, ASEAN, SAARC, the Organisation of American States, the Arab League, the Organisation of Islamic Cooperation and the Pacific Islands Forum with a view to encouraging the consolidation of regional human rights mechanisms. With regard to the Association of Southeast Asian Nations (ASEAN), Howard Loewen[18] has argued that a clash of cooperation cultures comes about in both structures of interregional collaboration between Asia and Europe, with minor variations owing to the institutional framework; whereas diverging attitudes on the question of democracy and human rights between the EU and ASEAN have led to a transitory standstill in cooperation, the flexible institutional means of ASEM seem, at first sight, to have alleviated the disruptive effects of such dialogues. Yet, informality has not removed the issues from the agenda, as the continuing disagreements over Myanmar's membership in ASEM clearly specify. Divergent cooperation cultures—in particular the non-intervention norm preferred by the Asian ASEM members—hence play a significant role in explaining the obstructive nature of the interregional human rights and democracy dialogue between Asia and Europe.[19]

Whereas the African Union has in its Charter on Human and Peoples' Rights as commitment that the Member States shall adhere to the principles of human and people' rights and freedoms contained in the declarations, conventions and other instruments adopted by the African Union and the United Nations and their duty to promote and protect human and peoples' rights and all freedoms and taking into account the importance traditionally attached to these rights and freedoms in

[17]The fact that Bosnia and Herzegovina was the first country in the region to decriminalise defamation back in 1999 was a hallmark in its media reform. Mijatović said: What I see today goes against these standards and the country's OSCE commitments to develop and protect media freedom and freedom of expression. Such issues should be resolved in an open dialogue, conducive to reconciliation. See OSCE. http://www.osce.org/fom/104930. Accessed 4 March 2015.

[18]Howard Loewen, 'Democracy and Human Rights in the European-Asian Dialogue: A Clash of Cooperation Cultures?, GIGA Working Paper No. 92, December 2008.

[19]See GIGA Research Programme: Transformation in the Process of Globalisation from the institute of GIGA.

Africa[20] The ACP-EC Partnership Agreement (the Cotonou Agreement), signed in 2000, provides the latest framework for a more than 20-year partnership for development aid to the 77 African, Caribbean and Pacific independent countries, funded mainly by the European Development Fund (EDF). Revisions in 2005 and further on have provided for a stronger political foundation to ACP-EU development cooperation. Political dialogue is one of the key aspects of the revised arrangements. New issues which had previously been outside the scope of development cooperation, such as peace and security, arms trade and migration, were addressed. The element of good governance was included as an "essential element", the violation of which could lead to the partial or complete suspension of development cooperation between the EU and the country in violation like the case concerning restrictive measures against Zimbabwe.[21]

5.4 The Application of General Principles of EU Law and International Law in Trade Cooperation Agreements

Inclusive and sustainable economic growth is crucial to long-term poverty reduction and growth patterns are as important as growth rates. To this end, the EU should encourage more inclusive growth, characterised by people's ability to participate in, and benefit from, wealth and job creation. The promotion of decent work covering job creation, guarantee of rights at work, social protection and social dialogue is vital. On the other hand, development is not sustainable if it damages the environment, biodiversity and natural resources and increases the exposure/vulnerability to natural disasters. Economic growth needs a favourable business environment. The EU should support the development of competitive local private sectors by building local institutional and business capacity, promoting SMEs (Small and Medium Enterprises) cooperatives, supporting legislative and regulatory framework reforms and their enforcement (including for the use of electronic communications as a tool to support growth across all sectors), facilitating access to business and financial services and promoting agricultural, industrial and innovation policies. This will also allow developing countries, especially the

---

[20]The Human Rights Strategy for Africa is a guiding framework for collective action by the African Union, No. 8.

[21]If a Party considers that the other Party has failed to fulfil an obligation stemming from respect for human rights, democratic principles and the rule of law referred to in Article 9, a process of consultation then ensues; if the consultations do not lead to a solution acceptable to both Parties, if consultation is refused, or in cases of special urgency, "appropriate measures" may be taken. These procedures, under Article 96, are intended as a measure of last resort and can only be invoked when Cotonou's "essential elements" are deemed to have been breached and all possible options provided through regular political dialogue have been exhausted. The aim of the process is to focus on the specific measures to be taken by the Party concerned to remedy the situation and thus arrive at a solution acceptable to the Parties.

poorest, to harness the opportunities offered by globally integrated markets. Better and more targeted Aid for Trade and trade facilitation must accompany these efforts.[22]

For example, the "Duty-free access to the EU market to 16 developing countries"; on 9 December 2008, the EU decided to give 16 developing countries duty-free access to its market for around 6400 tariff lines, under the EU's special incentive arrangement for sustainable development and good governance (GPS+). This provides an important incentive to developing countries to ratify and effectively implement a broadly defined set of international standards in the fields of human rights, core labour standards, sustainable development and good governance. As it is mentioned above, the EU has developed its external relations based on human rights over the years and as a result, its influence on world events has tended to become a good deal broader. Most of its human rights clause is provided in its trade or cooperation agreements. The EU can thus play a leading role in the development of human right clauses in the WTO system. In this context the EU's human rights clause provides a model and alternative for WTO in settling human rights-related trade issues.[23]

5.5 *Facilitating International Trade and Fostering Sustainable Development*

Regional integration can spur trade and investment and therefore foster peace and stability. The EU should support regional and continental integration efforts (including South–South initiatives) through partners' policies in areas such as markets, infrastructure and cross border cooperation on water, energy and security. In the early 1990s regarding the Latin American regional development, the trend was in the American Continent to unify the interest by the creation of the Mercado Común del Sur (Mercosur) which has as objective to establish a common market with free movement of goods, services and productive factors among its members and at the same time, to enable their competitive insertion in the world economy.

In the paper by Andrea Lucas Garin,[24] a study was made on the process of regional integration that the Mercosur has been developing, which has become a support for stability of the region, since the skeleton of economic interests and relationships has been growing under its protection and has created a regional forum that has advanced in the need to address topics of regional political dimension, such as Human Rights. The said paper continues to point out that because the

[22]See para 3 of the Commission's communication COM(2011)637final on the "Agenda for Change".

[23]See Der-Chin Horng 2003.

[24]At the VIII World Congress Constitutional Law on Constitutional Principles at Mexico 6-10 December 2010, Prof. Andrea Lucas Garin's paper 'Human Rights and Regional Integration in Mercosur: a bipolar relationship'.

process of economic integration inevitably reaches areas of action that has consequences in the realization of Human Rights within the countries involved. The conclusion was that there is an interrelation between the Mercosur Law and Human Rights Law, what can be noted as the constitutionalization of the Mercosur as Alston explains the idea of constitutionalization of the WTO (World Trade Organization) which has incorporated Human Rights into its institution.[25] Governance at all levels and, thus including trade, is crucial for regional development into the multilateral trading system, and for the creation of an attractive business environment in which investment and trade can thrive. It is therefore vital to economic development, without which poverty and poverty-related problems cannot be tackled. Only if developing countries have adequate institutional capacities and are willing to put in place a transparent, predictable and effective legal, regulatory, judicial and institutional environment, and are in a position to enforce rules and regulations, will they be able to attract sufficient domestic, regional and international investment.[26]

In relation to its own trade policy, the EU provides developing countries with preferential access to the EU market under the Generalised System of Preferences (GSP). This system aims to support development by according lower tariff levels to goods from developing countries than those applied to industrialised partners. However, these preferences may be withdrawn (as is currently the case for Myanmar) in cases of clear governance failures such as the use of prison, labour slavery and violation of the right of association. Furthermore, the GSP also provides positive incentives through additional preferences to countries which have incorporated certain ILO conventions into national law and/or which ensure sustainable management of their forests. Thus through positive and negative incentives the EU seeks to encourage good governance in trade-related areas.

6 Conclusions

There is an interrelationship between the eradication of poverty and Government compliance with rules of International Law/EU Law on the one hand (in particular, general rules of EU Law) and on the other hand the granting of financial aid and/or technical assistance. The promotion of sustainable development is also related to regional trade integration and at the same time respecting regional good governance, the rule of law and human rights (whether or not universal or regional). By non-compliance with general rules of international law/EU Law, appropriate measures can be taken against a Government which were agreed upon by the donor Party on the one hand and the recipient Party on the other hand. For example, Article 96 of the Cotonou Agreement foresees that in cases of violation

[25]See Alston 2002, pp. 815–844.

[26]See COM(2002)513final, 18 September 2002.

of one of those essential elements one party can invite the other party to hold consultations (a similar procedure had been introduced for the first time in 1995, through Article 366a of the revised Lomé IV Convention). Suspension of cooperation is in this context a measure of last resort. In the context of EU restrictive measures, it is questionable whether sanctions which are one of the EU tools to promote the objectives of the Common Foreign and Security Policy (CFSP) are legally applicable to third countries. This means the question whether these sanctions are applicable to be qualified as extraterritorial, whereas the nature of these sanctions is designed to have political effects in third countries. In general one might state that these restrictive measures are only legally applicable within the jurisdiction of the EU. As regards the process of regional integration one can compare the process of integration of Mercosur much like that of the European Union, which did not explicitly include from the outset of its existence the purpose to protect Human Rights, because the objectives of the founding agreements were economic, pursuing to build a common market with an institutional structure or intergovernmental features. The development of Human rights inside Mercosur as well as that of the EU came into existence through expressed programmatic ways (legal activities and developed programmes) and/or based on provisions of general rules of International Law/EU Law.

Documents

EU documents

The Future Approach to EU Budget Support to Third Countries COM(2011)638final Brussels, 13 October 2011

EU Strategic Framework and Action Plan on Human Rights and Democracy, Luxembourg 25 June 2012, 11855/12

EU Blending Facilities: Implications for Future Governance Options (European Think-Tanks Group| January 2011)

"Study Millennium Development Goals and beyond 2015: A strong EU engagement" Directorate-General for External Policies of the Union Directorate B Policy Department

Phedon Nicolaides and Anne-Marie Suren, 'The rule of law in the EU: what the numbers say. www.eipa.eu

EU Commission documents

Proposal for a Decision of the European Parliament and of the Council "European Year of Development", COM(2013)509final, Brussels, 10 July 2013 SWD(2013)265final

EC Communication: "Increasing the impact of EU Development Policy: an Agenda for Change" Brussels, 3 October 2011, COM(2011)637final, SEC(2011)1172final, SEC(2011)1173final

Conclusions Council on fundamental rights and rule of law and on the Commission 2012 Report on the Application of the Charter of Fundamental Rights of the European Union JUSTICE and HOME AFFAIRS Council meeting Luxembourg, 6 and 7 June 2013./

Proposal for a Regulation of the European Parliament and of the Council establishing for the period 2014-2020, the Rights and Citizenship Programme, Brussels, 15 November 2011 COM(2011)758final, 2011/0344 (COD)

UN reports

Side Events Related to the 2013 Special Event of the President of the General Assembly to follow-up efforts made towards achieving the Millennium Development Goals (as of 19 July 2013)

ECOSOC 2013—Coordination Segment Speaking points by EU Delegation for the Panel debate on Partnerships for productive capacity and decent work Friday 5 July 2013

ECOSOC (1-4 July 2013) Statement European Union High-level segment Annual Ministerial Review on the theme "Science, technology and innovation, and the potential of culture, for promoting sustainable development and achieving the Millennium Development Goals"

ECLAC: Latin America and the Caribbean in the World Economy 2013 (A sluggish post crisis, mega trade negotiations and value chains; scope for regional action)

ECLAC: Review of Cariforum-EU EPA—Implications for the British and Dutch Caribbean OCTs.

Press releases of EU council

Conclusions on the first anniversary of the EU Strategic Framework and Action Plan on Human Rights and Democracy and the appointment of the EUSR for Human Rights

The Overarching Post 2015 Agenda—Council conclusions General Affairs Council meeting Luxembourg, 25 June 2013

Conclusions on "local authorities in development" Brussels, 22 July 2013

European Union Strasbourg, 12 June 2013 A 314/13 Statement by EU High Representative Catherine Ashton on EEAS Review

EUROPEA2 U2IO2 Strasbourg, 12 June 2013, A 313/13 Remarks by EU High Representative Catherine Ashton on the EU annual report on human rights

Remarks by EU High Representative Catherine Ashton to the Inter parliamentary Conference (IPC), Vilnius, 5 September 2013

Francis Fukuyama, "What is Governance?", Working Paper 314, January 2013, Center for Global Development

Laurent Pech, "The Rule of Law as a Constitutional Principle of the European Union" Working Paper Series 04/09, Jean Monnet Center for the International and Regional Economic Law & Justice

International Centre for Trade and Sustainable Development, Assessing the Effectiveness of Aid for Trade: Lessons from the Ground July 2013 Issue Paper No. 29

Ministerie van Buitenlandse Zaken, Directie Westelijk Halfrond, report on Mercosur 1997

Overseas Development Institution (ODI) London, Report on a conference for EU Change-makers held at ODI, London, on 24 & 25 June 2013, "EU development cooperation: Where have we got to? What's next?"

References

Alston P (2002) Resisting the merger and acquisition of human rights by trade law: a reply to Petersmann. Eur J Int Law 13(4):815–844

Brandtner B, Rosas A (1998) Human rights and the external relations of the European Community: an analysis of doctrine and practice. Eur J Int Law 9(3):468–490

Horng D-C (2003) The human rights clause in the European Union's external trade and development agreements. Eur Law J 9(5):677–701

EU Enlargement, Its Impact at the European and National Level, and the Case of Albania

Alfred Kellermann

Abstract From 2006 onwards, Albania has been working on agreements with the EU about joining, but it has not joined the EU at this moment. However, in July 2014 Albania received the EU candidate status. Albania's constitution provides for the transfer of legislative powers to supranational organizations and no provisions in its constitutions are inconsistent with EU membership. The problem lies in the fact that some provisions do not exclude a possible negative interpretation, due to their openness. The biggest problem for Albania in joining the EU, according to the author, lies in the separation of powers, especially with regard to the judiciary. Although the independence is guaranteed, politics still have many ways to intervene, for example, via political nominations. Furthermore, case law is not being published. Some more positive signs of Albania's attitude towards the supremacy of EU law lie in the way it has implemented the European Convention for the Protection of Human Rights and Fundamental Freedoms. The Constitutional Court uses this convention to invalidate Albanian laws that are in conflict with provisions of this European Convention. In addition, Part Seven of the 1998 Constitution regulates normative acts and international agreements, stipulating that an international agreement that has been ratified by law has superiority over laws of the country.

Former Senior Policy Advisor and Head of EU Department at the TMC Asser Institute in The Hague, The Netherlands.

A. Kellermann (✉)
The Hague, The Netherlands
e-mail: alfred.kellermann@gmail.com

F.A.N.J. Goudappel and E.M.H. Hirsch Ballin (eds.), *Democracy and Rule of Law in the European Union*, DOI 10.1007/978-94-6265-066-4_10

Contents

1 Review of the Progress Made by Albania to Meet the Priorities for the EU Candidate Status

Albania signed a Stabilisation and Association Agreement (SAA) with the EU on 12 June 2006. The SAA provides a framework of mutual commitments on a wide range of political, trade, and economic issues. The Agreement has been ratified by 27 EU Member States and entered into force in April 2009. Albania presented its application for membership of the EU on 28 April 2009.[1] The Council on 11 December 2012 welcomed the progress made by Albania to meet the 12 key priorities laid out in the Commission's Opinion of 2010. In order to give an answer to the question of why the EU refused several times to give Albania the candidate status, I analyzed the impact of EU accession on Albania drafted in the period 2010–2012 based on documents and information by institutions.[2] An identical analysis was made in 2005 and following for many other New EU Member States and (Pre) Candidate countries in the Publication "Hopes and Fears."[3] This analysis[4] was made as follows. Firstly on the expected EU impact on the National Constitution, secondly, the EU impact on the role of the Judiciary, thirdly, the EU Impact on the Executive and fourthly, the EU Impact on the National Parliament. After answering questions and making analyses of the legal situation with regard to Albania in the following section, it may be easier to understand why some of the key priorities were not yet implemented in the Albanian legal order.

[1]SEC(2010)1335, Brussels 9 November 2010.

[2]Kellermann 2007a.

[3]Kellermann et al. 2006.

[4]Kellermann 2007b, c. Europian Nos. 12, 13 and 14 (Periodical of the Albanian Ministry of European Integration produced by GTZ) Including three articles on the impact of EU accession on the Albanian legal order (2) and the Reform Treaty signed at Lisbon (1), by A. Kellermann.

2 National Constitution of Albania[5]

Articles 121–123 of the Albanian Constitution, as approved by the Albanian Parliament on 21 October 1998, provide for ratification of international agreements, their effect in the Albanian Legal order, and the transfer to international organizations of state powers for specific issues. International treaties, being part of the national legal order pursuant to the Constitution of Albania, are to be applied by Albanian courts, and may, at least in theory, create individual rights.[6]) During the ratification process of the SAA, the issue of whether regulatory powers have to be transferred to the Stabilisation and Association Council will rise.

The Albanian Constitution, in Article 123, provides for the transfer of legislative powers to supranational organizations, although there is no confirmation in the constitutional practice so far. However, the question still remains whether it would be better to introduce into Article 123 of the Constitution an explicit legal basis for membership in the EU, which would provide for the transfer of powers on the EU institutions, and at the same time make clear that the legal norms they adopt will have direct effect in the Albanian legal order and are supreme to national law.[7]

Yet, there are no provisions in the Albanian constitution which are *prima facie* inconsistent with EU membership. The constitution sets out a reasonable framework for a democratic government system run in accordance with the rule of law. Therefore, the Treaties of Lisbon (Treaty on European Union and Treaty on the Functioning of the EU and the Charter of Fundamental Rights of the EU) may be ratified without formal amendments of the Constitution. However, certain constitutional provisions, due to their open wording, do not exclude interpretation that may create an obstacle for EU membership. It would therefore be useful to amend these constitutional provisions in order to exclude interpretation contrary to European law. It is assumed that Albania will best express its genuine desire for full membership of the EU by meeting the constitutional requirements for membership.[8]

As for a legal basis for EU membership of Albania, it needs to be noted that the Albanian constitution defines sovereignty (Article 1) as belonging to the people and also defines independence (Article 3). Such a constitutional definition of the state sovereignty and independence is ill adapted to the conditions of EU membership. In this respect the constitution could for instance provide for a shared exercise of the state sovereignty within institutions of the EU. Such a provision would provide for the procedure of ratification of the Treaty of Lisbon.

---

[5]Kellermann 2008a, pp. 183–218.

[6]See Europian No. 12, 2007, p. 12. See also report prepared by Ditmir Bushati LL.M, Founding Director of the European Movement in Albania, since 2013 Minister of Foreign Affairs of Albania.

[7]See Europian No. 12, 2007, p. 12. Legally not necessary however for European political reasons advisable.

[8]See Europian No. 12, 2007, p. 12.

Of course, the legal status of European law in future, both primary and secondary legislation, is not yet defined in the Albanian legal system. There is no differentiation between the legal rules of European law, what is at this stage understandable, as Albania is not yet an EU Member State. Despite the fact that EU law has direct effect in the Member States, implementation of European law would need to be able in Albania. Like it exists for international law in Article 122 of the constitution, there is also a clear need to adopt new constitutional rules in order to make European law an integral part of national law. Also, there is a need to differentiate them from international treaties and general rules of international law. Certainly, such a differentiation should recognize the specific legal nature and character of European law, and does not necessarily have to change the position of international law in the Albanian legal order. In other words, legal rules of European law, both primary and secondary, should be explicitly given legal authority and their supremacy and possibility of direct effect should explicitly be mentioned.[9]

Although the relationship between the legislative and executive branch is not of direct concern for Albania's EU membership, proper allocation of powers may significantly influence the efficiency of fulfillment of Albania's commitments and obligations. The ZELA Law of 8 July 2004 gave special legislation on the role of the Assembly as the highest legislative body in the Stabilisation and Association process, aiming at designing and observing the Albanian EU integration process.

According to Article 3, the Council of Ministers regularly sends information to the Parliament on the work done with the EU institutions and its assessments especially regarding draft agreements and draft acts related to EU obligations. However, the need for the government to take part in the decision-making at EU level calls for a change. It is desirable to provide for direct constitutional authority which would give the government the constitutional basis for making such decisions, and for implementing them in national law, when required by European law. This would preferably be accompanied by a simultaneous obligation to inform the Parliament regularly about such regulatory activities. For example, this could be the case with the Joint Committee Decisions of the Interim Agreement (IA).

For the judiciary, however, more measures will be necessary. Issues of constitutional jurisdiction in cases of EU membership, or in cases of a collision with EU obligations are not unique to the Albanian legal system and it will be possible to build on the experiences of comparable legal systems, such as German and Italian systems. The jurisdiction of the Constitutional Court is regulated in Article 131 of the Constitution. The Constitutional Court has been given a clear Constitutional authority to decide ex ante on compatibility of international treaties with the Constitution. The consequence of a declaration of compatibility will

[9]See Europian No. 12 2007, p. 13. Legally not necessary however for European political reasons advisable.

be a presumption of the conformity of the treaty with the constitution; possible ex ante constitutional review of the accession treaty would make future obligations as to the constitutionality of Albania's EU membership more difficult. Secondly, EU membership will require amendment of procedural rules of the Constitutional Court in order to bring it in line with the Simmenthal requirements, thus availing ordinary courts of recourse to *exceptio illegalitatis* in case of incompatibility of national laws and implementing regulations with legal rules of European law. In case that legislation is incompatible with European law, the constitutional court will, under the Simmenthal rule, have an obligation to apply national law without having to wait for the law to be set aside. In other words, European law requires ordinary courts to by-pass the concrete constitutional review.

Thus, there are several provisions in the Albanian constitution which will have to be amended in order to comply with the requirements of the *acquis*. Also there are a number of other provisions which are not contrary to the *acquis* as such, but need to be amended for other reasons, ranging from non-clarity to doctrinal imperfection. For the purpose of this analysis we can identify two different categories of constitutional provisions that are actually or potentially incompatible with the requirements of EU membership.

The Constitution guarantees, in Article 45, the right to vote for Albanian citizens. Although the constitution is silent on this point, it does not explicitly exclude to give non-nationals the right to vote. The provisions should not explicitly exclude EU citizens from the right to vote, however, as far as requirements of membership in the EU are concerned, right to vote on local elections, being a participatory right, has to be guaranteed to all EU citizens *expressis verbis*. The constitutional provisions should be broad enough to extend to requirements of Article 22 of the Treaty on the Functioning of the EU (TFEU) subject to which "Every citizen of the Union residing in a Member State of which he is not a national shall have the right to vote and to stand as a candidate at municipal elections in the Member State in which he resides, under the same conditions as nationals of that State." Constitutional amendment of these provisions should make direct universal suffrage of EU citizens residing in Albania at local elections in Albania possible.

As stated above, Articles 121–123 of the Constitution state, ratified and published international treaties which are in force form part of the Albanian legal order and are supreme to Albanian laws. However, the hierarchy is not entirely defined, having in mind the multitude of different legal sources that exist in the Albanian legal order. A clearer constitutional provision as the one in Article 116 would be welcome in this respect. Additionally, as already mentioned, express reference to the effect and status of EU law in the Albanian legal order should be added in the Constitution together with the express legal basis for EU membership for European integration political reasons.

3 The Role of the Judiciary (National Courts) in Albania

Despite all this, the judiciary seems to be the weakest link in Albania's fragile system of separation of powers. The principle of independence of the judiciary is provided for in the constitution and in the relevant legislation. However, political nominations and other forms of political interventions hamper the effective independence.[10] The judicial culture of Albanian courts can be best described as positivist formalist approach to the law, the situation that is not uncommon in other former communist countries, some of which are new Member States of the EU. The procedures remain lengthy and poorly organized. The interpretation of the law is mostly textual, and depends on legal dogmas, representing a world of their own, not necessarily matching the reality.[11] The social context is rarely taken into context in the judgments, and even more, rarely mentioned. Although expressly empowered by the Constitution, judges rarely apply the Constitution directly when deciding cases. Even the Constitutional Court gives a very narrow and formalistic interpretation of the Constitution. The biggest shortcoming of the Albanian judicial and, more widely, legal system is the missing tradition of publication of case law.

Based on the belief that judges have nothing to do with law creation, that the law is written in the Statutes and that the case law is therefore irrelevant, the court decisions were not regularly published. Only occasionally some judgments were published, and even than not the entire judgments, but only excerpts that whoever prepared the publication deemed to be relevant.

The Albanian judicial organization consists of three levels: general courts, courts of appeal, and the high court as the final national instance in civil and criminal cases. The Constitutional Court decides on the conformity of laws and other regulations with the constitution. Appointments of judges to the courts and courts of appeal are less affected by political interference, to the extent that the president upon proposal of the High Council of Justice, a largely professional entity, appoints them. The High Court and Constitutional Court members as well as the State Prosecutor are more exposed to political pressure. The fragile separation of the powers of the state and political intimidation of the judiciary has largely undermined any effective legal prosecution of abuse of office.[12] Most allegations of high level corruption that were disclosed in media investigations have not been translated into cases before the courts. In the cases that have been officially investigated, few have led to convictions, and when there were convictions it was only of

---

[10]Source: discussions in Tirana with journalists, civil servants from Ministries and the European Movement.

[11]See Europian No. 13, 2008, p. 12.

[12]Source: discussions in Tirana with journalists, civil servants from ministries and European Movement.

low-level officials. As the judgments were rarely published, not only was the current legislation not known outside the judiciary, but the judges themselves did not know what the other judges' positions on different aspects of law were. The uniformity of legislation, the most important task of the Constitutional Court, had therefore to be ensured in some other way. This was and still is done at the sessions of the judges of Constitutional and High Court, at which the joint positions of the "correct interpretation" of law are accepted.[13]

A solution could be that the Albanian courts could apply the Stabilisation and Association Agreement (SAA) and Interim Agreement directly and/or indirectly. The SAA entered into force in 2009 as mentioned above. The Interim Agreement (IA) entered already into force on 1 December 2006. This Interim Agreement allows the trade provisions of the SAA to come already into force. Under the IA, Albania also commits aligning with EU standards in several trade-related fields. The EU expects that Albania will consequently profit from an unlimited free access to the EU Market. The courts could apply the Interim Agreement and the Joint Decisions taken by the Joint Committee in implementing the IA, since it has now been in force for several years. However, there is no information available about direct effect of and references to the IA. We could however imagine that such a case concerning the standstill provisions of the IA could emerge. For example, I found that the excise duty of raki is lower than the excise duty on grappa. This conflicts with Article 21 SAA on the prohibition of fiscal discrimination. One could imagine that the importer of grappa could make a case out of it referring as well as to Albanian constitutional law (Article 122) and to European law. In other words the Albanian courts could apply the IA directly or indirectly. The Albanian Parliament adopted at the initiative of the Albanian Government, the Law on the Implementation of the SAA and Interim Agreement. The law accepted a dualist approach, which may be unconstitutional, but its constitutionality has not been questioned yet. The Law envisages that decisions of the Stabilisation and Association Council have to be either ratified by the Parliament or enacted in the form of an internal law or transformed into an act of the Government in order to have effect in the Albanian Legal order. The same can be said about the Joint Committee Decisions of the IA. In other words they are not directly applicable, although on the basis of the SAA itself, Acts of the Association Council, as such, are published in the Albanian Official Journal and therefore, according to the Constitution, the Albanian courts have authority to apply the SAA and IA.

The SAA could even have a pre-accession effect. Although no case has yet been initiated before a court in an EU Member State in which an Albanian national is involved and where a preliminary ruling is requested on the interpretation of the SAA or Interim Agreement, I could imagine that such a case could soon or later be

[13] Gjevori2008; Kellermann 2008b.

decided since the SAA has entered in 2009 into force. For this, Article 46 SAA, in Title V, Chapter I—Movement of Workers can be used as an example. This provision holds the following:

> Subject "to the conditions and modalities applicable in each Member State:-treatment according to workers who are Albanian national and who are legally employed in the territory of a Member State shall be free of any discrimination based on nationality as regards working conditions, remuneration or dismissal to its own nationals; …."

The provision does not give a right to legal employment. However, once the worker is legally employed he has the right of equal treatment with EU nationals regarding working conditions, remuneration, and dismissal. Many Albanian nationals legally employed in EU Member States may enforce their rights before national courts in EU Member States to enforce their rights. Another example is Article 49 SAA on Establishment and following, which guarantees equal conditions of establishment for Albanian and Community companies in the Community and Albania. These rights are somewhat identical to the rights which Polish and Slovak nationals used to enforce their rights on equal treatment in case of establishment.

The question remains whether the judiciary has already embraced the principle of supremacy and direct effect of European law. As Albania is not yet an EU Member State, European law as such does not apply (except for the SAA and Interim Agreement). In the pre-accession stage, it is possible to ask whether courts apply these principles in relation to the SAA/IA Agreements and whether they make difference between the SAA itself and the decisions of the Stabilisation and Association Council as secondary association law.

An indication of the possible attitude towards supremacy and direct effect of primary EU law in the Albanian legal order may be the judicial application of the European Convention on Human Rights and Fundamental Freedoms (ECHR), to which Albania is party. The Albanian Constitutional Court has developed a practice of applying the European Convention as a basis for invalidating Albanian Laws which were contrary to the European Convention provisions. The Court also used the European Convention as an interpretative tool, and quoted the case law of the European Court of Human Rights. Supremacy of the European Convention in relation to Albanian laws did not prove problematic, as the Albanian Constitution expressly envisages supremacy of international treaties in relation to ordinary laws.[14] The Constitutional Court has developed a well-established practice that non-conformity of Albanian laws with an international treaty represents a breach of the principle of the rule of law and is contrary to the Constitution.

Integration with the EU and potentially EU membership authorizes Albanian courts to directly apply secondary association law that is capable of creating direct

[14]See Europian No. 13, 2008.

effects subject to the criteria developed by the European Court of Justice. Even if courts will interpret SAA as allowing direct application of secondary association law, they may not apply Albanian legislation (in this case the Law on the implementation of SAA) by themselves. According to the Albanian Constitution on the Constitutional Court and the Law on the Courts, they must stay the procedure, refer such question to the Constitutional Court, and await its decision. Non-recognition of direct effect of secondary association law, additionally to being contrary to the monistic constitutional choice of Albania, is also not in line with the case law of the European Court of Justice.

In a more practical sense, membership of the EU itself will not cause any changes in the organization of the judiciary in Albania. It is clear from the case law of the European Court of Justice that EU law does not interfere with the organization of justice in the Member States,[15] provided that there is always a competent court that can hear action based on European law and providing that the judicial protection is empowered to offer effective protection according to the European standards. Although an organizational change will not be necessary, the requirement of effectiveness of the legal protection will provoke changes in the procedural sphere. Some new procedures and practices will have to be accepted also for participation in the judicial cooperation in the EU, i.e. for use of the preliminary rulings procedure and possible for participation in the field of judicial cooperation. The application of this case law of the European Court of Justice demands two things from the national judges: firstly they need to be familiar with the case law of the ECJ and keep themselves informed, and secondly and equally important they have to be prepared to a creative role demanded from them by European law.

Yet, in order to become 'European judges', the national judges need to be familiar with European law, understand not only as a set of written rules but including also case law, interpreting these rules as well as the principles of European law which relate to their application and interpretation. For this to be achieved it is necessary to educate all the judges—present and future—in European law. Up to today the number of Albanian judges who did have a sufficient training in EU law is very small.

For accession respect for human and civil rights is also necessary. Respect for civil rights is enshrined in the Albanian Constitution and in the Conventions that Albania has ratified. The office of the ombudsman is Albania's main institution for civil rights, which has played an active role in monitoring the human rights situation. Due to a political stalemate the election of the new ombudsman in 2010 was delayed.

[15]See Europian No. 14, 2008, p. 12.

4 The Role of the Executive (Government and Administration) in Albania

The government and ruling coalition consisting of the Democratic Party and the Socialist Movement for Integration remained in place and stable during 2012. In March and June 2012, a government reshuffle took place. The Albanian government has adopted a national plan to implement the Partnership priorities and the SAA. The Plan has formed part of the new National Strategy for Development and Integration (NSDI). The NSDI will feed into the Integrated Planning System (IPS) through which national and donor resources will be allocated.

Fulfilment of all the obligations stemming from the SAA represents the start of serious reforms of public administration as well as of society as a whole in order to facilitate adjustment to the political, economic and legal standards of the EU.

The Ministry of European Integration (MEI played a key role in the revision of the Action Plan to address the Opinion's key priorities,) in cooperation with the Parliamentary Committee for European Integration. The Action Plan has been improved by clarifying the content of the measures and specifying deliverables. A monthly monitoring mechanism was smoothly implemented. There has been progress in updating the National Plan for the implementation of the SAA (NPISAA), and this plan has been approved by a Council of Ministers' decision. There has been some progress in coordinating processes for aligning legislation with the *acquis*. The MEI has continued working on legislative gap analysis. An IT system for legal approximation (IMS) has been introduced.

In order to ensure the coordinated and timely implementation of the SAA, many mechanisms for coordination, monitoring, and reporting have been set up. State administration bodies, in the preparation of legislative documents which approximate the legislation of Albania with the *acquis communautaire* pursuant to Article 70 SAA, are obliged to submit together with the legislative act a completed statement on the harmonization and a parallel review of the conformity of the provisions of the proposal of the act with the provisions of the relevant legal Community acts. This so-called *Compatibility Statemen*t gathers essential information in respect of the compatibility of a draft proposal of an act with the relevant SAA provisions as well as with the relevant EU legislation.

In order to have an effective harmonization, as effectively as possible, in addition to the Compatibility Statement, administrative authorities fill out a *Table of Concordance*, which is in fact a parallel review of the conformity of the provisions of the (draft) proposal with provisions of the relevant EU legislation acts. In April 2007, the Prime Minister of Albania passed a Decision on the Establishment of Working Groups for the Harmonization of the Albanian Legislation with the acquis. There has been only moderate progress regarding the coordination of the EU integration process. Comprehensive and sustainable capacity development of the 35 interinstitutional working groups in 2012 and further improvement of policy coordination among institutions is necessary. The policy-making and legislative drafting processes in line ministries are still subject to shortfalls in prior analytical work and there is not enough transparency or consultation with relevant stakeholders. Staff turnover and weaknesses in analytical capacity have had an impact on the quality of legislation drafted. More attention should be paid to the implementation and enforcement of legislation.

There is also a role for parliament in this. Since the country's first pluralist elections in 1991, Albania has maintained a parliamentary democracy. The Albanian constitution provides the main institutional infrastructure for democratic governance. The country's 2009 elections, however, represented a major drawback in Albania's march toward more democratic norms, as the results produced a dangerous radicalization between opposition parties asking for an investigation into alleged election fraud, and the governing majority refusing their requests.[16] The failure to investigate existing allegations of corruption that involved current ministers shows the continued collapse of an already weak rule of law. According to the Albanian Constitution the Assembly, the national parliament is the highest body of state power and exercises oversight over the executive and institutions it establishes. However, the contested elections of 2009 and the subsequent boycott of the opposition have hampered the functioning of the parliament.

For purposes of the process of integration into the EU, changes in the internal structure and parliamentary procedure were introduced since 2004. These changes are reflected in the Law of 8 July 2004 referred to as the ZELA law. This law describes the responsibilities of the Council of Ministers in the EU decision-making procedures and the Law Approximation process (Article 3). Parliament has set up the *European Integration Committee* (CEI), which consists of a chairman, vice chairman, and members, composed according to the proportional representation in the Parliament. The European Integration Committee of the Albanian Parliament has a key role in the legislative process.

Progress was further made in the functioning of parliamentary procedures, with the adoption of a considerable number of acts, including laws, decisions, resolutions and declarations. In a significant number of cases these were approved by consensus. Progress was also noted in terms of improving public consultation in the legislative process. Under its new chairman, the Committee on European Integration was actively involved with the Ministry of Integration in developing and monitoring relevant parts of the Action Plan.

However, work needs to continue to further improve the functioning of the Parliament. The working calendar of the parliament does not always give enough time to standing committees for proper review and for public hearings on draft law, which, as a result, is often adopted in an expedited manner potentially to the detriment of the quality. Draft legislation is often not accessible to the public. Further efforts are required to strengthen the parliament's oversight function, including reinforcing the use of interpellations with members of the government and written questions and answers. Some progress was made in strengthening the

[16]Source: opinions and discussions with journalists, (staff) members of parliament and civil servants of ministries, and European Movement).

administrative capacity of the parliament Secretariat through training of staff and expert advice, including international experts.

This means that there is political will to give the Parliament considerable powers in EU affairs, especially since the Treaty of Lisbon strengthened the role of national parliaments in EU decision-making. The Albanian parliament will have at least advisory influence over the Government's position in the Council. The issue of a Parliamentary role in EU affairs is of large importance not only for the democracy in the country, but also for effective EU membership. Thus, as mentioned above, the public debate on the role of parliament and government in EU affairs has been opened. It could be made part of the debate on the possible constitutional changes necessitated by EU membership.

5 The New Accession Approach of the EU

All this needs to be placed in the framework of the new accession approach of the EU. Enlargement remains a key policy of the EU. However after the recent accessions, the EU has strengthened its criteria for accession. This is the so-called new approach for accession which is now applicable to Albania. At a time when the European Union faces major challenges, the enlargement process continues to reinforce peace, democracy, and stability in Europe and allows the EU to be better positioned to address global challenges and pursue its strategic interests. The prospect of accession stimulates Albania to develop political and economic reforms, transforming societies, consolidating the rule of law, and creating new opportunities for citizens and business. These reforms are necessary in order to receive the candidate status.[17]

Strengthening the rule of law and democratic governance remains crucial for Albania to come closer to the EU and later to fully assume the obligations of EU membership. The new approach to negotiations on the judiciary and fundamental rights and on justice, freedom, and security, resulting from the experience of previous accession negotiations, has put rule of law issues, including the fight against organized crime and corruption, at the center of the EU's enlargement policy. The new approach provides for the above-mentioned issues to be tackled early in the enlargement process, and reaffirms the need for solid track records of reform implementation to be developed throughout the negotiation process, with the aim of ensuring sustainable and lasting reforms. The new approach envisages incentives and support to the candidate countries, as well as corrective measures, as appropriate. In the new Union's approach for accession, the rule of law is now firmly anchored at the heart of the accession process. The Council also welcomes

[17]Kellermann 2009. Article was written in English but translated for publication in Albanian language afterwards.

the cooperation with Europol in this area, as well as the closer interaction with Member States, and the Commission's intention to reinforce its assessments and reporting to the Council on organized crime for each Western Balkans country, on the basis of specific contributions prepared by Europol.

The importance of protecting and ensuring the enjoyment of the full range of human rights is now underlined, including the rights of persons in Albania belonging to minorities, and without distinction as to the sexual orientation or gender identity of persons, including the right to freedom of assembly, expression and association, and the importance of promoting a culture of tolerance. Furthermore, the work on improving social and economic inclusion of vulnerable groups, including the Roma, should continue, in particular through the EU Framework for National Roma Integration Strategies.

On 11 December 2012, the Council welcomed the progress made by Albania to meet the 12 key priorities laid out in the Commission's 2010 Opinion. The 12 key priorities concerned the following areas:

- the proper functioning of parliament;
- adopting reinforced majority laws;
- appointment procedures and appointments for key institutions;
- electoral reform;
- the conduct of elections;
- public administration reform;
- rule of law and judicial reform;
- fighting corruption;
- fighting organized crime;
- addressing property issues;
- reinforcing human rights and implementing anti-discrimination policies;
- improving the treatment of detainees and applying recommendations of the Ombudsman.

The improved dialogue between the government and the opposition, after the November 2011 agreement, has allowed Albania to make good progress towards fulfilling the political criteria for membership of the EU. Albania delivered on a set of reforms against the twelve key priorities, particularly addressing the proper functioning of the parliament, electoral reform and appointments of key officials. The European Commission assessed that Albania has met four of the key priorities and was well on its way towards meeting two others. Albania's continued constructive role in the region was welcomed.

However, good progress is not enough. The Council underlined the need to further intensify efforts, particularly in the area of the reform of the judiciary in order to strengthen its independence, efficiency and accountability, fight against corruption and organized crime, protection of all minorities, as well as the implementation of reforms. The successful conduct of Parliamentary elections in 2013 was a crucial test for the smooth functioning of the country's democratic institutions. Sustainable political dialogue and continued efforts in all the areas covered by the key priorities will remain essential to implement reforms necessary for Albania's EU future.

The opening of accession negotiations was considered by the European Council, in line with established practice, once the Commission had assessed that Albania has achieved the necessary degree of compliance with the membership criteria and had met in particular the 12 above-mentioned key priorities set out in the 2010 Commission's Opinion. Sustained implementation of reforms and fulfilment of all the key priorities was required for Albania to open accession negotiations with the EU and to receive the candidate status. The necessary degree of compliance with accession criteria included, according to the Council inter alia: conducting elections in line with European and international standards; strengthening the independence, efficiency and accountability of judicial institutions; determined efforts in the fight against corruption and organised crime; effective measures to reinforce the protection of human rights and anti-discrimination policies, including in the area of minorities, and their equal treatment; and implementation of property rights.

6 Evaluation of Albania's Application for EU Candidate Status

In order to give an answer to the question of why the EU had refused several times to give Albania the candidate status, first an analysis and assessment of the impact of EU Accession for Albania had to be made for the constitution, judiciary, government, and parliament. The recommendations were based moreover on my experiences, during the years 2006–2008 when I was EU Team Leader of an EU project to strengthen the capacity of the Albanian Ministry of European Integration. Secondly afterwards the main Agreements and recent documents regarding Albania's application for EU Membership have been reviewed.

From the analysis of the previous desk-research and the Commission Progress Report 2012, the European Commission had to conclude that Albania had not met all key 12 priorities. According to the new approach, the EU Council was not yet satisfied in 2012 with good progress and partial implementation of accession criteria. Taking into account the disappointing experiences with the accession of Bulgaria and Romania, the degree of compliance with the accession criteria had increased after 2007. In the new approach and vision of the European Council and its Member States, all the requirements to become a candidate EU Country must be fully met. That is in my opinion the reason why Albania had not received the EU candidate status in 2012.

Not receiving the candidate status was just a formality but not a tragedy. Switzerland and Norway are not EU Member States; however, these countries have a modern effective society and are happy with their position. More important than just the formality of candidate status, is the full implementation of the accession requirements by Albania which result in the political and economic reforms, transformation of the society, consolidation of the rule of law and the creation of new opportunities for Albanian citizens and business.

7 EU Candidate Status for Albania

Finally, since June 2014, the Republic of Albania is an official candidate for accession to the European Union. At the General Affairs Council meeting in Luxembourg on 24 June 2014 the Ministers from the EU Member States have agreed—based on the recommendation by the European Commission—to grant EU candidate status to Albania, subject to endorsement by EU heads of states at the forthcoming European Council in Brussels. Being recognized as an EU candidate country has a number of implications for Albania. Candidate status does not mean that the EU will automatically start accession negotiations with Albania, which is a subsequent step in the EU integration process, to which additional progress in the key priorities, is required.

References

Gjevori A (2008) The rights of non-member state nationals under the EU association agreements. Europ J Law Reform 10(3):339–382

Kellermann AE, Czuczai J, Blockmans S, Albi A, Douma WTh (eds) (2006) The impact of EU accession on the legal orders of new EU member states and (pre-)candidate countries: hopes and fears. Asser Press, The Hague, T.M.C

Kellermann A (2007a) Impact of EU Accession on the legal order of Albania. REVISTA E drejta parlamentare dhe politikat ligjore [Parliam Law Legal Polic Rev] 2007(1):4–35

Kellermann A (2007b) European experiences of good governance. REVISTA E drejta parlamentare dhe politikat ligjore [Parliam Law Legal Polic Rev] 2007(3)

Kellermann A (2007c) Report on guidelines for an effective approximation of Albanian legislation with the acquis communautaire. REVISTA E drejta parlamentare dhe politikat ligjore [Parliam Law Legal Polic Rev] 2007(3)

Kellermann A (2008a) Guidelines on the quality of EU legislation and its impact on Albania. Europ J Law Reform 10:183–218

Kellermann (2008b) Legal effects of EU Association Agreements for non EU Member State nationals. REVISTA E Drejta parlamentare dhe politikat ligjore [Parleam Law Legal Polic Rev] 2008:4–63

Kellermann A (2009) Accession Negotiation Techniques for Albania. REVISTA E Drejta parlamentaredhe politikat ligjore [Parliam Law Legal Polic Rev] 2009:1–21

Part III
Policy Areas

European Ruling on Pensions: A Second Warning for the Netherlands

Hans van Meerten

Abstract The Hogan Judgment of the ECJ found that each EU state is liable for a minimum level of pension benefit commitments. The claimants in this case found that Ireland had not properly transposed Article 8 of Directive 2008/94 into national law. This Directive protects employees when their employer becomes insolvent. The Irish Court asked the ECJ whether a causal link between loss of pension benefits and insolvency of the employer was necessary for the Directive to be applicable and if the Irish State was liable if transposing Article 8 was done incorrectly. The ECJ concluded that causality between the employer's insolvency and the loss of pension rights of the employee was not necessary. This case was preceded by several others in which the interpretation of the Directive and the liability of the state were under discussion. The Dutch government has transposed the Directive into several national Acts. Although many consider this transposition to be sufficient, the author mentions several reasons why a situation similar to the Irish case can also happen in this country. In his conclusion, the author emphasizes the danger of the statement that the Netherlands has provided sufficient safeguards to prevent the Irish situation. The Hogan case can have severe implications for the Netherlands, warns the author, especially when reducing and discounting pension accruals and benefits.

Dr. H. van Meerten is a lawyer with Clifford Chance LLP, The Hague, and writes in a private capacity. This contribution is a translated and slightly amended version of an article which appeared in Dutch *Pensioen Magazine*, 2013.

H. van Meerten (✉)
Clifford Chance LLP, The Hague, The Netherlands
e-mail: Hans.vanMeerten@CliffordChance.nl

F.A.N.J. Goudappel and E.M.H. Hirsch Ballin (eds.), *Democracy and Rule of Law in the European Union*, DOI 10.1007/978-94-6265-066-4_11

Contents

1 Introduction

The considerable influence of the European Union on 'our' pensions is an issue that was discussed at length in different contributions.[1] The fact that non-compliance with European law can lead to state liability has been known for some time, but the fact that the non-functioning (or at least not sufficiently) of the second pillar can also lead to state liability has come as a surprise to many. This contribution focuses on the implications of and background to the recent *Hogan* judgment of the European Court of Justice ("ECJ").

This judgment found that the State, i.e. any Member State of the EU, is liable for a minimum level of pension benefit commitments if the pension fund has no resources to satisfy such benefits in the event of the employer's insolvency. This Irish case is also interesting because it deals with the ubiquitous economic crisis. All the same, and as per usual, lawyers have different opinions on the impact of this judgment on the Dutch situation.

2 The Issue[2]

The claimants in the main proceedings against the Irish State were ten former employees of 'Waterford Crystal', an undertaking based in Waterford, Ireland, most of whom had not yet reached their retirement age. For the claimants, one of the conditions of employment was that they join one of the defined benefit

[1] Van Meerten 2012.

[2] The body of facts is derived from the case itself and the commentary of the Dutch Ministry of Foreign Affairs, www.minbuza.nl/ecer. Accessed 10 March 2015.

supplementary pension schemes set up by their employer (in EU lingo: a supplementary system of social security benefits with awarded benefits). In early 2009, a receiver was appointed for Waterford Crystal and it was found to be insolvent. The supplementary pension schemes set up by that company were wound up on 31 March 2009.

According to their actuary, the claimants would only receive between 18 and 28 % of the actual value of their accrued old-age pension rights. The actuary retained by Ireland found that this percentage was between 16 and 41 %. This did not matter very much as neither calculation approached the 49 % referred to by the ECJ in the judgment in *Robins and Others* (detailed below).[3] The claimants in the main proceedings subsequently brought an action against Ireland, claiming that Ireland had not properly transposed Article 8 of Directive 2008/94. By contrast, Ireland maintained that it had adopted, both before and after the judgment in *Robins and Others*, numerous measures designed to protect the interests of beneficiaries of supplementary occupational pension schemes. As the Irish High Court took the view that interpretation of the provisions of Directive 2008/94 was necessary, it decided to stay the proceedings and refer seven questions to the ECJ for a preliminary ruling. In essence, these questions asked whether there had to be a causal link between the claimants' loss of their pension benefits and the insolvency of their employer for the Directive to be applicable and whether the Irish State would be liable if it were established that Article 8 had not been transposed correctly.

In the judgment in *Hogan* the ECJ provides an answer to these questions. Before discussing these answers it may be useful to elaborate briefly on some (recent) EU legal principles.

3 The Legal Framework

We have known ever since 1963 that European law prevails over national law and thus over the Dutch Pensions Act. This case involves a Directive. Member States—to whom it is addressed—have to transpose a Directive into national law within a certain period of time. A Directive does not, in principle, have legal effect before the end of the transposition period. In principle, because the concept of interpretation 'in a manner consistent with the wording and purpose of the Directive' obliges the Member States, both before and after transposition, to interpret national law in a manner consistent with the wording and purpose of the Directive where possible.[4] EU citizens can rely on the Directive if it has direct effect, i.e. if the Directive confers rights on them that are sufficiently clear.

[3]ECJ 25 January 2007, Case No. C-278/05, *Robins*.

[4]See Van Meerten 2009.

In a recent case, the ECJ confirmed that the effect of interpretation in a manner consistent with the wording and purpose of the Directive must be considered before the direct effect.[5] If a dispute cannot be resolved by an interpretation in a manner consistent with the wording and purpose of the Directive, citizens may rely on the direct effect of the Directive and have national law declared inapplicable. In a judgment of 2012, the Dutch Supreme Court found that in the interpretation in a manner consistent with the wording and purpose of the Directive the options that the text of the national Act transposing the Directive offers prevail over the legislative history of that Act.[6]

3.1 Directive 2008/94

This Directive of the European legislature of 22 October 2008 intends to protect employees when their employer becomes insolvent.[7] A key recital of the Directive is recital 3, which reads:

> It is necessary to provide for the protection of employees in the event of the insolvency of their employer and to ensure a minimum degree of protection, in particular in order to guarantee payment of their outstanding claims, while taking account of the need for balanced economic and social development in the Community. To this end, the Member States should establish a body which guarantees payment of the outstanding claims of the employees concerned.

Article 8 of the Directive, what the case before the ECJ was about, reads: "Member States shall ensure that the necessary measures are taken to protect the interests of employees and of persons having already left the employer's undertaking or business at the date of the onset of the employer's insolvency in respect of rights conferring on them immediate or prospective entitlement to old-age benefits, including survivors' benefits, under supplementary occupational or inter-occupational pension schemes outside the national statutory social security schemes".

3.2 State Liability

In 1991, in the judgment in *Francovich and Others*, the ECJ recognized the principle of state liability for the loss and damage caused to individuals as a result of breaches of European law that may be attributed to the State.[8] According to the

[5]ECJ, Case No. C-97/11, *Amia SpA*.

[6]Dutch Supreme Court 21 September 2012, No. AB 2012/367, with commentary by Widdershoven.

[7]Directive 2008/94/EC, pp. 36–42.

[8]ECJ 19 November 1991, Cases C-6/90 and C-9/90, *Francovich* (para 37).

ECJ, this principle is 'inherent in the system of the Treaty'. Since then, this principle has been elaborated in more detail on various occasions. It applies to all breaches of European law of which the act or omission forms a part, irrespective of the State body, thus including, for instance, the Dutch Central Bank.[9] A breach of European law by a Member State will be attributed to a government body and result in the obligation to make good loss and damage caused to the individuals suffering injury if:

a. the rule of law infringed should be intended to confer rights on individuals;
b. the breach should be sufficiently serious; and
c. there should be a direct causal link between the breach and the damage caused to the individuals.[10]

If these conditions are met, the failure to take measures to transpose a Directive to attain the result prescribed by this Directive within the period laid down for that purpose will *as such* constitute a serious breach of European law and may give rise to a right of reparation for individuals suffering injury. The ECJ came to this conclusion in the judgment in *Dillenkorfer*.[11]

3.3 The Robins Case

As stated above, this case dealt with a similar issue to the *Hogan* case. The *Robins* case involved a British final salary scheme which in some cases entailed an obligation for members to contribute a percentage of their salary whilst the employer had to contribute at a rate necessary to enable the benefits to be maintained and provided. This case too turned on the interpretation of Article 8 of Directive 2008/94. The claimants argued that Article 8 imposed an *obligation of result* and the Advocate-General shared their view. The ECJ, however, did not. Although it did find, for the first time, that 49 % of the pension benefits to which the claimants were entitled was a minimum level, it ruled at the same time that the considerable discretion allowed to the Member States is an important criterion in determining whether or not attaining this constituted a sufficiently serious breach of European law. According to the ECJ, that was not the case here: "It is apparent from consideration of the first question that, on account of the general nature of the wording of Article 8 of the Directive, that provision allows the Member States considerable discretion for the purposes of determining the level of protection of entitlement to benefits".

[9]For the case law and further interpretation of this issue see the commentary of Schutjes, JGR 2009/7 ECJ, 16 October 2008, Case C-452/06.

[10]See, in particular, Case C-278/05, *Robins*, para 69 and the case law cited there.

[11]Joined Cases C-178/94 and others, *Dillenkorfer*.

According to the ECJ, a Member State can only be held liable for the incorrect transposition of a provision on a finding of manifest and serious disregard by that State for the limits set on its discretion.[12] According to the ECJ, neither the parties in the main proceedings, nor the Member States which had submitted observations, nor the Commission had been able to suggest with precision the minimum degree of protection that in their view is required by the Directive. Thus the United Kingdom was not held liable, in part because the European Commission had submitted dated information.

4 The Judgment

The ECJ reached a conclusion in a remarkably swift manner. It found that:

1. Directive 2008/94/EC of the European Parliament and of the Council of 22 October 2008 on the protection of employees in the event of the insolvency of their employer must be interpreted as meaning that it applies to the entitlement of former employees to old-age benefits under a supplementary pension scheme set up by their employer.
2. Article 8 of Directive 2008/94 must be interpreted as meaning that State pension benefits may *not* (emphasis added by *HvM*) be taken into account in assessing whether a Member State has complied with the obligation laid down in that article.
3. Article 8 of Directive 2008/94 must be interpreted as meaning that, in order for that article to apply, it is sufficient that the pension scheme is underfunded as of the date of the employer's insolvency and that, on account of his insolvency, the employer does not have the resources to contribute sufficient money to the pension scheme to enable the pension benefits owned to the beneficiaries of that scheme to be satisfied in full. It is not necessary for those beneficiaries to prove that there are other factors giving rise to the loss of their entitlement to old-age benefits.
4. Directive 2008/94 must be interpreted as meaning that the measures adopted by Ireland following the judgment of the Court of Justice of the European Union of 25 January 2007 in Case C-278/05 *Robins and Others* do not fulfil the obligations imposed by that Directive and that the economic situation of the Member State concerned does not constitute an exceptional situation capable of justifying a lower level of protection of the interests of employees as regards their entitlement to old-age benefits under a supplementary occupational pension scheme.

[12] At [75], Case C-278/05. This requirement could also be regarded as an elaboration of the requirement of conferring rights.

5. Directive 2008/94 must be interpreted as meaning that the fact that the measures taken by Ireland subsequent to *Robins and Others* have not brought about the result that the plaintiffs would receive in excess of 49 % of the value of their accrued old-age pension benefits under their occupational pension scheme is in itself a serious breach of that Member State's obligations.

5 The Dutch Situation

The Netherlands has transposed the Directive into various Acts, including the Dutch Unemployment Insurance Act. Some argue that the Netherlands offers sufficient statutory protection to preclude a situation such as the Irish one. Reference is, for example, made to the combination of provisions laid down in the Dutch Pensions Act and Section 64(1)(c) of the Dutch Unemployment Insurance Act: the takeover by the Dutch Employee Insurance Agency ["UWV"] of the pension contributions payable by the employer to the pension administrator.[13]

There are several reasons to disagree with this. In as early as 2007, Amrish Ritoe drew attention to the implications of the judgment in *Robins*.[14] He described the takeover obligation of contributions of an insolvent employer by the UWV in some cases as 'a drop in the ocean' and warned, even then, that the Netherlands might not have transposed Article 8 of the Directive correctly. In at least one regard his contribution is still extremely current, i.e. the discount options of pension funds (Section 134 of the Dutch Pensions Act). The benefits of members of pension schemes can be reduced and discounted in all kinds of ways—by pension funds and the government—even during the accrual phase: no indexation, restructuring, reducing the accrual percentages, increasing the contributions, increasing the retirement age, bringing in new pension rights, etc. Quite apart from the employer's insolvency, these mechanisms can result in pension funds paying less than 49 % of the value of the pension scheme commitments.

Thus Pikaart tried to calculate the level of the old-age pension, including the state pension ["AOW"] (even though the 49 % in the *Hogan* ruling is exclusive of AOW) for a 30-year old.[15] He arrived at 57 %. According to Pikaart, Knot, currently the President of the Dutch Central Bank, had already shown that an annual accrual of 1.75 % over 40 years and the averaging over various average indexations, during the accrual, from 0 to 3 % can result in a theoretically expected end result of 48 % for a 30-year old. These calculations date from before the credit crunch, when the average *nominal* coverage ratio of pension funds was still around 150 % in lieu of the current average of around 95 %.

[13]Lutjens 2013.

[14]Ritoe 2007.

[15]Pikaart 2013 (the online version was consulted for this article).

In many cases the *realistic* coverage ratio is much lower. And the assumption that an employee will constantly be employed over a period of 40 years does not hold true for the younger generations. What is more, short-term employment contracts in sectors that employ many young people, such as the employment agency industry, the retail trade and the cleaning sector, have led to many pension entitlements remaining below the commutation threshold. This means that pension benefits for younger generations will on average be much lower. In addition, no account is taken here of the calculations made by Kocken and others, which show that an ageing, underfunded pension fund may well reach rock bottom within 20 years if government policy remains unchanged.[16] And finally, the discounts relating to the bringing in of new pension rights over old ones *plus* the effects of the UFR calculation method, considered artificial by many economists, would still have to be factored in.

In other words, given the highly problematic state of our pension funds, and the fact that several years ago it was also postulated that it was inconceivable that funds would have a considerable funding shortfall and would have to be restructured, the statement that Dutch legislation provides sufficient safeguards to preclude situations such as the Irish one is a very risky statement indeed. Even without an insolvent employer the minimum level of 49 % is conceivable.

5.1 Obligation of Result

The second reason why this is a risky statement is the following one. It could be argued that the judgment in *Hogan* is not really new. Many issues were already clear and at first glance the judgment in *Hogan* appears to be a reiteration of the judgment in *Robins*. This is incorrect as well. It is true that many findings were a logical consequence of European law, but it nevertheless appears to be a permanent trend that in the assessment of State liability the causality requirement is no longer factored in. In its judgment in *Robins* the ECJ drew a great deal of attention to the requirement of a 'sufficiently serious breach' without discussing the other requirements for state liability.[17] Nor did the ECJ find that a causal link between the loss of pension rights and the employer's insolvency was required. From the aforementioned requirements of State liability, the ECJ examined only the requirements at a and b.

Unlike in the Robins case the ECJ did however find that Article 8 of the Directive entailed an obligation of result. The mere fact that a minimum level of protection is not attained—in this case due to the employer's insolvency—leads to state liability. At the hearing the Netherlands, just as Ireland and in line with the *Robins* judgment, argued that the Directive imposes a best efforts obligation on the

[16]Kocken 2010.

[17]Bruyninckx 2007.

Member States, but to no avail.[18] Whilst in its judgment in Robins the ECJ still found that the Member State involved could only be held liable on a finding of manifest and serious disregard by that State for the limits set on its discretion, and the ECJ offered some pointers as to when that would be the case, the judgment in *Hogan* for the most part fills in that discretion. That makes the parameters within which State liability can be determined clearer (once again).

This gives rise to the interesting question of whether the obligation of 49 % must also be performed without an insolvency of the employer, e.g. in the event of a de facto insolvency of the pension fund. Lutjens does not think so.[19] It is however worth pointing out that the ECJ noted in its judgment in *Hogan* that Article 8 of the Directive gives rise to a general obligation to protect the interests of employees. It would not be a huge stretch to place the pension fund, as the manager of deferred wages, within the scope of the Directive.

The judgment is also 'new' because the ECJ made it clear that the consequences of the financial crisis ought not to play a part in the financing of the pension system. In the Netherlands this is cited by some people as an argument for the poor performance of pension funds.[20] In the ECJ's opinion, this is (put bluntly) irrelevant. All in all, as affirmed by Voogsgeerd too, a dynamic development is noticeable in the case law of the ECJ as regards Article 8 of the Directive.[21]

6 Conclusion

The judgment in *Hogan* contains new elements and could have considerable implications for the Netherlands. In the case of an employer's insolvency, no causal link has to be established between the employer's insolvency and the loss of pension rights. A breach of an obligation of result suffices for State liability. This is a second warning for the Netherlands. And this is all the more cogent in view of the considerable criticism of Europe by (some parts of) the pension sector. It is 'forgotten' or simply not mentioned that 'EU involvement' is aimed at facilitating the protection of members of pension schemes: payment of 49 % of the pension benefit commitments is an absolute minimum threshold. If a pension fund drops below this threshold, the Member State is automatically liable. Whether this development will lead to a European guarantee fund, it is certainly desirable, but as yet

[18] www.minbuza.nl.

[19] Lutjens 2013.

[20] As evidenced by the radio interview of 18 July 2013 with Mr Riemen, director of the Pension Federation [*Pensioenfederatie*] for BNR. He claimed that the financial markets were to blame for the poor performance of the pension funds. Incidentally, the low interest rate is only one of the many reasons for the discounts.

[21] See the commentary of H.H. Voogsgeerd to Case C-398/11, LJN BX9899.

unclear.[22] It is in any event positive that Dutch pension funds and the Dutch government are warned to be cautious about reducing and discounting pension accruals and benefits.

Case law, legislation and documents

Case law

ECJ 19 November 1991, Case C-6/90 and C-9/90, *Francovich*

ECJ 8 October 1996, Case C-178/94 and others, *Dillenkorfer*

ECJ 25 January 2007, Case C-278/05, *Robins*

ECJ 24 May 2012, Case C-97/11, *Amia SpA*

Dutch Supreme Court 21 September 2012, No. AB 2012/367, with commentary by Widdershoven

Case law commentaries

Voogsgeerd HH to Case C-398/11, LJN BX9899

Schutjes, JGR 2009/7 ECJ, 16 October 2008, Case C-452/06

Directives

Directive 2008/94/EC of the European Parliament and of the Council of 22 October 2008 on the protection of employees in the event of the insolvency of their employer, OJ L 283, 2008

References

Bruyninckx TB (2007) De voorwaarde van causaliteit als obstakel voor gemeenschapsaansprakelijkheid in staatssteunzaken. NTER 11:232–237

Kocken T (2010) Aandacht voor uitkeringsfase, IPN October/November:24–25

Lutjens E (2013) Bescherming pensioenaanspraken bij insolventie. Tijdschrift voor Pensioenvraagstukken 3:44–48

Pikaart M (2013) Lusten en lasten van de generaties in het pensioenstelsel. De Actuaris 20(4):40–41 (the online version was consulted for this article)

Ritoe JA (2007) Bescherming tegen betalingsonmacht van werkgever kan beter. PensioenMagazine No. 6

Van Meerten H (2009) Iets over richtlijnconforme interpretatie. Tijdschrift voor Financieel Recht 10:377–379

Van Meerten H (2012) Europa en ons pensioen: enkele overpeinzingen. PensioenMagazine No.1

[22]See the questions raised in the Dutch Parliament by Omtzigt and the answers given by the government, Dutch Lower House [TK] 2012–2013, Appendix, 2530. See also my opinion published in Dutch national newspaper *Het Financiële Dagblad* on 27 May 2013.

Over the Edge: European External Policy in Evolution

Monica den Boer

Abstract The external policies of the EU are mostly focused on its neighbouring regions. The EU's expansion of these external policies is backed by several assumptions. Leading assumptions consist of a correlation between failed states, crime and terrorism and of the idea that crime and terrorism do not stick to borders and are therefore semi-uncontrollable and mobile. The author also argues that there is therefore no longer use to distinct between EU citizens and citizens outside of the EU. Although the EU counts fewer deaths than Iraq or Syria, the EU suffers from crimes such as trafficking in human beings and cybercrime. The EU's external policy is also based on the asymmetry of income, employment, education and liberty, which draws many people from surrounding areas to Europe. Furthermore, it is based on the concept of interdependency. Globalization implies that the EU is connected economically to other countries. The European Crisis Management shows the connection between the internal and external side of justice and home affairs, for example in the areas of counter-terrorism and organized crime. The author mentions three instruments the EU uses to perform activities in this area. Firstly, the regulatory instrument, which is meant to normalize the conduct of the target partners. Secondly, the incentive instruments, which are non-coercive by nature. Thirdly and most preferable, the capacity tools that activate individuals and groups to make decisions. The major challenge for the EU, according to the author, is shaking off its reputation of internal fragmentation, because

Professor of Comparative Public Administration at the Vrije Universiteit Amsterdam and professor at the College of Europe in Bruges. Academic dean of the Police Academy of the Netherlands.

M. den Boer (✉)
Vrije Universiteit Amsterdam, Amsterdam, The Netherlands
e-mail: monicadenboer@gmail.com

M. den Boer
College of Europe, Bruges, Belgium

M. den Boer
Police Academy of the Netherlands, Apeldoorn, The Netherlands

F.A.N.J. Goudappel and E.M.H. Hirsch Ballin (eds.), *Democracy and Rule of Law in the European Union*, DOI 10.1007/978-94-6265-066-4_12

this reduces its external credibility. The EU has to create a long-term strategy, particularly for peace operations and slowly integrate national policing actors in its external programmes.

Contents

1 Introduction

Nowadays one can hardly imagine that two decades ago, European police cooperation resembled a barren landscape with hardly any legal instruments, agencies or practices which enable police forces in the EU Member States to engage in cross-border policing. Despite the adoption of a variety of bilateral and multilateral agreements, such as the Benelux Treaty, the European Community was primarily inspired by an economic drive and the facilitation of the free movement of goods. During the last 25 years a significant evolution has taken place, which would not have happened had the political leaders and senior executive not been so relentless in their construction of a Fortress Europe. In particular the Schengen Agreements, which brought about a compensatory framework for the free movement of persons in Europe, has contributed enormously to the possibility to engage in cross-border law enforcement practices, including information exchange, hot pursuit, controlled delivery and surveillance. This was seemingly only the beginning of a hyperactive period of regulation and law-making, during which the area of police cooperation was both deepened through a process of gradual agencification and widened by means of accession and standardization of procedures throughout the European Union. Today, the landscape is full of agencies like Europol, Frontex, Eurojust and Cepol. For the Member States, there are significant consequences in terms of legal implementation, technical infrastructure, professionalization and finances.

The vast expansion of internal policing in the European Union tends to overshadow the growth of external policing activities of the European Union in third countries.[1] The Tampere Programme—which laid the first foundations for the

[1] For a chronological reconstruction, see T. Balzacq, *The external dimension of EU justice and home affairs: tools, processes, outcomes*. Brussels, CEPS Working Document No. 303, 2008.

Area of Freedom, Security and Justice—threw a line towards the external dimension of justice and home affairs cooperation. A quick gloss at the world map of risks, failed states and corruption, suffices to detect a missionary role for Europe in its surroundings. Yet, Europe is far from alone in its endeavour to expand its potential as global policing actor, as it has partly been preceded, partly been accompanied by other multilateral organizations, such as—most prominently—the United Nations, but also the OESCE and NATO. External security efforts are closely associated with the domain of development aid and security sector reform. Though the EU is the biggest donor of development aid around the world, it has specific interest in neighbouring regions, especially the Maghreb, West Africa, Balkan countries and ENP countries. The individual Member States have concentrated a lot of their bilateral effort on former colonial countries like Indonesia.

The expansion of EU's external policing efforts is buttressed by a number of assumptions—some of them more explicit than others. Leading documents in which the EU portrayed its strategy of preventive security engagement and in which it framed internal and external security threats as a growing amalgam were for instance the EU Security Strategy which was adopted by the Council in 2003 and renewed in 2008.[2] Meanwhile, the EU has built its External Action Service (EAS) which is the administrative pillar underneath an impressive array of external security programmes, some of which we will discuss below. The threats were smartly knit together in a self-justificatory discourse which was hard to argue with. A document stemming from 2005 defined the main challenge by addressing several key thematic priorities: "In order to meet the expectations of its citizens the European Union must respond to the security threats of terrorism, organized crime, corruption and drugs and to the challenge of managing migration flows. If the EU is to be effective in doing so it needs to work with countries outside the EU".[3] This argument was pivotal in positioning JHA as a central priority in the external relations of the European Union: "The development of the area of freedom, security and justice can only be successful if it is underpinned by a partnership with third countries (…) which includes strengthening the rule of law, and promoting the respect for human rights and international obligations".[4]

---

[2]The EU Security Strategy was flanked by the 2002 US National Security Strategy, the 2004 UN High Level Panel on Threats, and several national security strategies at the level of the EU Member States.

[3]Council of the European Union, *A Strategy for the External Dimension of JHA: Global Freedom, Security and Justice*, Brussels, 30 November 2005. Doc. 14 366/3/05. http://register.consilium.europa.eu/doc/srv?l=EN&t=PDF&gc=true&sc=false&f=ST%2014366%20 2005%20REV%203&r=http3A2F%2Fregister.consilium.europa.eu%2Fpd%2Fen%2F05%2 Fst14%2Fst14366-re03.en05.pdf. Accessed 30 December 2013.

[4]Id.

2 Leading Assumptions

So, what are those assumptions behind the stretching of Justice and Home Affairs beyond the edge of the European Union? First, there are concerns about gaps in the security in the direct geographical neighbourhood of the European Union. The Balkan wars are an example of how a conflict spreads regionally, of how difficult it has turned out to contain it, and of how it has produced a long-term security hangover for the whole of Europe, including the displacement of persons to other countries and the magnitude of human suffering and. Hence, the potential of a spillover effect from insecurity in another region is potentially significant in is duration and size. Together with countries like the United States, Canada, Australia and New Zealand, the EU countries harbour a haven of peace and stability, at least when one compares this with the vast number of fragile countries around the world which are beaten by semi-permanent situations of ungovernability and which are rife with tension, conflict and war. Hence, one of the other assumptions is that this global asymmetry needs to be countered and possibly solved. Europe—which has been aptly captured by Deirdre Curtin as an "emerging security actor" seeks to define a role for itself in which it is responsible for policing no-man's land. The world is full of so-called "ungoverned spaces" and "safe havens", in which the competent—or not-so competent—authorities fail to guarantee the basic services for citizens and demonstrate little or no interest in supervising the equal distribution of goods, services and rights. Countries or regions which have had a long-term conflict have enormous difficulty in recovering and are often characterized by perpetual post-conflict chaos. Ill-functioning economies, black markets, vast unemployment and a lack of educational and emancipatory opportunities often produce communities that are stuck in insecurity.

Hence, the leading assumption is that one situation infects the other, that there is a strong correlation between failed states, crime and terrorism. Critical questions about this leading assumption are not often raised: is the external security prophecy a legitimate paradigm, and if so, what is the evidence? Do external security actors like the EU and the UN only look at the dark side of life and are bleak prospects about chronic insecurity perhaps used as a unifying rhetoric to endorse the normative dimension of Europe's mission?

Another leading and perhaps rather collectively unifying assumption is that crime and terrorism do not stick to borders. Those threats have become semi-uncontrollable, mobile and fluid phenomena without ideological proprietors. "Franchise terrorism" and copy-catting have become easier with information and communication technology: the cyber-jihad is one of Europe's recently defined common threats. As Europe seeks to carve out a Venus-profile rather than a Mars-profile for itself, it has sought to emphasize the preventive aspects of its external security efforts as part of a wider spectrum of possible interventions. The prevention of crime, terrorism and irregular migration is to be performed both inside and outside Europe's borders, at least, such is the mantra that the EU has amplified in many of its policies. The exchange of information on crime and terrorism is no longer a matter for EU countries themselves, but for the wider community of external partners with whom the EU engages. The collection of intelligence and evidence, the disruption of illegal activities and the bringing to justice of perpetrators of crime and terrorism have become main strands in recent anti-crime and terrorism strategies.

Thirdly, it makes no longer sense to draw a distinction between the security of citizens inside and outside the European Union—or does it? Despite separatist terrorism in some EU Member States there are relatively low levels of crime, and stunningly, these levels have generally declined despite the impact of the economic crisis and soaring levels of unemployment. As argued above, the European Union has remained one of the safest regions on earth, despite tough confrontations between citizens and police, violent demonstrations, school shootings and isolated acts of terrorism. And yes, we should take into account a warning by The Economist that there is a "troubling similarity" between 2014 and 1914, which is complacency: "(...) the European Union, which came together in reaction to the bloodshed of the 20th century, is looking more fractious and riven by incipient nationalism than at any point since its formation".[5] It is hard to convince citizens in Europe that their security—on the whole and for a considerable period of time—has been much better than the security of many of their fellow citizens in the world. Iraq, Syria, Afghanistan, Pakistan and many other countries have been subjected to high levels of violence. The death toll in Iraq has been consistently high since the departure of the American troops. But the nexus between transnational crime and terrorism and levels of victimization of citizens in Europe has not been the subject of much attention within the theatres of national politics: trafficking in human beings is a transnational crime by which many countries in Europe are hit and which produces high numbers of victims, particularly amongst women and children. Europol estimates that 100,000 women and children are victims of human trafficking and that the trafficking of drugs causes serious health, social and economic problems. Cybercrime produces thousands if not millions of victims in Europe each year, due to identify fraud and theft, cyber exploitation and several other offences. Governments receive far less tax income than they should do if there had not been such high levels of VAT-fraud, costing the administrative authorities in the Member States billions of tax revenue on an annual basis. Hence, one of the assumptions underneath the externalization of justice and home affairs is that Europe needs to address the causes and the beginnings of criminal chains: at least it should be far more effective than waiting until crime washes upon Europe's shores.

Given Europe's relatively stable and safe climate, it is an attractive region for those who want to study and work. The asymmetry in income, employment, education and liberty between Europe and surrounding regions is so high that it has become a destiny for those that seek a happier future. Unfortunately free access to the European Union is hard to be gained, despite several visa-waiver programmes

[5] "Look back with angst", *The Economist*, 21 December 2013.

for students and workers. There has been an active policy of discouragement which has been reinforced by readmission agreements with third countries, refugee centres outside Europe's borders, the reinforcement of external border controls and surveillance and several other agreements. In part this may have given rise to opportunities for criminal entrepreneurs who sweep up desperate migrants who are keen on travelling to a destination in the European Union. The human tragedies that result from this form of exploitation, including the most disheartening deaths of migrants at sea, display a counter-effect which Europe does not want: it portrays Europe as an impenetrable paradise for the happy few. Those 500 million Europeans or so who live in this gated community do however do not stay in those numbers: Europe faces a rather steep demographic decline as female reproduction is relatively low compared to other regions. Hence, the EU is caught between a welcoming and an inhospitable face when it concerns immigrants. Like the Scottish would say when you stand on someone's doorstep: "You will have had your tea yet?" In a clever but ambiguous move the EU has declared migration as one of those Justice and Home Affairs issues which has an external dimension to it. On the one hand, the EU seeks to maximize the benefit of legal migration and integration, by promoting safer remittances and temporary and circular migration. Whilst on the other hand, the EU pursues a rather ruthless expansion of its maritime surveillance capacity through the construction of Eurosur, intensifies document security, and imposes particular demands on third countries when it concerns border control standards.

A final smart card which is thrown into the game of externalization of security is the interdependency card: we cannot do it on our own and we need you—third countries—as a co-producer to solve the problem at heart. Globalization itself already implies that countries, communities and economies are intrinsically interconnected. Unilateralism may sound convincing to the national electorate but is an unwise step in a world which has been soldered. Without being all too explicit on the assumption that the EU Member States themselves bear the brunt of responsibility when it concerns the demand for illegal goods and services, there is obviously a lot to say against going for it on one's own. Indeed, in this interconnected world it makes little or no sense to contemplate the liberalization of drugs markets if not all others make a move as well. The flipside argument is that criminalization of services—exemplified by the penalization of consumption of prostitution services in Sweden—may be useful, but what about the waterbed effect that may be caused by it? Will it not result in a displacement of criminal activity to other countries? Hence, global interconnectedness brings with it international interdependency of Europe's security.

3 Tangoing Internal and External Security

The growth of the European Crisis Management operations illustrates the intricate dance between the internal and the external side of justice and home affairs, in particular of the policing efforts. Didier Bigo[6] already published this prophecy about two decades ago, namely that the two hitherto compartmentalized areas of security would be folded into one security amalgam. An important dimension in Europe's external outreach is talk. Distilling, finding, moulding, defining and instilling a common ground has become an indispensable aspect of the way Europe formulates its external security policies, programmes and instruments. The European Union cautiously seeks to avoid the image of a security actor that seeks to impose its ideas on others. Co-production and consensus are important levers in the externalization discourse. In order to reach levels of common sense, it is important that partner countries recognize, understand and endorse the art and nature of the commonly defined threat, be it terrorism or drugs trafficking. Like in a dance which becomes gradually more intimate, the EU shows itself as the patient and understanding lover before it enters the stage of fiancée, when things suddenly become more serious and conditional for the candidate partner. The incentive becomes either a carrot or a stick, depending on the eagerness of the other state to become more intimate. Third countries are moved to a position where they are slowly but surely spoon-fed with the expectation that they adopt and implement international standards and human rights obligations, knowing that in the end there will be a prize of being praised and treated as a privileged partner. The beauty of this approach is that every country feels and is being treated differently. The European Neighbourhood Programme, which applies to 16 different countries, is for instance built on a differentiated and flexible approach, with chapters on justice and home affairs specifically tailored and designed to fit the individual needs of the partner country.

Interoperability, mutual recognition, standardization, convergence and even harmonization are core concepts in the strategies which are advocated by the European Union in order to align third countries with the European internal security domain. For countries inside Europe, accession to the European Union is potentially an attractive prospect. It is regarded by the EU as an effective way to align justice and home affairs standards in candidate countries with those that have already been adopted and implemented by EU Member States. Also, operational cooperation and coordination can benefit from the alignment process. As said earlier, the European Neighbourhood Programme and its financial instruments provide an incentive to countries in the direct surroundings of the European Union:[7] the Action Plans with the individual countries have considerable JHA components,

---

[6]Didier Bigo, When Two Become One: Internal and External Securitisations in Europe. http://didierbigo.com/students/readings/When%20Two%20Become%20One.pdf. Accessed 30 December 2013.

[7]Lavenex and Wichmann 2009, pp. 83–102.

and the emphasis in this process lies on the actual implementation agenda. With the United States of America, the European Union has started a transatlantic strategic partnership, which has culminated in several instruments, including the Container Security Initiative, the provision of PNR-data and financial intelligence in view of counterterrorism, as well as a police cooperation agreement. With sub-Sahara and West-African countries, the EU engages in a range of programmes on counterterrorism, drugs trafficking and police reform. The outer ring of effort in the externalization of security is for instance India with whom the EU engages in high-level dialogue.

4 External Policing as An Art of Diplomacy

EU engagement with other countries in the domain of Justice and Home Affairs is comprehensive in the sense that it is stretched across different fields including counterterrorism, organized crime, corruption, managed migration, drugs, human rights and access to justice. This implies for instance that the EU JHA agencies––Europol, Eurojust, Frontex and Cepol—have effectively been tasked with an international (read: external) policing role.[8] Liaison officers are pivotal actors in this context, and they have to ensure levels of operational cooperation with priority countries. Meanwhile, the EU is gradually moving into defence issues as it seeks to expand its role in civil–military cooperation. Obviously there is a financial side to this choice, which in passing brings up the question of to what extent the EU spending on external security efforts should be complementary to national spending on development aid, security sector reform and capacity building programmes. JHA external activity is subject to regular monitoring (18 months) and some activities in which the EU engages have already been subjected to an audit by the European Court of Auditors. In many ways, the European Union pursues a strategy of "responsibilization", in which countries and regional organizations assume responsibility to control jointly identified security voids.

Balzacq[9] aptly distinguishes a number of instruments by means of which the EU seeks to perform activities in the external realm of justice and home affairs. The most commonly used technique by the EU to achieve the externalization of internal security is that of a regulatory instrument: Action Plans, Communications by the Commission, Council Declarations and ordinary Community legislation, the most important objective of which is to "normalize" the conduct of the "target partners". Secondly, the EU employs incentive instruments, which are "typically non-coercive". Thirdly, the EU uses "capacity tools", which are the most preferred ones: individuals, groups and organizations are being capacitated in order to make

[8]See for instance Europol's external role in counter-terrorism, Kaunert 2010, pp. 652–671.

[9]See T. Balzacq, *The external dimension of EU justice and home affairs: tools, processes, outcomes*. Brussels, CEPS Working Document No. 303, 2008, p. 13.

decisions and to undertake activities, mostly through information, training and other resources. An example of the latter is the financing of border management practices in third countries.

On a more fundamental level, restlessly waiting for an answer lies in the question of whether and to what extent the EU employs these instruments for the externalization of justice and home affairs—in particular through external policing—as a transformative vehicle for state-building or other purposes. The French philosopher Foucault would have argued that harmonization (of state governance) is conducted through discourses, laws and administration, while Manners would say that the external reach of the EU in the security domain is a way for Europe to export its "normative power". Rather convincingly, Ryan argues that international policing may be a power strategy to secure the power connections between the centre (EU) and the periphery. Power is transferred through the dissemination of a single, homogenizing idiom, which is the foundation for a vocabulary that encapsulates the entire empire, even in its most remote corners.

Appealing as these general theoretical perspectives may be, one may arrive at the sobering conclusion that a genuine harmonization has been far from completed. Yet, from the outside, Europe looks like a space which the former diplomat from Singapore, Mr Mahbubani, characterizes as the "great convergence" project. And indeed, when one looks around wearing pink spectacles, a great deal of mutual recognition, standardization and convergence has been achieved in the area of internal security, certainly when one looks at border control practices, information-sharing and common strategic intelligence. If this convergence process is to be rolled out across other countries and regions across the globe, this process of external security convergence will almost surely be accompanied by a series of rather unsettling convulsions.

5 Drawing the Line

A major challenge for the EU is to shake off its reputation of being internally fragmented and chronically indecisive. If it fails to do so, it will hinder its external credibility and consequently it will undermine the goodwill and support so drastically needed for realizing sustainable effectiveness. A necessary step to be made by the EU is to actually devise a coherent and long-term strategy, particularly for peace operations. Such a move will help the EU to get rid of its reputation as an ad hoc actor or quick fixer that seeks to maintain maximum flexibility in each and every conflict it faces.

A first start towards a more stable and credible reputation has been made in the area of EU crisis management capacity. Treaty Articles that allow rapid decision-making in crisis management are Article 41.3 on the creation of a start-up fund and Article 44 on entrusting a task to a group of Member States. These provisions facilitate able and willing Member States to proceed with deploying operations. EU Crisis Management Procedures were revised in June 2013. However, since the inception of CDSP, the EU has not been keen on using crisis management procedures in Eastern vicinity.[10]

Soon the EU will no longer be able to take recourse to its relatively luxury position of being the girl looming in the shadows of the dancing room. The USA has clearly indicated that it shifts its security focus towards Asia, providing ample space to Europe to propel itself as primary security actor in adjacent regions. Yet, as Biscop and Van Langenhove[11] argue, Europe neither has the power nor perhaps the aspiration to become a global "cop". This means that the EU faces a perfect political momentum for realizing maximum potential in its neighbourhood, that is, Eastern Europe, the Caucasus, the Maghreb and the Middle-East. But also the "neighbours of the neighbours" ought to reside under Europe's responsibility (Sahel, Horn of Africa, Gulf region and a part of Central Asia), because these areas are very volatile and extremely susceptible to conflict with a potentially high spillover effect to Europe.[12] Hence, instead of aspiring to be a global cop, Europe certainly has potential to boost its role as regional cop, given its growing experience with capacity building and security sector reform programmes.

As a strategizing actor, the EU will probably stretch the concept of neighbouring countries, whilst ensuring that it will not run into capacity problems itself and making local actorship a crucial ingredient for soft security interventions. Making muscle is another challenge for Europe as it has to make a step from relatively small-scale crisis management interventions to large-scale ones. The latest missions of the European are focused on the maintenance of order and stability: EUCAP SAHEL Niger was launched in 2012 to support Nigerian police forces with the training of their officers in counterterrorism and organized crime, while more recently under EUTM Mali 500 military officers have been responsible for training officers of the army in Mali. EUBAM Libya is directed towards supporting the Libyan authorities with securing their borders, in order to prevent irregular migration and border traffic, whilst in Congo, EUPOL DR Congo was focused on police reform.[13]

Gradually, national policing actors from the EU Member States are pulled into these kinds of external programmes of the EU. It means that law enforcement professionals in the Member States have to be adequately prepared for their mission by means of training and professionalization. Both Europol and Cepol, as well as national law enforcement institutions carry a serious responsibility in pre- and post-mission guidance and in building knowledge and research about related issues. With all its twists and turns, European external policing has become firmly engrained in the externalization of EU Justice and Home Affairs.

[10]Biscop and Fiott 2013.

[11]Biscop and Van Langenhove 2013, pp. 23–27.

[12]Biscop and Van Langenhove 2013, p. 25.

[13]See Martinelli 2006, pp. 379–339.

References

Biscop S, Fiott D (eds) (2013) The state of defence in Europe: state of emergency? Egmont Royal Institute for International Relations, Brussels

Biscop S, van Langenhove L (2013) Europese vredesoperaties: waar is de strategie? Int Spectator 67(12):23–27

Kaunert C (2010) Europol and EU counterterrorism: security actorness in the external dimension. Stud Conflict Terrorism 33(7):652–671

Lavenex S, Wichmann N (2009) The external governance of EU internal security. J Eur Integr 31(1):83–102

Martinelli M (2006) Helping transition: the EU police mission in the Democratic Republic of Congo (EUPOL Kinshasa) in the framework of EU policies in the great lakes. Eur Foreign Aff Rev 11(3):339–379

Confiscation of Proceeds from Crime: a Challenge for Criminal Justice?

Ladislav Hamran

Abstract At the international level, the United Nations, the Council of Europe, the institutions of the European Union have adopted a significant number of instruments to enhance the fight against crime, including organised crime, and to minimise the negative consequences produced by (organised) crime for national economies and for society. Individual States have also adopted legislative and non-legislative measures to combat (organised) crime. One of the legislative measures is the implementation of legislation related to confiscation of the proceeds of crime. Practice shows that the law-enforcement authorities have often difficulties to identify, freeze and confiscate the proceeds of crime. Despite several decades of effort, the European Union and its Member States must keep paying a lot of attention to this problem. This article generally describes this problem and briefly explains the different confiscation models applied in different EU Member States; as well as the result of this situation in the field of international judicial cooperation. In the vast majority of the Member States there are no statistics available concerning proceeds of crime. Therefore to assess the efficiency of the law-enforcement authorities in the fight against organised crime, based on the criteria of confiscated proceeds of crime, is a challenging task. We believe that confiscation of criminal assets should not only be seen as a key indicator of success in terms of protecting national economies, but it should also be seen in terms of enforcement of the rule of law.

L. Hamran is a prosecutor of the General Prosecution Office of the Slovak Republic and National Member for the Slovak Republic at Eurojust, The Hague. Presented opinions are exclusively the author's and do not represent the official position of the Slovak Republic, Eurojust or other institutions.

L. Hamran (✉)
Eurojust, The Hague, The Netherlands
e-mail: lhamran@eurojust.europa.eu

F.A.N.J. Goudappel and E.M.H. Hirsch Ballin (eds.), *Democracy and Rule of Law in the European Union*, DOI 10.1007/978-94-6265-066-4_13

Contents

1 Introduction

The majority of crime is committed for profit. About 70 % of recorded crime is acquisitive.[1] As different studies show, the profits generated by organised crime are huge. Based on a study, undertaken by the United Nations Office on Drugs and Crime (UNODC) to estimate illicit financial flows resulting from drug trafficking and other transnational organised crimes,[2] the overall best estimates of criminal proceeds are close to USD 2.1 trillion in 2009 or 3.6 % of global GDP.[3]

The UNODC study also estimates that the largest source of income for transnational organised criminals comes from illicit drugs, which account for some 20 % of all crime proceeds, about half of transnational organised crime proceeds, and 0.6–0.9 % of global GDP.[4] The World Bank and the UNODC estimate that the cross-border flow of the global proceeds from criminal activities, corruption and tax evasion is estimated at between USD 1 trillion and USD 1.6 trillion per year.[5] The amount of proceeds of crime reported by individual Member States of the European Union is alarming. In Italy, for example, the profits of organised crime in 2011 were estimated at EUR 150 billion.[6] EU sales of illicit drugs generate an estimated EUR 100 billion per year.[7] According to a report issued by the Centre for the Study of Democracy, organised crime in Bulgaria generates EUR 1.7 billion in revenue each year.[8] Although the data referred to above cannot be confirmed, they suggest the severity of the problem and the extent of organised crime.

To enhance the fight against organised crime and to minimise the threats posed by it both to national economies and to society, the United Nations, the Council of Europe and the institutions of the European Union have adopted a significant number of international treaties and other legal acts. Over recent decades, individual states have also adopted legislative and non-legislative measures to combat

[1]Recovering the Proceeds of Crime, Cabinet Office, Performance and Innovation Unit report, June 2000, p. 6.

[2]Estimating illicit financial flows resulting from drug trafficking and other transnational organized crimes, United Nations Office on Drugs and Crime, Vienna, 2011.

[3]Ibid., p. 7.

[4]Ibid.

[5]Stolen Asset Recovery (StAR) Initiative: Challenges, Opportunities, and Action Plan, The International Bank for Reconstruction and Development/The World Bank, 2007, p. 1.

[6]http://europa.eu/rapid/pressReleasesAction.do?reference=IP/12/235&. Accessed 10 March 2015.

[7]Ibid.

[8]Ibid.

organised crime. One of these legislative measures is the implementation of legislation related to the confiscation of the proceeds of crime.

However, as practice shows, law enforcement agencies have often difficulty in identifying, freezing and confiscating the proceeds of crime. For example, an analysis undertaken by the UK Home Office suggests that approximately GBP 2 billion is theoretically available for seizure in the United Kingdom, with a further GBP 3.3 billion of proceeds sent overseas.[9] The estimated annual level of asset is GBP 125 million.[10]

For these reasons, among others, more attention needs to be paid to the identification, freezing and confiscation of the proceeds of crime across the European Union. Therefore, documents of strategic importance have been created to address the confiscation of criminal proceeds, such as the Internal Security Strategy in Action: Five steps towards a more secure Europe.[11] On 13 March 2012, the European Commission submitted to the European Parliament and the Council a proposal for a Directive on the freezing and confiscation of the proceeds of crime to strengthen the systems for freezing, managing and confiscating criminal assets across the European Union.[12]

The current situation indicates that several decades of effort have not produced satisfactory results, possibly due to the failure to establish a direct link between specific property and specific crime. In order to confiscate property, the criminal legislation of many countries requires the establishment of a link between specific proceeds and specific acts that constitute the essential elements of a crime. Under the standard of conviction-based confiscation system, a convicted offender is sentenced, *inter alia*, to forfeiture of assets—property obtained through unlawful criminal conduct.

In response to the problems described above, and taking into consideration the complexity of financial flows, trade patterns used by perpetrators of crime to disguise the origin of money, and the extent and degree of organisation of crimes, some EU Member States have implemented confiscation systems to provide for the confiscation of property without a prior criminal conviction.[13] These systems are generally referred to as civil because they allow for the recovery in civil proceedings, before civil courts and applying civil standard of proof (balance of probabilities). Civil confiscation proceedings are initiated against the asset itself (*in rem*).

In civil proceedings, the court concludes that property has been obtained through unlawful conduct. Sufficient evidence to instigate criminal proceedings or establish a link between the property and a related crime or criminality in general

---

[9]Dubourg and Prichard 2007, p. 76.

[10]Ibid.

[11]Communication from the Commission to the European Parliament and the Council, COM(2010)673final.

[12]7641/12 DROIPEN 29 COPEN 57 CODEC 656 + ADD 1 + ADD 2.

[13]By passing Act No. 575/1965, Italy was the first country to implement a preventative confiscation system in continental Europe.

is lacking. Therefore, the confiscation is civil by nature but with an indirect link to the crime or criminality. This system requires that, initially, the competent authority of the Member State must prove the indirect link before a civil court. The Member State may then allow the burden of proof that the asset has been obtained legally to "shift" to the defendant. Only a few EU Member States—Bulgaria,[14] Ireland,[15] Italy,[16] Slovenia,[17] the Slovak Republic[18] and the United Kingdom[19]—have implemented civil confiscation systems. Estonia uses a variation of this model. Civil confiscation models are deviation from the "classical" criminal forfeiture,[20] where proceedings are commenced against a person (*in personam*). This model requires a criminal trial and conviction for a specific criminal offence. The requirement of a criminal conviction means that the prosecuting authority must prove guilt "beyond reasonable doubt".

In practice, the implementation of the two confiscation systems illustrated above has divided countries into two groups which represent two different legislative regimes. Both models have their variations. Some countries have implemented a so-called extended confiscation, which allows them to confiscate property in criminal proceedings without establishing a direct link between the property and the crime for which the convicted person is sentenced.[21] In this situation, a court convicts a specific person of a crime and also awards a decision on the confiscation of property, when either the national court believes that the property was obtained through similar unlawful conduct of the person convicted, committed before the actual conviction, or the value of the property of the person convicted is disproportionate to the person's legal income and the national court concludes that the property has been obtained through unlawful conduct of the person convicted. Establishing a direct link between the property and the offence is not necessary if the court concludes that part of the person's property was obtained through other unlawful conduct, for which the court finds the person guilty.

There is a difference also between countries applying civil forfeiture regimes. For instance the Slovak Republic has adopted Act No. 101/2010 Coll. on Demonstrating the Origin of Property (the "Property Origin Act"). The Act is based on principle of "unexplained wealth" where a comparison of the actual property of a person is made against the income declared by that person so as

[14]Act on the forfeiture to the exchequer of unlawfully acquired assets.

[15]Proceeds of Crime Act, 1996.

[16]See above n. 13.

[17]Forfeiture of Assets of Illegal Origin Act.

[18]Act No. 101/2010 Coll. on Demonstrating the Origin of Property.

[19]The Proceeds of Crime Act 2002.

[20]The terms "confiscation" and "forfeiture" are used in this article interchangeably.

[21]Council Framework Decision 2005/212/JHA on Confiscation of Crime-Related Proceeds, Instrumentalities and Property provided the legal ground for such a model and the Member States should have adopted the necessary measures to comply with this Framework Decision by 15 March 2007.

to establish a clear disproportion between the actual and declared property. Establishing an indirect link to a crime is unnecessary. In these cases, the burden of proof that the property has been obtained lawfully lies with the defendant, meaning that the relevant civil court considers in this case whether the person has obtained the property lawfully. Where the court concludes that the person has obtained the property through unlawful conduct, the court will make a decision that the property thus obtained shall be confiscated by the State.

Some EU Member States cannot be clearly classified under any of the confiscation systems described above. These Members States have implemented either more than one confiscation system, or a combination of more confiscation systems. In addition to the confiscation systems already mentioned, some of the EU Member States apply different administrative proceedings to confiscate property obtained through unlawful conduct. For example, in Hungary any property obtained through unlawful conduct could be confiscated in the frame of tax proceedings. The burden of proof may change in those proceedings and the person concerned is required to demonstrate that the property was obtained lawfully.

From the existence of different legislation on confiscation more significant problems in the field of international judicial cooperation could be predicted, especially in cases of conflict between the two very different confiscation models (the civil and the criminal model). This fact was confirmed by the results of a recently published report of Eurojust on non-conviction-based confiscation.[22] In this project, particular attention was paid to international judicial cooperation in the civil law confiscations. In view of the above, perhaps it does not seem surprising that only a few EU Member States applying civil confiscation system would obtain the requested assistance, due to a lack of any legal basis in civil matters to handle such requests in other EU Member States or due to the fact that the action sought would be contrary to the fundamental principles of the legal system of the requested EU Member State.[23]

The main reason for rejection of the requests for mutual legal assistance (hereafter "MLA") in the civil recovery cases is that no criminal proceedings or investigation is ongoing in the requesting state. The vast majority of countries applying civil confiscation regimes according to their legislation must provide an indirect link to a crime or criminality. However, the requests for MLA are not issued in that particular criminal case, but in the civil proceedings.

The competent judicial authorities of countries implementing civil confiscation regimes use the Council of Europe Convention on laundering, search, seizure and confiscation the proceeds from crime[24] as the legal basis for judicial cooperation with another state (hereafter "the Strasbourg Convention"). Although, the Strasbourg Convention in Article 7 Section 1 obliges the parties to cooperate to the widest extent possible for the purposes of investigations and proceedings aiming at

[22]Report on non-conviction based confiscation (General Case 751/NMSK-2012), Eurojust 2013.

[23]Ibid., p. 13.

[24]Convention on laundering, search, seizure and confiscation the proceeds from crime, CETS: 141, entry into force 1 September 1993.

the confiscation of instrumentalities and proceeds, it is important to underline that this particular legal instrument does not cover civil confiscation. It is evident that the Convention concerns criminal confiscation of specific items of property representing proceeds or instrumentalities, as well as confiscation of proceeds consisting in a requirement to pay a sum of money corresponding to the value of proceeds.[25]

Due to the recurring problems in mutual legal cooperation under the Strasbourg Convention in civil confiscation matters, some of the EU Member States implementing civil confiscation model started to use Council Regulation (EC) No. 44/2001 on jurisdiction and the recognition and enforcement of judgments in civil and commercial matters[26] (hereafter "the Brussels Convention") as the legal framework for international cooperation. Those countries refer to Article 1 Section 1 of the Brussels Convention which provides that the Regulation shall apply in civil and commercial matters whatever the nature of the court or tribunal. Those countries believe that civil confiscation orders can be recognised in other Member States without any special procedure being required.[27]

However, the European Court of Justice in several judgments already provided the interpretation of the term "civil and commercial matters". It is important to mention the Irini *Lechouritou* case,[28] the, which explicitly defines that the term "civil and commercial matters" does not cover disputes resulting from the exercise of public powers by one of the parties to the case, as it exercises powers falling outside the scope of the ordinary legal rules applicable to relationships between private individuals. In other words, the Regulation can be applied only for disputes between private individuals.[29]

The High Court of Ireland in the matter of Section 16(B)(4) of the Proceeds of Crime Act, 1996 between *Criminal Assets Bureau and Jackson Way Properties Limited* came to the same conclusion. In this particular case, the Criminal Assets Bureau was seeking an order according to Proceeds of Crime Act 2000 directing the defendant to pay an amount equivalent to the amount by which the court determines that the defendant has allegedly been corruptly enriched. The basis upon which the defendant was seeking to set aside the order was based upon a claim which falls within the scope of the Brussels Convention. The Court concluded that the Brussels Convention can be used essentially in matters in which private rights and obligations of individuals are in question. The Court reached a conclusion that proceedings brought by the Criminal Assets Bureau are not criminal proceedings, however, that does not mean that the proceedings, which are civil proceedings

[25]See Article 2 Section 1 of the Strasbourg Convention.

[26]Official Journal of the European Communities, L12/1, 16 January 2001.

[27]For more details, please see ch. 3 of the Council Reg. (EC) No. 44/2001.

[28]Case C 292/05, *Irini Lechouritou and Others v. Dimosio tis Omospondiakis Dimokratis tis Germanias*, 15 February 2007.

[29]For further details see also Cases *The Netherlands v. Ruffer*, No. 814/79, *LTU v. Eurocontrol*, No. 29/76.

under Irish law, are necessarily to be identified as civil or commercial matters for the purposes of the Brussels Regulation. The Court also stated that the Criminal Assets Bureau exercises its public law powers and it is clear that a private individual could not bring an application for a corrupt enrichment order as the Criminal Assets Bureau does not exercise private law rights. This specific case example very well demonstrates the difficulties which the judicial and law-enforcement authorities are confronted when exercising their civil confiscation cases.

Only recently, the Supreme Court of the United Kingdom handed down its judgment in *Perry and others v Serious Organised Crime Agency* (hereafter "SOCA"). The Supreme Court ruling can be perceived as one of the most important judgments since the Proceeds of Crime Act was adopted in 2002 in the United Kingdom. The Supreme Court in this case ruled that the jurisdiction to make a civil recovery order or a freezing order was limited only to property located in the United Kingdom. The ruling has serious consequences on civil recovery cases led by SOCA under Part 5 of the Proceeds of Crime Act 2002. The Supreme Court came to the conclusion that civil recovery proceedings "in respect of property outside the jurisdiction would involve the assertion of an exorbitant jurisdiction *in personam* without any basis in international law. They would also be likely to prove ineffective". The Supreme Court of the United Kingdom also added that the Proceeds of Crime Act must be interpreted in the light of the Strasbourg Convention whereas the Part 5 of the Proceeds of Crime Act 2002 (civil recovery) focuses on recovering criminal property rather than punishing a particular defendant and unlike Parts 2, 3 and 4 of the Proceeds of Crime Act, it does not contain provisions relating to foreign enforcement.

The before mentioned judgments from two common law countries, which undoubtedly have significant experience in civil recovery, remind us of the difficulties and legal barriers in that particular field of mutual legal cooperation.

Most EU Member States do not have such civil confiscation systems in place. As a result, only some Member States would be able to execute a request for MLA from a Member State applying the civil system. Most EU Member States would encounter difficulties in executing requests for legal assistance at the stage of identifying and freezing the property concerned, before even considering the difficulties in recognising confiscation orders issued by foreign courts.

Without any doubt, this situation may affect the overall effectiveness of the civil confiscation systems, particularly when the property is situated within the territory of a Member State applying a system other than the civil confiscation system. Undeniably, the problems described above have contributed to the relatively modest percentage of confiscated proceeds of crime. Alarming statistics are not relevant only to cross-border organised crime cases but also to domestic investigations and prosecutions of acquisitive crime.

To assess the efficiency of law-enforcement authorities in the fight against organised crime, based on the criteria of confiscated proceeds of crime, is a challenging task. In the vast majority of the EU Member States, there are no statistics available in this regard. The study "Assessing the effectiveness of EU Member States' practices in the identification, tracing, freezing and confiscation of criminal assets", prepared by Matrix Insight for the European Commission, confirmed the lack of data in this regard. The study continues that "it was not clear whether this was because data were not collected or Member States' governments were unwilling to publish what they had".[30]

Mutual evaluation between the EU Member States and Member States of the Council of Europe confirmed that a lot of countries do not even consider the criteria of the confiscated proceeds of crime as the efficiency criteria for their criminal policy or performance of the competent authorities.

It is clear that the development of a functioning system focused on identification, seizure and confiscation of illegally obtained property requires several years of efforts. It is evident that the proceeds of crime have negative social consequences and represent serious threats against democratic principles. Therefore we believe that confiscation of criminal assets is not only a key indicator of success in terms of protecting national economies, but it should be also seen in terms of enforcement of the rule of law.

Case law, legislation and documents

Case law

LTU Lufttransportunternehmen GmbH & Co. KG v. Eurocontrol, Reference for a preliminary ruling, European Court of Justice, 14 October 1976, 29-76

The Netherlands v. Ruffer, Reference for a preliminary ruling, European Court of Justice, 16 December 1980, 814/79

Legislation

Strasbourg Convention on laundering, search, seizure and confiscation the proceeds from crime, CETS. 141, entry into force 1 September 1993

Proceeds of Crime Act, 1996, Ireland

Council Regulation (EC) No. 44/2001 of 22 December 2000 on jurisdiction and the recognition and enforcement of judgments in civil and commercial matters

Proceeds of Crime Act, 2002, Ireland

Council Framework Decision 2005/212/JHA on Confiscation of Crime-Related Proceeds

Proposal for a Directive of the European Parliament and of the Council on the freezing and confiscation of proceeds of crime in the European Union7641/12 DROIPEN 29 COPEN 57 CODEC 656 + ADD 1 + ADD 2

Slovak Act No. 101/2010 Coll. on Demonstrating the Origin of Property ("Property Origin Act")

[30]Matrix insight—European Commission Directorate-General Justice, Freedom & Security, Assessing the effectiveness of EU Member States' practices in the identification, tracing, freezing and confiscation of criminal assets, Final Report, June 2009, p. 72.

Press releases and other information from the institutions
Official Journal of the European Communities, L12/1, 16 January 2001
Communication from the Commission to the European Parliament and the Council, COM(2010)673final.
'Crime does not pay: cracking down on criminal profits', European Commission Press Release 2012. http://europa.eu/rapid/pressReleasesAction.do?reference=IP/12/235&. Accessed 10 March 2015

Reports
Recovering the Proceeds of Crime, Cabinet Office, Performance and Innovation Unit report, June 2000, p. 6
Stolen Asset Recovery (StAR) Initiative: Challenges, Opportunities, and Action Plan, The International Bank for Reconstruction and Development/The World Bank, 2007
Matrix insight—European Commission Directorate-General Justice, Freedom & Security, Assessing the effectiveness of EU Member States' practices in the identification, tracing, freezing and confiscation of criminal assets, Final Report, June 2009
Estimating illicit financial flows resulting from drug trafficking and other transnational organized crimes, United Nations Office on Drugs and Crime, Vienna, 2011
Report on non-conviction based confiscation (General Case 751/NMSK-2012), Eurojust, 2013

Reference

Dubourg R, Prichard S (2007) The impact of organised crime in the UK: Financial Revenues and Economic and Social Costs. Home Office, London

European Union's Readmission Policy in the Post-Stockholm Programme Era

Türkan Ertuna Lagrand

Abstract As the post-Stockholm Programme era is approaching, it is a good time to be thinking of how to go further with the European Union's readmission policy, which should not only represent an effective tool for combating illegal immigration, but also reflect EU's commitment to respect for human dignity, freedom and respect for human rights. This article aims at highlighting the main areas requiring improvement in the post-Stockholm era regarding the negotiation, implementation and monitoring phases of European readmission agreements.

Contents

1 Introduction

The Stockholm Programme comes to an end in 2014. It is a good time to be thinking about how the area of Freedom Security and Justice will be shaped in the post-Stockholm era. As opposed to earlier multiannual programmes, all having followed major treaty changes, for the first time the post-Stockholm Programme

T.E. Lagrand (✉)
Policy Advisor at the European Parliament, Rotterdam, The Netherlands
e-mail: tertun@gmail.com

F.A.N.J. Goudappel and E.M.H. Hirsch Ballin (eds.), *Democracy and Rule of Law in the European Union*, DOI 10.1007/978-94-6265-066-4_14

will come at a time when such drastic changes in EU law and structure have not taken place.[1] This situation presents a great opportunity to take stock of the functioning of various policy areas and concentrate on how these can be improved. Accordingly, the post-Stockholm Programme should represent a maturity stage for the EU in the area of Freedom, Security and Justice, in which already existing policies should be refined taking into account the implementation so far. In this context, EU readmission agreements should be one of the priorities in the post-Stockholm period; their aims, how they are negotiated, implemented and monitored should be re-evaluated thoroughly, as was requested by the Stockholm Programme itself. The EU approach towards readmission agreements should reflect the EU's commitment to respect for human dignity, freedom, democracy, equality, the rule of law and respect for human rights as highlighted in the Treaty on European Union as well as represent effective, functioning tools in combating illegal immigration.

This contribution aims at highlighting the main issues regarding the negotiation, implementation and monitoring of EU readmission agreements with a view to specify the aspects of the readmission agreements policy of the EU which require improvement so as to contribute to the debate towards the post-Stockholm period.

2 Readmission Agreements in General

Readmission agreements, which are the key tools in combating illegal immigration, facilitate the return of irregular migrants back to their countries of origin, or to the countries through which they are believed to have transited. While the obligation to readmit one's own nationals already exists under customary international law[2] the readmission of persons who are not nationals of the requested state is a thorny issue. The latter, due to the blurry personal and territorial competence a state has over third country nationals, leads to legal questions as to the authority of states under international law.[3] This article will leave this theoretical discussion aside and focus on the current practice of readmission agreements. What this entails at the EU context is agreements which 'impose reciprocal obligations on the contracting parties to readmit their nationals and also, under certain conditions, third country nationals and stateless persons.'[4]

[1]'The Stockholm Programme: What's next?', European Policy Centre Information Paper, 11 July 2013.

[2]Hailbronner 2000, p. 482.

[3]'European Commission evaluation of EU readmission agreements. Some comments and questions', MIGREUROP, http://www.statewatch.org/news/2011/apr/eu-migreurop-readmission-en.pdf. Accessed 19 December 2014.

[4]Communication on the Evaluation of EU Readmission Agreements, COM(2011)76final, 23 February 2011.

European readmission agreements, which were initially used to enable the expulsion of undesirable persons to their countries of nationality or former nationality in the nineteenth century, have transformed into tools for regulating migratory flows in the 1950s and 1960s.[5] In the early 1990s, a 'renaissance' of readmission agreements was seen since internal border controls were to be abolished and expulsion and readmission to countries outside the common area became important.[6]

Since there was no competence yet for the European Union to conclude readmission agreements with third countries, a standard approach was adopted by the Commission as to the common features which should be included in bilateral readmission agreements concluded by EU Member States.[7] This first step concerning the conclusion of readmission agreements was followed by the drawing up of guiding principles regarding the implementation of bilateral readmission agreements.[8] The former Community competence to conclude readmission agreements was introduced by the Treaty of Amsterdam and the Commission was thereby empowered to negotiate and conclude readmission agreements with third countries. Ten years after the entry into force of the Amsterdam Treaty, the Lisbon Treaty entered into effect, making the European Parliament's consent a requirement for the conclusion of EU readmission agreements,[9] as well as necessitating the immediate and full information of the European Parliament of all stages of the procedure.[10]

The Stockholm Programme, which covers the years 2010 through 2014, stipulates the importance of monitoring the implementation of readmission agreements in order to ensure their effective implementation as well as of the conclusion of effective and operational readmission agreements, on a case by case basis, be it at Union or bilateral level. It suggests that in order to make action against illegal immigration more effective, focus should be on, among others, facilitating readmission by promoting support measures for return and reintegration, capacity building in third countries. The Stockholm Programme has also asked for an evaluation of the EU readmission agreements to be presented by the Commission, including the ongoing negotiations, and for the Commission to propose a mechanism to monitor the implementation of readmission agreements. This evaluation should then lead to the Council defining a renewed and coherent strategy on

[5]Coleman 2009, pp. 12, 14.

[6]Ibid., p. 17.

[7]Council Recommendation of 30 November 1994 concerning a specimen bilateral readmission agreement between a Member State and a third country, OJ C 274, 19 September 1996, pp. 20–24.

[8]Council Recommendation of 24 July 1995 on the guiding principles to be followed in drawing up protocols on the implementation of readmission agreements, OJ C 274, 19 September 1996, pp. 25–33.

[9]In accordance with the procedure laid down in Article 218 TFEU.

[10]Article 218(10) TFEU.

readmission.[11] The call contained in the Stockholm Programme was initially answered by the Commission by the sending out of questionnaires to Member States and third countries, which resulted in the drafting of the Communication on the Evaluation of EU Readmission Agreements.[12]

2.1 Negotiation of European Readmission Agreements

The EU enters into readmission agreements for essentially the same reasons that motivate the majority of its actions in the fields of asylum and immigration: 'the will to strengthen external borders in order to sustain internal free movement within.'[13] Indeed, when it comes to the efficient management of migration flows into the European Union, readmission agreements are seen as a necessary tool, in the sense that they are important elements in tackling irregular migration by facilitating the swift return.[14]

When one looks at the countries which the EU has readmission agreements with, such as Ukraine, Albania, Russia, Moldova, Georgia, as well as the countries with which a similar process is under way such as Turkey,[15] Armenia[16] and Azerbaijan,[17] it does seem as though Fortress Europe is being reinforced with a moat around it, or rather a 'buffer zone' in order to externalize the migration pressure. Indeed, geographical proximity of a country as well as migratory pressure exerted from or via a country are among the criteria which the EU uses in determining which states to sign readmission agreements with.[18] The aim is the facilitation of the swift return of irregular migrants to their countries of origin or transit.

From a migration management point of view, it is completely understandable why the EU-side wishes to conclude readmission agreements. Yet, for the third countries, a readmission agreement in itself is to a great extent an economic, social and political burden. Sending countries are generally less developed countries in comparison to the EU Member States. Next to the costs directly incurred due to readmitting citizens and third country nationals, there are also indirect costs of

---

[11]The Stockholm Programme—an open and secure Europe serving and protecting citizens, OJ C 115, 4 May 2010, pp. 30–31, 6.1.6. Effective policies to combat illegal immigration.

[12]COM(2011)76final, 23 February 2011.

[13]'An EU-Turkey Readmission Agreement—Undermining the rights of migrants, refugees and asylum seekers?', Euro-Mediterranean Human Rights Network, http://www.euromedrights.org/eng/wp-content/uploads/2013/06/En_TurkeyReadmis_Pb_web.pdf. Accessed 10 March 2015.

[14]Communication on the Evaluation of EU Readmission Agreements, COM(2011)76final, 23 February 2011.

[15]The EU—Turkey Readmission agreement initialed on 21 June 2012.

[16]The EU—Armenia Readmission agreement is signed on 19 April 2013.

[17]The EU—Azerbaijan Readmission agreement is initialed on 29 July 2013.

[18]Council Conclusions on criteria for the identification of third countries with which new readmission agreements need to be negotiated, 16 April 2002.

readmitting citizens such as loss of remittances.[19] For countries whose economy remains dependent on remittances, readmission agreements will actually mean the facilitation of weakening of national economy.

It is for this reason that readmission agreements are presented to third countries coupled with incentives, such as special trade concessions, technical cooperation and assistance, increased development aid or visa facilitation in order to induce countries in the Southern Mediterranean and Africa to cooperate on readmission.[20] It can be said that the bargaining positions of the two sides are far from equal, since the EU-side presents the signing of the readmission agreement as a condition of granting the expected benefits. Consequently, readmission agreement negotiations take place between the EU, which expects to externalize migration pressure through the agreement, and the third country, which expects various other benefits from the EU in return of signing the readmission agreement. It is due to this trade-off during negotiations that concerns which should be central to all agreements on migration, such as the fundamental rights of the migrants, do not receive enough attention in readmission agreements. In this regard, Turkey's situation is an interesting example. Turkey and the EU have initialled a readmission agreement on 21 June 2012 in exchange of the prospect of visa-free travel for Turkish nationals into the EU, which the Turkish side wants to be implemented simultaneously as the readmission agreement.[21]

Turkey, the only EU candidate country with no visa-free travel for its citizens, has been bringing this issue forward for many years already. Considering this together with the fact that Turkey–EU relations have been experiencing a rough patch for the last few years, it will undeniably be a major success for any government that manages to secure visa-free travel for Turkish citizens. When the stakes are this high, the human rights aspects of readmission agreements are overshadowed during negotiations by the gains partner countries expect to obtain. It is therefore important that the main incentives that will be proposed by the EU should relate to the readmission agreement itself and not to other issues which are usually tremendously important for the partner country, making them disregard the actual administrative, financial and social burden of signing a readmission agreement.

In the negotiation phase, the European Union is fixated at signing the readmission agreement and thereby achieving its aim of combating irregular migration to such an extent that it is counterproductive. This is because the EU does not take into consideration the special needs of individual countries and follows a rather non-flexible approach. 'The European Commission pursues a standardized approach in negotiating readmission agreements and proposes a more or less

[19]Remittances are the portion of migrant workers' earnings sent home to their families. See Lagrand 2010, pp. 125–129.

[20]Cassarino 2010.

[21]See: http://www.hurriyetdailynews.com/turkey-studying-annotated-roadmap-for-visa-liberalization-with-eu.aspx?pageID=238&nid=50696, http://europa.eu/rapid/press-release_MEMO-12-477_en.htm. Accessed 19 December 2014.

similar structure.'[22] The consequences of this disregard of the situation and of the needs of the third country demonstrate themselves in the implementation phase of the agreement when the third country acts reluctant or simply unable to readmit. A further concern arising out of this situation does not even hit the radar of the EU, and that is the human rights of the readmitted migrant. However, for readmission agreements to function in an effective way, both sides to the agreement should be satisfied with its conditions. A more flexible approach which takes into consideration the special circumstances in the third country will add to the well-functioning of the readmission agreement, and prevent the EU from entering into agreements which do not offer any concrete benefits in the implementation stage.

Instead, the partner country should be seen as a part of the solution. It has been suggested that, in order to prevent the partner country from having to struggle to send the third country national whom it had to readmit to his/her country of origin,[23] the EU could assist the partner country in signing readmission agreements with countries of origin, since it has more leverage.[24] In any event, to contribute to the well-functioning of a readmission agreement, research should be done as to the real costs of readmission and it should be determined what the burden will be on the partner country. This is crucial due to the fact that 'the high costs stemming from the concrete implementation of the agreement make the extent of the actual cooperation highly uncertain.'[25] In this regard, burden sharing becomes a relevant issue in order to conclude agreements which do actually work in practice.

In determining what would be the best way to share the burden it is also decisive to know if the country is a source country or a country of transit. If the partner country will be readmitting predominantly its own nationals, the granting of development aid might be an appropriate approach.[26] When it comes to countries of Eastern Partnership with which there is intensive institutional cooperation, the readmission agreements should be reformed in a way as to provide more institutional assistance to deal with the issue. The EU also has an incentive to do this since these countries are in the direct proximity of the EU and it is more pressing to have well-functioning readmission agreements. Essentially for transit countries, EU support could comprise aspects such as assistance in concluding readmission agreements with source countries, financial support for the building and operating of reception centees, cooperation in establishing an asylum system which complies with international standards and a mechanism which facilitates the sharing of best practices concerning immigrant integration.

[22]Tokuzlu 2010, p. 19.

[23]It must be noted that such a system of chain readmission puts the migrants in an even more vulnerable position, increasing the danger of refoulement.

[24]'Turkiye-AB Iliskilerinde Geri Kabul: Hangi Sartlarda?', International Strategic Research Organization (USAK) Reports No. 10-02, March 2010, p. 41.

[25]Cassarino 2010.

[26]Tokuzlu 2010, p. 9.

Financial assistance for implementing the readmission agreement is presented by the commission as an incentive with great potential.[27] However, it should not be forgotten that financial assistance to the partner country is not a favour, but a necessity. In many cases it is crucial in order to make sure that the readmitted third country national has dignified treatment, and that there are adequate reception facilities. So far, the funds provided for partner countries have not been enough. Depending on the relationship between the partner country and the EU, readmission assistance can be provided under the Instrument for Pre-Accession Assistance, the European Neighbourhood and Partnership Instrument or the Thematic Programme for cooperation in the areas of migration and asylum. These funds are already limited though, which led the Commission to state that financial assistance 'could be quite efficient as leverage, provided the money offered is substantial and comes on top of what has already been programmed or promised under the relevant EU geographic programmes.'[28]

Probably one of the most problematic issues about the negotiation phase of EU readmission agreements is that we actually do not know much about them. The Commission conducts the readmission negotiations with very little transparency. 'This has prevented political institutions and the civil society from expressing their concerns in due time about the agreement prior to the initialling of the agreement, and has also prevented them from conducting extensive research on the issue.'[29] Even the European Parliament, which cannot make any amendments to the text of the EU readmission agreements but has to give its consent to them, does not have access to the negotiation phase of these agreements. More transparency, especially towards the European Parliament, but also towards the civil society would contribute immensely to making EU readmission agreements more human rights-sensible.

An important issue concerning the negotiations of readmission agreements with third countries is in fact the entering into negotiations on this subject with certain countries. Concluding readmission agreements with countries which do not have functioning asylum systems endangers the human rights of those returned and brings EU's credibility to question when it comes to human rights in the world. In this regard, the EU should make sure that the countries it signs readmission agreements with have laws in effect on foreigners, asylum and immigration based on human rights principles, that they have ratified the relevant international instruments and also that they are correctly implemented.[30] If it is important for the EU

[27]Communication on the Evaluation of EU Readmission Agreements, COM(2011)76final, 23 February 2011.

[28]Ibid.

[29]'An EU-Turkey Readmission Agreement—Undermining the rights of migrants, refugees and asylum seekers?', Euro-Mediterranean Human Rights Network, http://www.euromedrights.org/eng/wp-content/uploads/2013/06/En_TurkeyReadmis_Pb_web.pdf. Accessed 19 December 2014.

[30]'Readmission Agreements: a Mechanism for Returning Irregular Migrants', Parliamentary Assembly of the Council of Europe, Report dated 17 March 2010.

to enter into readmission agreements with a country which does not have an acceptable level of protection, the first step should be assisting the country to reach standards satisfactory to the EU. The negotiations for a readmission agreement should start after such a level is reached. Establishing such a layered system would slow down the negotiation phase but would contribute not only to upholding human rights and thereby to the credibility of the EU in the international arena but also to establishing a readmission system that actually functions.

2.2 Implementation of European Readmission Agreements

After being concluded, the EU readmission agreements are implemented at a bilateral level between EU Member States and the third countries concerned. The actual return process is carried out by the Member State. 'EU readmission agreements cannot be isolated from a predominantly bilateral system of cooperation on readmission in which most Member States are currently involved. Paying attention to this bilateral system is key to understanding the real challenges facing the development of a common readmission policy based on the fundamental rights principles that the Union seeks to advance in its external action.'[31] In this regard it is useful to study the functioning of the bilateral readmission agreements between Member States and third countries to draw lessons for future readmission agreements that will be negotiated and concluded between the EU and third countries.

The implementation of the 'highly dysfunctional'[32] readmission agreement between Greece and Turkey should have been thoroughly studied in the course of negotiations of the EU readmission agreement with Turkey. Such a study would have revealed that unless structural changes are introduced and effectively implemented both in Turkey and in Greece, the EU readmission agreement, which will mainly be implemented between these two countries, will be destined to remain as another dysfunctional readmission agreement. 'Turkey accepts a small percentage of readmission requests by Greece and incidents of refoulement are well-documented.'[33] Greece, on the other hand, is also responsible for serious human rights breaches. Migrants arriving from Turkey are sometimes pushed straight back to Turkey. These push-back operations are done in ways including abandoning migrants in the middle of the sea on unseaworthy vessels or leaving them on the Turkish side of the land border with tied hands.[34]

---

[31]Cassarino 2010.

[32]'An EU-Turkey Readmission Agreement—Undermining the rights of migrants, refugees and asylum seekers?' Euro-Mediterranean Human Rights Network, http://www.euromedrights.org/eng/wp-content/uploads/2013/06/En_TurkeyReadmis_Pb_web.pdf. Accessed 19 December 2014.

[33]Ibid.

[34]'Frontier Europe: Human Rights Abuses on Greece's Border with Turkey', Amnesty International, July 2013.

Push-back operations not only endanger the lives of migrants but they also represent violations of the non-refoulement principle. They are done against groups of migrants, while asylum is a process that requires a case by case examination. Collective expulsions are prohibited by EU law including in the case of irregular border crossings.[35] Preventing Member States from performing push-back operations has proven to be difficult. Italy's practice of intercepting migrants at sea and returning them to Libya without assessing their need for protection has previously been condemned by the European Court of Justice.[36] Nevertheless, the practice has not been abandoned. Recently, Italy has been ordering commercial ships to conduct push-back operations.[37]

These examples illustrate the fact that violations of principles of international law and human rights violations may occur on both sides of the readmission operation. The violations on the EU-side are not limited to Greece and Italy. It has been reported that both Hungary and Slovakia have deported unaccompanied minors back to Ukraine and many migrants who have been returned to Ukraine from these two countries have indicated that they had asked for asylum upon arrival but their request had been ignored by the Hungarian and Slovakian authorities.[38] While this is the case in some EU Member States, we have very little data on the human rights violations on the side of the partner countries.

It has already been indicated above that negotiating readmission agreements with countries which do not have functioning asylum systems is inviting human rights violations and threatening EU's credibility. To date, the EU has not been attentive towards the level of asylum protection or human rights records of the countries it signed readmission agreements with. Pakistan, for example, with which the EU has a readmission agreement, is not a state party to the 1951 Geneva Convention relating to the status of refugees. The implementation of the readmission agreement should be subject to careful scrutiny in order to make sure human rights violations do not occur. The EU should have mechanisms in place to assist such countries in dealing with the readmission requests.

For readmission agreements already concluded with countries with no adequate laws on asylum and immigration based on human rights principles, or those who have not ratified the relevant international instruments, the human rights safeguards in readmission agreements would have been functional. However, current EU readmission agreements do not offer any provisions guaranteeing the human

---

[35]Ibid.

[36]'An EU-Turkey Readmission Agreement—Undermining the rights of migrants, refugees and asylum seekers?', Euro-Mediterranean Human Rights Network, http://www.euromedrights.org/eng/wp-content/uploads/2013/06/En_TurkeyReadmis_Pb_web.pdf. Accessed 10 March 2015.

[37]See http://migrantsatsea.wordpress.com/2013/08/13/italy-conducted-defacto-push-back-of-migrants-by-ordering-cargo-ship-to-rescue-and-transport-migrants-to-libya/. Accessed 19 December 2014.

[38]'Buffeted in the Borderland: the Treatment of Asylum Seekers and Migrants in Ukraine', Human Rights Watch, December 2010, http://www.hrw.org/sites/default/files/reports/ukraine1210WebVersion.pdf. Accessed 19 December 2014.

rights of those readmitted. The reason lies in the Union's reading of readmission agreements as human rights neutral agreements which only facilitate the return.[39] 'The EU considers EURAs as technical instruments bringing procedural improvements to cooperation between administrations. The situation of the person subject to readmission has not been regulated, leaving those issues to relevant international, EU and national applicable law.'[40] In the lack of applicable international or national laws, this approach brings human rights to jeopardy. It is due to this risk that any EU readmission agreement should be fully in compliance with human rights standards which the EU adheres to and contain explicit human rights safeguards and guarantees against refoulement.

> They must contain clear provisions protecting the rights of migrants and asylum seekers. These must include their rights to liberty and freedom from arbitrary detention; protection against torture or other ill-treatment; their rights to access to a fair and satisfactory asylum procedure and protection from return to a country or territory where he or she would be at risk of serious human rights violations.

The human rights concerns arising out of readmission agreements are escalated due to the 'accelerated procedure'. Accelerated procedure allows the authorities to expel unauthorized persons apprehended in border areas within a maximum time limit (two days) without a formal readmission application and without the need to provide evidence based on the commonly agreed list of documents. Under the accelerated procedure, the statement of a border officer suffices to provide evidence and readmit the person within 48 h.[41]

> The inclusion of an accelerated readmission procedure for migrants found in border areas also increases the risk of migrant rights being violated. Not only does this type of procedure strongly reduce possibilities for asylum seekers to apply for refugee status (…) but it also hampers means of judicial protection, such as access to effective legal remedies against deportation or rejection of the asylum application.[42]

Especially in the case of a group of irregular migrants being caught in the act of crossing borders, accelerated procedure is applied to a group of persons collectively even though such expulsions are prohibited under EU law, decreasing the possibility of allowing individuals to apply for asylum.

Apart from risks to human rights inherent to the accelerated procedure, there are also additional concerns arising out of the implementation of the readmission agreements. Based on the bilateral readmission agreement with Turkey, Greek authorities conduct sweep operations in urban areas, apprehend migrants without

---

[39] 'Readmission Agreements: a Mechanism for Returning Irregular Migrants', Parliamentary Assembly of the Council of Europe, Report dated 17 March 2010.

[40] Communication on the Evaluation of EU Readmission Agreements, COM(2011)76final, 23 February 2011.

[41] Cassarino (2010).

[42] 'An EU-Turkey Readmission Agreement– Undermining the rights of migrants, refugees and asylum seekers?', Euro-Mediterranean Human Rights Network.

giving them a chance to explain their situation and send them back to Turkey. There have been reported cases of asylum seekers, who had left their asylum seeker cards at home at the time of their apprehension being sent back to Turkey even though they had been living in Greece for years.[43] It is due to these threats it poses to the right of asylum that the implementation of accelerated procedure requires heavy scrutiny.

In fact, the European Union does not have much experience with accelerated procedure, and the Member States' use of accelerated procedures is extremely low.[44] This is also why the Commission has suggested not to include them in future EU readmission agreements.[45] The Commission hereby aims at accelerating the negotiation phase of readmission agreements by excluding issues which typically do not occur very often. If this would mean that future readmission agreements will not allow accelerated procedures, this would have been a worthy suggestion. However, the Commission recommends that in the future, accelerated procedure should be dealt with not in readmission agreements but in the bilateral implementing protocols. This would further weaken the situation of migrants by putting Member States in charge of not only implementing the accelerated procedure but also of formulating the clause. Accelerated procedure is too sensitive of an aspect of readmission agreements to be left solely to the competence of Member States. Furthermore, accelerated procedure will definitely be widely used once the readmission agreement with Turkey is concluded and implemented judging by its already frequent use by Greece under the bilateral agreement. The shortcomings of the current bilateral system should be evaluated by the Commission and safeguards should be designed in order to prevent human rights violations caused by the application of accelerated procedures.

In conclusion, the implementation of readmission agreements very often gives rise to the violation of the rights of migrants, refugees and asylum seekers. 'The practical implementation of the agreements has resulted in frequent human rights violations on both sides, including violation of the right to asylum and of the non-refoulement principle.'[46] In order to make sure that future EU readmission agreements will not share the same fate, a monitoring system should be put in place identifying human rights violations on both sides of the readmission operation.

---

[43]'Frontier Europe: Human Rights Abuses on Greece's Border with Turkey', Amnesty International, July 2013.

[44]Communication on the Evaluation of EU Readmission Agreements, COM(2011)76final, 23 February 2011.

[45]Ibid.

[46]'An EU-Turkey Readmission Agreement– Undermining the rights of migrants, refugees and asylum seekers?', Euro-Mediterranean Human Rights Network, http://www.euromedrights.org/eng/wp-content/uploads/2013/06/En_TurkeyReadmis_Pb_web.pdf. Accessed 19 December 2014.

2.3 Monitoring of European Readmission Agreements

The current system does not supply us with thorough data concerning the readmission procedure, let alone the situation of migrants who are readmitted to third countries. Even though the return directive requires that Member States provide for an effective forced-return monitoring system,[47] such a system does not exist by which all Member States would collect and categorize data relating to readmission. While some Member States collect detailed figures on specific aspects of readmission, others can only estimate the number of readmission applications per third country per year and different Member States include different cases under the same headings.[48] It is clear that an effective readmission policy cannot be formulated without adequate and coherent data. The type of data collected and the categorization of the collected data should be standardized among Member States with the coordination of the Commission in order to reach healthy statistical information to base policy on.

A monitoring system is needed not only in terms of operability but also in terms of respect for the Union's fundamental values.[49] Consequently, such a monitoring system should scrutinize Member State practice to ensure that the rights of asylum seekers are respected as well as to observe the human rights situation of migrants readmitted to third countries. It is also important to know to what extent returnees make renewed attempts to migrate.[50] Without sufficient information on identifying problematic areas, the EU runs the risk of continuing to sign a series of readmission agreements which are not effective, or which result in grave human rights violations.

In practice, it is the individual Joint Readmission Committees that possess the tools of monitoring the application of the relevant EU readmission agreement. Each EU readmission agreement envisages the establishment of a Joint Readmission Committee (JRC) comprising representatives of the European Commission, assisted by experts from the Member States, and representatives of the third country.[51] The task of the JRC is to promote regular exchanges among the individual Member States and the third country on issues regarding the application and interpretation of the agreement.[52] In this context, provided some struc-

---

[47]Directive 2008/115/EC, 16 December 2008 on common standards and procedures in Member States for returning illegally staying third-country nationals, OJ L 348/98, 24 December 2008, Article 8(6).

[48]Communication on the Evaluation of EU Readmission Agreements, COM(2011)76final, 23 February 2011.

[49]Cassarino 2010.

[50]'Readmission Agreements: a Mechanism for Returning Irregular Migrants', Parliamentary Assembly of the Council of Europe, Report dated 17 March 2010.

[51]Cassarino 2010.

[52]Ibid.

tural changes are introduced, the JRC could be transformed into an effective mechanism for monitoring readmission agreements. These structural changes should focus on including European Parliament representatives[53] and civil society in the JRC mechanism.

The Treaty of Lisbon has granted the European Parliament the power to give consent to, among others, European readmission agreements. It is self-evident that unless the European Parliament is well informed about the implementation, as well as the negotiations of readmission agreements, the Parliament's consent will not amount to anything other than an appearance of democratic legitimacy. So far, the European Parliament has not been sufficiently informed about the implementation of the readmission agreements and the treatment of third country nationals who have been readmitted to partner countries. In this respect, the European Parliament should be fully informed about issues such as whether the principle of non-refoulement is being respected on both sides of the readmission agreement, whether third country nationals are being subjected to arbitrary detention and if they have access to minimum social and economic rights. Since the Commission has so far been reluctant in providing the Parliament with such essential data, the representatives of the European Parliament should be involved in the monitoring by taking part in Joint Readmission Committees.

It has been asserted even by the Commission that the participation of independent NGOs in the JRC should be considered since readmission agreements have possible interaction with human rights and international protection standards.[54] The benefits of monitoring by independent NGOs have been widely supported.[55] The Commission has also suggested to set up a monitoring mechanism focusing on 'post-return', gathering information about the situation of persons readmitted and to realize this by tasking an international organization with monitoring the situation in each partner country and reporting back to the Joint Readmission Committee.[56]

[53]Cassarino 2010; MIGREUROP:'European Commission evaluation of EU readmission agreements. Some comments and questions', http://www.statewatch.org/news/2011/apr/eu-migreurop-readmission-en.pdf. Accessed 19 December 2014.

[54]Communication on the Evaluation of EU Readmission Agreements, COM(2011)76final, 23 February 2011.

[55]'Readmission Agreements: a Mechanism for Returning Irregular Migrants', Parliamentary Assembly of the Council of Europe, Report dated 17 March 2010; MIGREUROP:'European Commission evaluation of EU readmission agreements. Some comments and questions', http://www.statewatch.org/news/2011/apr/eu-migreurop-readmission-en.pdf. Accessed 19 December 2014.

[56]Communication on the Evaluation of EU Readmission Agreements, COM(2011)76final, 23 February 2011.

3 Conclusion

The negotiation, implementation and monitoring phases of EU readmission agreements hold features which not only cause the effectiveness of readmission agreements to be debatable, but also lead to human rights violation. It is essential to initiate an inclusive debate with all stake holders, ahead of the post-Stockholm period, and rethink the European approach towards readmission. This article has highlighted some of the thorniest issues regarding the current readmission policy and practice of the European Union.

The negotiation of readmission policies should be made more transparent, especially towards the European Parliament, which gives consent to EU readmission agreements without having the chance to amend the texts of these agreements. This is why the Parliament should be involved in the process from the beginning. The agreements should also become more flexible, taking into consideration the specific needs of individual third countries, instead of the current approach offering essentially a similar structure to all partner countries. During the negotiation phase, the real cost of the readmission agreement should be realistically calculated and incentives should be based on this projection instead of the approach which has prevailed to date, presenting the signing of a readmission agreement as a consideration for other benefits such as trade concessions. In signing readmission agreements, the level of human rights protection, especially the existence of a functioning asylum system in the partner country should be one of the criteria the EU focuses on. If the third country does not offer a level of protection acceptable to the EU, the first step should be to assist the country in reaching this level.

In order to improve the implementation of EU readmission agreements, the current EU and bilateral readmission agreements of Member States should be studied in order to identify problematic issues. There are widespread violations of the principle of non-refoulement committed by Member States, especially in the course of push-back operations and the implementation of the accelerated procedure. The accelerated procedure should be strictly regulated, which is why, contrary to what has been suggested by the Commission, they should not be only dealt with in bilateral implementing protocols but be included in future readmission agreements as well.

Human rights violations do not only take place on the EU-side of the readmission operation, but also in partner countries once the persons are readmitted. A monitoring system should be set up in order to scrutinize the operability of readmission agreements as well as their human rights implications on both sides of the readmission agreement. This could be done by involving the European Parliament and NGOs in Joint Readmission Committees.

Readmission agreements may have become an indispensable tool in combating illegal immigration, but this does not suggest that the current European policy is an acceptable one. There is certainly room for improvement in terms of effectiveness and human rights implications. An inclusive debate should be initiated by the European Commission in achieving a new European readmission policy that equally focuses on both aspects.

Documents

Council Recommendation of 30 November 1994 concerning a specimen bilateral readmission agreement between a Member State and a third country, OJ C 274, 19 September 1996, pp 20–24

Council Recommendation of 24 July 1995 on the guiding principles to be followed in drawing up protocols on the implementation of readmission agreements, OJ C 274, 19 September 1996, pp 25–33

Council Conclusions on criteria for the identification of third countries with which new readmission agreements need to be negotiated, dated 16 April 2002.

Directive 2008/115/EC of 16 December 2008 on common standards and procedures in Member States for returning illegally staying third-country nationals, OJ L 348/98, 24 December 2008.

The Stockholm Programme – an open and secure Europe serving and protecting citizens, OJ C 115, 4 May 2010, pp 1–38

Parliamentary Assembly of the Council of Europe (2010) Readmission agreements: a mechanism for returning irregular migrants

Communication on the Evaluation of EU Readmission Agreements, COM(2011)76final of 23 February 2011

International Strategic Research Organization (USAK) (2010) Turkiye-AB Iliskilerinde Geri Kabul: Hangi Sartlarda? USAK Report No. 10-02

References

Cassarino JP (2010) Readmission Policy in the European Union. European Parliament Directorate-General for Internal Policies

Coleman N (2009) European readmission policy: third country interests and refugee rights. Martinus Nijhoff Publishers, Leiden

Hailbronner K (2000) Immigration and asylum law and policy of the European Union. Kluwer Law International, The Hague

Lagrand TE (2010) Immigration law and policy: the EU acquis and its impact on the Turkish legal order. Wolf Legal Publishers, Nijmegen

Tokuzlu LB (2010) Burden-sharing games for asylum seekers between Turkey and the European Union, EUI Working Papers, RSCAS 2010/05, Robert Schumann Centre for Advanced Studies, European University Institute, Badia Fiesolana

Das regionale Privatrecht und die Harmonisierung des Privatrechts in der Europäischen Union

Viola Heutger

Abstract Die europäische Integration schreitet voran. Dennoch ist festzustellen, dass die Harmonisierung einhergeht mit dem Wunsch nach mehr Autonomie in einigen europäischen Regionen. Die Komplexität dieser Entwicklung beginnt bereits bei der Definition, was in Europa als Region verstanden wird. Diese Unabhängigkeitsbestrebungen einiger Gebiete umfassen nicht nur das Verfassungs- und Verwaltungsrecht, sondern auch das Privatrecht.

Contents

1 Einleitung

In der Diskussion über Unabhängigkeitsbestrebungen von Regionen stehen meist die verfassungsrechtlichen und europarechtlichen Aspekte zentral. Als Beispiel für Länder, in denen Gebietsteile mehr Autonomie fordern, worden Schottland

---

V. Heutger (✉)
Lehrbeauftragte Für Europäische Rechtsgeschichte, Türkisch-Deutschen Universität, Istanbul, Turkey
e-mail: viola.heutger@gmail.com

F.A.N.J. Goudappel and E.M.H. Hirsch Ballin (eds.), *Democracy and Rule of Law in the European Union*, DOI 10.1007/978-94-6265-066-4_15

und Flandern näher vorgestellt. Was den Bürger wirklich bewegt, das ist allerdings deutlich im Privatrecht zu sehen. Dieser Bereich des Rechts steht dem Bürger am Nächsten und ist ein Indiz dafür inwieweit Bürger selber für ihre Rechte aufkommen wollen und das Recht, welches ihre Rechtsverhältnisse regelt, mitgestalten wollen. Der Gedanke der Parteiautonomie und der Selbstregulierung entspringt dem Privatrecht. Rechtsstaatliches Denken darf daher auf keinen Fall nur auf das Verfassungsrecht beschränkt sein.

Das Recht auf regionale Selbstbestimmung ist tief verankert in den Grundgedanken der Europäischen Union. Euregios wurden geschaffen, Minderheiten werden geschützt, lokale Selbstverwaltung gefördert. Bisher wurde allerdings dem regional unterschiedlichen Privatrecht wenig Aufmerksamkeit gewidmet. Neben der fortschreitenden unionsweiten Harmonisierung ist Raum für die Entwicklung regionaler Besonderheiten in den verschiedensten Bereichen, auch im Privatrecht.

Mit dem Begriff Regionen werden zumeist geografische Besonderheiten und lokale Spezialitäten assoziiert. Regionale Produkte wie Zuckerbrot aus Friesland oder Whisky aus Schottland werden geschützt.[1] Immer mehr Gruppen beschäftigen sich mit der regionalen Identität der Bürger. Im internationalen Dialog wird Europa sogar als Model einer regionalen Entwicklung gesehen.[2]

Das Subsidiaritätsprinzip unterstützt regionale Belange und sagt: Gesetzgebung und Ausführung sollen so dicht wie möglich beim Bürger stattfinden. Ausnahmen sind nur die exklusiven Befugnisse der Union oder wenn Maßnahmen auf Unionsniveau zieltreffender sind als Maßnahmen auf nationalem, regionalem oder lokalem Niveau. Der Vertrag von Lissabon bestätigt und verankert dieses Subsidiaritätsprinzip als einen der zentralen Grundsätze der Europäischen Union.[3] In der Praxis heißt das, dass bei gemeinsamer Kompetenz von Union und Mitgliedstaaten, wie zum Beispiel im Verbraucherrecht, eine höhere politische Instanz nur dann tätig wird, wenn die ihr untergeordnete Ebene die Aufgaben nicht erfüllen kann und eine höhere Ebene ein besseres Resultat erreichen kann. Daher ist es nicht möglich das gesamte Recht der Mitgliedstaaten zu vereinheitlichen. Nur jene Bereiche dürfen vereinheitlicht werden, die in den Verträgen genannt

[1]So wird in der EU zwischen der geschützten Ursprungsbezeichnung, der geschützten geografischen Angabe und der garantiert traditionellen Spezialität unterschieden. Ein eigenes Logo weist auf diese Schutzbezeichnungen hin, http://ec.europa.eu/agriculture/foodqual/protec/logo_en.htm. Zugriff 10.3.2015.

[2]Im internationalen Kontext ist dieses Modellwirkung allerdings vor allem auf große regionale Zusammenschlüsse zu beziehen, wie z.B. Mercosur, Andean Community und ACP Regionen. Dazu Pietrangeli 2009, pp. 10 ff.

[3]Article 5 Absatz 3 des Vertrags über die Europäische Union (EUV).

werden, und auch dann nur, wenn ein bestimmtes gemeinsames Ziel auf Unionsebene besser erreicht werden kann als auf nationaler oder regionaler Ebene. Immer wieder muss daher ausgelotet werden, wieweit regionale Selbstbestimmung gehen kann. In einigen Regionen der Mitgliedstaaten besteht ein Streben nach Autonomie und damit einhergehend dem Wunsch nach mehr Freiheit und Eigenheiten auch bei der Regelung von privatrechtlichen Problemen.

Auf einige Regionen, die derzeit nach mehr Autonomie streben und bereits über eigene Teilrechtssysteme verfügen möchte ich näher eingehen. Stellvertretend für andere ist dort eine Entwicklung im Gange, die als Trend gesehen werden kann.

2 Definition einer Region in Europa

Immer wieder sprechen wir von einem Europa der Regionen. Aber wenn man sich auf die Suche begibt, wie man nun so eine Region definieren könnte, so stößt man auf eine Vielfalt von Möglichkeiten. Betrachtet man die Definitionen, die verschiedene offizielle und inoffizielle EU-Einrichtungen bieten, so werden die Regionen unterschiedlich eingeteilt, je nachdem ob man sie mehr auf Grund von politischen oder administrativen Systemen sortiert, also nach Bundesländern, Provinzen und Gemeinden, oder auf Grund der Bevölkerungsdichte oder der Identität der regionalen Bevölkerungsgruppe, also ob es sich zum Beispiel um Friesen, um Flamen, Sorben oder Katalonier handelt.[4]

Regionen haben Anziehungskraft und sind identitätsbildend. So manch einer wollte schon gerne ein Europa von Regionen gestalten.[5] Innerhalb der Europäischen Union sehen wir deutlich neben der voranschreitenden Harmonisierung auch die verschiedensten Prozesse der Fragmentierung. Regionale Zusammenarbeit wird in den letzten zwei Jahrzehnten immer mehr gefördert. Der 'Ausschuss der Regionen', eine europäische Institution die durch den Vertrag von Maastricht 1993 errichtet wurde, strebt nach mehr Partizipation

[4]So spricht auch die Europäische Charta der Regional- oder Minderheitensprachen, SEV-Nr. 148, Strassburg 1992 und in Kraft seit dem 1.3.1998 von Regionen. Eine Definition ist allerdings auch in diesem Dokument nicht zu finden, ohne weiter zu differenzieren wird dort von Regionen Europas und Regionen der Staaten Europas gesprochen. Auch der Vertrag über die Arbeitsweise der europäischen Union sowie der Vertrag über die europäische Union bieten keine Definition, was unter einer Region verstanden wird.

[5]So dachte zum Beispiel auch Freddy Heineken, der große niederländische Bierproduzent, an eine Einteilung von Europa in Regionen. Er sah die bestehenden Mitgliedstaaten als ein Hindernis der Europäischen Integration. Er schuf eine Eurotopia, die Europa in 75 Regionen mit einer etwa gleich großen Bevölkerungsdichte verteilte. Bei seiner Einteilung folgte er den schon bestehenden Verwaltungseinheiten. Siehe Heineken 1992, p. 2.

der Regionen und beschäftigt sich vor allem mit Regionen im Gebiet der EU, die mit den politischen Provinzen, Gemeinden oder Ländern identisch sind.[6] Um das Privatrecht kümmerte sich der Ausschuss allerdings bisher nicht.[7]

Bei der Betrachtung der Karte der 'Versammlung der Regionen Europas', einem unabhängigen Netzwerk der Regionen in Europa, wird Europa aufgeteilt in Regionen, die manchmal mehr übereinkommen mit der regionalen Identität der Bewohner als mit der politischen Einteilung. Die Versammlung bezieht auch weit entfernt gelegene Regionen der EU, zum Beispiel in der Karibik, mit in ihr Programm ein.[8] Laut den Statuten der Versammlung der Regionen bezieht sich das Wort "Region"auf eine territoriale Autorität, die eine Stufe unter der nationalen Regierung mit seinen eigenen politischen Vertretern in Form einer gewählten regionalen Versammlung agiert.

Eine wirkliche Standarddefinition, was in der EU als Region angesehen wird, gibt es allerdings nicht. Aus den EU-Verträgen können wir nur ableiten, dass es hier in Europa als auch Übersee Regionen gibt. Diese Regionen befinden sich zwischen der lokalen und der nationalen Ebene und können auch grenzüberschreitend sein, wobei es sich dann um nationale Teilregionen in einer Grenzlage handelt. Bei den Euregios, wie die Europäischen Regionen zumeist genannt werden, handelt es sich um grenzüberschreitende Zusammenschlüsse auf kommunaler Ebene. Der nationale Anteil an einer Euregio kann also auch nur einen Teil eines Gebiets umfassen, welches im jeweiligen Nationalstaat als Region bezeichnet wird. Das eine Region keineswegs nur als Verwaltungseinheit fungiert, wird deutlich aus Art. 174 des Vertrags über die Arbeitsweise der Europäischen Union, der auch von Grenzregionen, Inselregionen als auch Bergregionen[9] spricht. Neben den Regionen in Europa haben einzelne EU-Mitgliedstaaten auch noch Regionen außerhalb Europas in überseeischen Gebieten. Hier wird jedoch der Begriff Region bei der Bezeichnung in der deutschen Vertragsversion vermieden und der Vertrag über die Arbeitsweise der Europäischen Union spricht in Art. 349 von Gebieten in äußerster Randlage. Andere Sprachversionen sprechen allerdings auch in Bezug auf diese Gebiete von Regionen, so zum Beispiel der französische und englische Vertragstext.

[6]http://cor.europa.eu. Die Arbeit ist vor allem gerichtet auf die Regionen, die innerhalb der EU im Kontinent Europa liegen, beinah gar nicht auf die Regionen von Dänemark, Frankreich, den Niederlanden und des Vereinigten Königreichs, die außerhalb des Kontinents liegen.

[7]Eine schriftliche Nachfrage bestätigte mir diesen Befund.

[8]http://www.aer.eu/de/veroeffentlichungen/tabula-regionum-europae.html. Zugriff 15.3.2015. Zur Stärkung des Regionalismus wurde diese Versammlung 1985 gegründet.

[9]So wurde auch schon intensiv über ein Grünbuch über die Bergregionen nachgedacht. Siehe auch die Stellungnahme des Europäischen Wirtschafts- und Sozialausschusses zum Thema Zukunftsperspektiven der Landwirtschaft in Gebieten mit bestimmten naturbedingten Nachteilen (Berg- und Inselgebiete sowie Regionen in äußerster Randlage) Amtsblatt Nr. C 120 vom 16/05/2008 S. 0047-0048.

Im 2. Annex des Vertrages über die Arbeitsweise der Europäischen Union werden verschiedene überseeische Länder und Gebiete genannt, die zu Frankreich, den Niederlanden, Dänemark und dem Vereinigten Königreich eine Beziehung haben. Wie bereits vermeldet verzichtet die deutsche Version des Vertrags auf den Begriff Region. Es wird von überseeischen Ländern und Hoheitsgebieten gesprochen. Art. 198 des Vertrages über die Arbeitsweise der Europäischen Union regelt die Assoziierung dieser Regionen mit der EU.[10]

Eine Definition des Begriffs Region liegt also nicht vor. Der Begriff "regionales Recht" wird allerdings oft gebraucht, er kann aber nicht einfach mit Hilfe eines juristischen Wörterbuches definiert werden. Der Begriff wurde auch einige Male gebraucht für die Andeutung des Rechtssystems eines besetzten Gebietes. Von regionalem Recht wird auch gesprochen, wenn man über größere Gebiete—eine Region der Welt—spricht, wie Lateinamerika oder Nordamerika. Oder hier in Europa über die BENELUX Länder. Hier liegt eine Region, anders als in den EU Verträgen, nicht zwischen der lokalen und der nationalstaatlichen Ebene.[11] Ebenso wird von regionalem Recht gesprochen, wenn man im globalen Rahmen an Handelsunionen, wie die OHADA[12] als Handelsorganisation in Afrika, an die Europäische Union[13] oder an den karibischen gemeinsamen Markt der CARICOM[14] Länder denkt.[15]

Regionen können also sowohl grösser sein als nationale Staaten. Regionen können aber auch ein Gebiet eines Staates sein. Regionen können außerdem im Sinne der Euroregios, wie zum Beispiel die Region um Aachen, Maastricht und Lüttich, verschiedene Teile von unterschiedlichen Staaten sein. Auf diese Euregios werde ich nicht näher eingehen. Ebenso nicht auf die Regionen die grösser als ein nationaler Staat sind. Ich möchte auf die Regionen innerhalb eines Staates eingehen und untersuchen, in wieweit diese durch ein eigenes Privatrecht zu einer Fragmentierung des Privatrechts innerhalb eines Nationalstaates beitragen.

3 Harmonisierung Versus Fragmentierung

Die EU strebt danach um nationales, regionales, und lokales Recht in Einklang zu bringen oder zumindest zu koordinieren im Hinblick auf eine spätere Harmonisierung und Vereinheitlichung. In Europa sind wir sowohl an geographische

[10]Einen guten Einblick in die Materie bietet Kochenov 2011. Sowie Murray 2012.

[11]Über die EU als Region siehe: The EU and World Regionalism, The Makability of Regions in the 21st Century, De Lombaerde and Schulz 2009.

[12]L'Organisation pour l'Harmonisation en Afrique du Droit des Affaires, siehe http://www.ohada.org.

[13]De Lombaerde and Schulz 2009.

[14]Caribbean Common Market, siehe http://www.caricom.org.

[15]Auf diese Art des regionalen Rechts möchte ich aber nicht weiter eingehen.

Fragmentierung, als auch an die Fragmentierung des Rechts gewöhnt. Es gibt mehr Rechtssysteme in der EU als Mitgliedstaaten. Auf die Fragmentierung des Privatrechts wurde in den vergangenen Jahren immer wieder hingewiesen.[16] Dabei dachte man allerdings meist weniger an regionale Zersplitterung, als an die Einteilung in Handelsrecht, Verbraucherrecht und das allgemeine Zivilrecht, sowie die Fragmentierung des Rechts in Bezug auf die verschiedenen Vertragstypen. Regionale Unterschiede lassen sich aber auch im Vertragsrecht sowie in anderen Bereichen des Privatrechts zurückfinden.

Aber die Fragmentierung ist noch nicht vollständig. Denn zum einen gibt es EU Mitgliedstaaten hier in unserer Nähe, die aus verschiedenen Gebietsteilen mit unterschiedlichen Rechtssystemen bestehen. Aber ebenso gibt es zum anderen EU Mitgliedstaaten, die teilweise auch noch Teil eines größeren Gebietes sind, mit Landesteilen sogar außerhalb Europas weit weg über See und jeweils mit unterschiedlichen Rechtssystemen.

4 Beispiele von Ländern mit Regionen mit verschiedenen Rechtsordnungen

Region, und spezifisch das 'Regionale Privatrecht' definiere ich als ein eigenständiges Privatrechtssystem, das nur Geltung in einem geografischen Teilbereich eines EU-Mitgliedstaates hat.[17] Ich möchte untersuchen, welchen Einfluss die Harmonisierung des Privatrechts auf diese Regionen hat und was für eine Wechselwirkung zwischen diesen Regionen und der Europäischen Union stattfindet. Zur Verdeutlichung meiner Ausführungen habe ich Beispiele aus EU Mitgliedstaaten gewählt, auf die die genannten Kriterien zutreffen. Mitgliedstaaten also, deren Bürger alle den gleichen europäischen Pass haben, die aber als Unionsbürger in Gebieten leben, wo unterschiedliche Rechtssysteme zu finden sind.

Ein prominentes Beispiel ist das Vereinigte Königreich. So haben wir im Vereinigten Königreich mit England ein *common law* Mitglied in der EU und mit Schottland ein Rechtssystem, welches wir den gemischten Rechtssystemen zurechnen würden.[18] So haben wir eine EU mit 27 Mitgliedstaaten und mindestens 28 Rechtsordnungen. Derzeit gibt es aber noch mehr Rechtsordnungen und es entstehen noch weitere Rechtsordnungen.

---

[16]So zum Beispiel van Smits 2011, p. 122.

[17]Kodifiziert in dem Sinne, dass eben nicht nur im nationalen Zivilrechtrecht nach regionalen Besonderheiten verwiesen wird, sondern dass diese Regionen wirklich über ein eigenes und von den anderen Gebietsteilen unterschiedliches Rechtssystem im Privatrecht verfügen.

[18]Eine kurze Einführung in das schottische Rechtssystem mit weiteren Literaturnachweisen bietet zum Beispiel Rainer 2002, pp. 252–253.

In Spanien hat sich Katalonien für ein eigenes Zivilgesetzbuch entschieden. Auch gibt es dort eigene Aufsichtsbehörden, wie zum Beispiel zum Verbraucherschutz. Hier geht die Selbstregulierung sogar soweit, dass sich bestimmte Regeln auf Bürger von Katalonien beziehen, unabhängig von ihrem Wohnsitz. Man ist Spanier mit einer regionalen Identität, Katalonier. So gibt es Besonderheiten zum Beispiel im Ehegüterrecht. Diese Regelungen sind sogar noch anzuwenden, wenn Katalonier im Ausland heiraten und sich dort wieder trennen wollen.[19] Eine derartige Regelung, die an die regionale Identität als Nationalität anknüpft kennen wir in anderen Regionen nicht. In Spanien sind noch mehr regionale Entwicklungen zu beobachten, so strebt man auch im Baskenland nach mehr Autonomie.

Regionalismus kann aber auch noch anders gelebt werden. Selbst in Ländern mit nur einem Gesetzbuch finden wir verschiedene Rechtsentwicklungen. Das Land Belgien kämpft mit innerstaatlichen Sprachgrenzen. So ist es dort so, dass Richter und Anwälte aus dem flämischen Teil die Entscheidungen ihrer Kollegen aus dem französischsprachigen Teilen kaum beachten und die Entscheidungen des deutschsprachigen Richters auch nicht in die Rechtsprechung des flämischen Kollegen Eingang finden.[20] In Flandern kämpft man um mehr Autonomie, auch erwägt man eigene Gesetzgebung.

27 Mitgliedstaaten bieten also weit mehr Diversität als man zunächst erwarten würde. Betrachtet man jedes Land der EU einzeln aus der jeweiligen Perspektive des Landes und seiner Regionen, so kommt eine erstaunliche Vielfalt zutage.[21] Die Vielfalt der Rechtssysteme ist noch nicht so groß wie jene der vielen regionalen und Minderheitssprachen, die neben den offiziellen 23 Amtssprachen gesprochen werden. Aber eine deutliche Entwicklungstendenz hin zu Diversität ist festzustellen. Man fordert generell mehr regionale Autonomie und die Schaffung eines eigenen Instanzenzuges. Einige Regionen kennen sogar schon eine absolute Selbständigkeit. So bleiben zum Beispiel alle Instanzenzüge in Schottland und geht es nicht weiter bis London.

5 Forderung nach mehr Mitbestimmung von Regionen

Es ist festzustellen, Regionen tragen zur Identität der dort lebenden Bürger bei. Regionen stehen dichter beim Bürger als Nationalstaaten oder die Europäische Union. Aufgrund von regionaler Identität entsteht oft die Forderung so viel wie

[19] Roca I Trias 1986, pp. 39–49, 48.

[20] Diese Auffassung beruht auf meiner persönlichen Erfahrung während einer Lehrstuhlvertretung an der Universität Hasselt im Frühjahr 2011.

[21] Abspaltungsbestrebungen, regionale Ausnahmen, Gebietsteile in Insellagen, die auch einen besonderen Status erhalten haben oder historische Verbindungen, wie zum Beispiel zu ehemaligen Kolonien Übersee.

möglich in der Region selber zu regeln. Eine Antwort auf diese Forderung sind die bestehenden regionalen Gesetzbücher oder Rechtsentwicklungen auch im Bereich des Privatrechts. Diese Autonomie setzt sich mehr und mehr auch in der Rechtsprechung durch. Die Forderung nach einem kompletten Instanzenzug in der jeweiligen Region mit eigener Gesetzgebung, wird in einigen Regionen bereits in die Praxis umgesetzt. Auch ist zu beobachten, dass in einigen Regionen eigene Aufsichtsbehörden entstehen wie Verbraucherschutzbehörden, Ämter für Markenrechte, Wettbewerbsautoritäten sowie Ombudsmänner. Allerdings sind Regionen durch ihre Gebietsgröße, die recht kleine Anzahl der Bevölkerung, Mentalitätsunterschiede und verschiedene finanzielle Ressourcen sehr schwer zugänglich. Nicht immer können Gesetze, Rechtsprechung und Verwaltungsstrukturen problemlos gefunden werden. Mehr Transparenz und ein vereinfachter Zugang zu den Informationen ist nötig.

Es wäre sehr hilfreich für die Regionen, wenn es eine Institution, wie z.B. das *European Law Institute* gäbe, wo alles Material gesammelt und analysiert werden könnte. Die Besonderheiten der Regionen sollten nicht vergessen werden. Sie sind ein Teil der europäischen Kultur und Geschichte. Die Regionen sollten im Sinne des Subsidiaritätsprinzips auch im Privatrecht mehr Beachtung finden. Durch spezifische Forschungs- und Dokumentationsprojekte sollten die bestehenden regionalen Privatrechtsordnungen besser zugänglich gemacht werden.

Neben internationalen Vereinheitlichungsinstrumenten, nationalen Regelungen und den stets mehr werdenden europäische Maßnahmen kommen nun auch noch regionale Bestrebungen mit ins Spiel. Die Beobachtung der Entwicklungen in den verschiedenen Mitgliedstaaten macht deutlich, dass regionale Entfaltungen in der Zukunft zunehmen werden und europäische Schritte mit Skepsis gefolgt werden und nur überzeugend lanciert werden können, wenn sie durch ein glaubwürdiges und transparentes Verfahren zustande kommen. Regionen sollte genügend Gestaltungsspielraum gelassen werden. Ihr Entwicklungspotential darf nicht unterschätzt werden, zumal nun der Regionalismus bis ins Privatrecht durchwirkt.

Ich schließe mit dem Fazit, dass bei der Rechtsharmonisierung mehr Zurückhaltung geboten ist. Regionale Interessen sollten mehr beachtet werden. Jegliches Eingreifen aus Brüssel kann kontraproduktiv sein und statt Harmonisierung innerhalb der Union vor allem zu Fragmentierung in einigen Staaten führen und die Entwicklung von Regionen hemmen. Besser wäre es die Rechtsentwicklung gut zu beobachten und festzustellen, ob sich bestimmte Grundgedanken auch in den Regionen wiederfinden.

Regionen sollten ein Mitspracherecht bei der Europäisierung des Rechts erhalten. Ebenso sollten die Rechte von Unionsbürgern in den einzelnen Regionen Europas sowie den überseeischen Gebieten nicht übersehen werden. Wollen wir weiter fortschreiten mit der Rechtsvereinheitlichung, dann sollten bei zukünftigen europäischen Rechtsharmonisierungsmaßnahmen die regionalen Interessen mitvergegenwärtigt werden.

References

De Lombaerde P, Schulz M (2009) The EU and world regionalism, the makability of regions in the 21st century. Ashgate, Farnham

Heineken AH (1992) The United States of Europe (a Eurotopia?), 2nd edn. De Amsterdamse Stichting voor de Historische Wetenschap, Amsterdam

Kochenov D (ed) (2011) EU law of the overseas, outermost regions, associated overseas countries and territories, territories sui generis. Kluwer Law International

Murray F (2012) The European Union and member state territories: a new legal framework, under the EU Treaties. T.M.C Asser Press, The Hague

Pietrangeli G (2009) Supporting regional integration and cooperation worldwide: an overview of the European Union approach. In: De Lombaerde P, Schultz M (eds) The EU and world regionalism, the makability of regions in the 21st century. Ashgate, Farnham pp. 9–44

Rainer M (2002) Europäisches Privatrecht, die Rechtsvergleichung. Peter Lang, Frankfurt am Main

Roca I, Trias E (1986) The Spanish system of federalism and self-government: regional law in Catalonia. Suffolk Trans Law J 10:39–49

Smits J (2011) Kodifikation ohne Demokratie? Zur Legitimität eines Europäischen (Optionalen) Zivilgesetzbuches. In: Joerges Ch, Pinkel T (Hgs.) Europäisches Verfassungsdenken ohne Privatrecht- Europäisches Privatrecht ohne Demokratie (ZERP Diskussionspapier 1/2011). ZERP, Bremen, pp. 119–132

Selected Legal and Policy Implications Arising from the EU–ICC Agreement of 2006

Gerhard Hafner

Abstract The cooperation between the EU and the ICC is regulated by the EU–ICC Agreement (2006) and deals with matters of mutual interest. It regulates cooperation and assistance, attendance to meetings, exchange of information, testimony, cooperation between the EU and the prosecutor and privileges and immunities. The Common Foreign Security Policy (CFSP) covers all ICC-related acts. With regard to sharing information, the ICC is held to ensure the regular exchange of information and documents. The central problem in this aspect, according to the author, is the delivery of sensitive information. The Agreement mentions two types of information. First, the type that could endanger the safety or security of former EU staff, proper conducts or any EU activity;. the second type is classified information that requires protection from unauthorized disclosure. The ICC decides on the retention of this information. The author questions whether this is appropriate, as the ICC decides if a transfer of information could endanger the EU. He claims that the EU should at least be involved in making this decision. The author concludes that since the Agreement is one-sided, uncertainty is created for the EU about how sensitive information would be treated by the ICC.

I am particularly grateful to Mr. Gregor Novak for his extremely valuable assistance.

G. Hafner (✉)
University of Vienna, Vienna, Austria
e-mail: gerhard.hafner@univie.ac.at

F.A.N.J. Goudappel and E.M.H. Hirsch Ballin (eds.), *Democracy and Rule of Law in the European Union*, DOI 10.1007/978-94-6265-066-4_16

Contents

1 Introduction

My contribution will discuss some of the issues relating to one of the principal foci of the EU's foreign policy, the International Criminal Court.[1] It will also draw on some personal experiences collected in the course of the negotiations leading up to the Rome Statute.[2]

2 History of the EU's Policy Towards the ICC

The engagement of the EU in the matter of the ICC resulted especially from the activities of the "like-minded group", a group of mostly small and medium sized States, but including—for historical reasons—also Germany.[3] This group sup-

[1]See on the EU's policy with respect to the International Criminal Court (ICC): Article 2 of the Council of the EU (11 June 2001) Common Position 2001/443/CFSP on the International Criminal Court; see also Ford 2011, p. 965 (analyzing expenditures on international criminal justice institutions by region, noting that European countries "will be the driving force behind spending by 2015"); see also generally J. Wouters and S. Basu S, *The Creation of a Global Criminal Justice System: the European Union and the International Criminal Court*. Leuven Center for Global Governance Studies Working Paper No. 26. http://www.law.kuleuven.be/iir/nl/onderzoek/wp/wp136e.pdf. Accessed 25 June 2013; Groenleer and Rijks 2009, as well as Strapatsas 2002.

[2]Rome Statute of the International Criminal Court (adopted 17 July 1998, entered into force 1 July 2002) 2187 UNTS 90 (Rome Statute).

[3]See e.g. Kirsch and Holmes 1998, pp. 3–39; Schabas 2011, pp. 18–19; Schiff 2008, pp. 70–71; Washburn 1999, pp. 367–368.

ported the establishment of the ICC ever since the draft of the Statute was submitted to the GA by the ILC in 1994.[4] By 1996, this group of ICC supporters already encompassed almost all member states of the EU—consisting of 15 members at the time—with the exception of the UK and France. Only after the Labor Party was voted into government in the UK and Tony Blair became the Prime Minister did that country join the group. This addition was mostly welcomed, particularly because the UK was the first permanent member of the Security Council to become a member. As of then, the group enjoyed the backing of two major States, namely Germany and the United Kingdom. Nevertheless, the position of the EU remained less than clear with regard to the ICC, and common statements were the exception even during the first half of the Rome Conference in June 1998. Nevertheless, since 1995, the EU had provided some funding to NGOs advocating the creation of the ICC.[5]

Only when Austria took over the presidency of the Council of the EU by the beginning of July 1998 did the situation change substantially. At that time, with the Rome Conference underway,[6] the presidency was called on to elaborate substantial common positions in favor of the ICC, guided also by the Political Committee (PC, later became the Political and Security Committee, PSC) acting within the Common Foreign and Security Policy (CFSP). After France had succeeded in obtaining the exception under Article 124 at the Rome Conference,[7] all EU member states were able to support the establishment of the ICC and voted in favor of the final text that was submitted to a vote on 17 July 1998.

Since that moment, the EU has become very active in its support of the ICC and the Court became a major target of its CFSP. The discussions in the EU on the topic were first held in the Working Party on Public International Law (COJUR), and subsequently in the ICC Sub-area of the Working Party (COJUR-ICC).

[4]UN ILC (1994) Draft Statute for an International Criminal Court. GAOR 49th Session Supp 10, 29.

[5]General Secretariat of the Council (May 2010) The European Union and the International Criminal Court. http://www.consilium.europa.eu/uedocs/cmsUpload/ICC_may%2010_internet.pdf. Accessed 25 June 2013, p. 16.

[6]The Rome Conference took place in Rome from 15 June to 17 July 1998.

[7]Article 124 (Transitional Provision) of the Rome Statute provides as follows: "Notwithstanding article 12, paragraphs 1 and 2, a State, on becoming a party to this Statute, may declare that, for a period of seven years after the entry into force of this Statute for the State concerned, it does not accept the jurisdiction of the Court with respect to the category of crimes referred to in article 8 when a crime is alleged to have been committed by its nationals or on its territory. A declaration under this article may be withdrawn at any time. The provisions of this article shall be reviewed at the Review Conference convened in accordance with article 123, paragraph 1."

3 Legal Acts Concerning the EU's Policy Towards the ICC

In the course of its policy in support of the ICC, the EU adopted various legal acts: the first legal act was the Common Position of 11 June 2001, which was followed by Common Positions, adopted in 2002 and 2003 and supplemented by a 2004 Action Plan.[8] Only after the Lisbon Treaty finally entered into force, the Council adopted a new Council decision on the ICC on 21 March 2011.[9] The legal nature of the most recent decision is that of a "decision defining [the EU's] position on a particular matter [...] not [requiring] a particular action to be carried out by the EU institutions".[10] These legal acts were supplemented by various conclusions and declarations emanating from the Council, and other EU institutions, reinforcing the EU's position with respect to the ICC.[11]

In 2006, the ICC and the EU concluded an agreement on cooperation and assistance, including an Annex governing the "release of EU classified information by the EU to an organ of the Court" (Article 9 and Annex).[12] On 31 March 2008, and on the basis of the Agreement, the joint EU–ICC "security arrangements for the protection of [exchanged] classified information" came into effect.[13]

4 The EU–ICC Agreement (2006)

The Agreement regulates a number of specific matters relating to cooperation and assistance "on matters of mutual interest". It raises several points worthy of discussion, particularly in light of the increasing engagement of the EU in crisis situations where the commission of crimes within the jurisdiction of the ICC has

[8]Council of the EU (28 January 2004) Action Plan to follow-up on the Common Position on the International Criminal Court. Doc. 5742/04. http://register.consilium.europa.eu/pdf/en/04/st05/st05742.en04.pdf. Accessed 25 June 2013.

[9]Council of the EU (11 June 2001) Common Position 2001/443/CFSP on the International Criminal Court; Council of the EU (20 June 2002) Common Position 2002/474/CFSP amending Common Position 2001/443/CFSP on the International Criminal Court; Council of the EU (16 June 2003) Common Position 2003/444/CFSP on the International Criminal Court; Council of the EU (21 March 2011) Council Decision 2011/168/CFSP on the International Criminal Court and repealing Common Position 2003/444/CFSP.

[10]Koutrakos 2013, p. 37 (noting that "Council Decision 2011/168/CFSP on the International Criminal Court" provides an example of a "decision defining its position on a particular matter [...] not require[ing] a particular action to be carried out by the EU institutions".).

[11]See General Secretariat of the Council (May 2010) The European Union and the International Criminal Court, n. 5 above.

[12]Agreement between the International Criminal Court and the European Union on Cooperation and Assistance, Doc. ICC-PRES/01-01-06, entered into force on 1 May 2006.

[13]Council of the EU (15 April 2008) Security Arrangements for the Protection of Classified Information Exchanged between the EU and the ICC, Doc. 8349/1/08. http://register.consilium.europa.eu/pdf/en/08/st08/st08349-re01.en08.pdf. Accessed 25 June 2013.

become conceivable. Accordingly, it cannot be excluded that persons engaged in an operation directed or staffed by the EU could be asked to appear before the ICC either as witnesses or, although this might rarely be the case, as suspects under a warrant of arrest. Even peacekeepers under UN command can be held responsible before the commission of such crimes since otherwise the Security Council would not have considered it necessary to take a decision for the exclusion of the jurisdiction of the ICC for such personnel in 2002 and 2003.[14] The Agreement has to be scrutinized with respect to both of the above scenarios.

In addition, questions have been raised as to the effect the Agreement could have on the likelihood that the US will join the ICC. It was argued that agreements providing for the transmission of classified documents from the ICC to the EU would put further obstacles in the way of an eventual accession by the US to the Rome Statute. If true, this fear creates a dilemma for the EU: on the one hand, the EU has consistently advocated universal accession to the Rome Statute, and the US's support for the ICC is seen as an important element in this strategy. On the other hand, the EU seeks to contribute to the day-to-day work of the ICC, and the exchange of information, which is usefully placed on a legal basis and can facilitate the ICC's work.

My contribution will first examine the competence of the EU to conclude an agreement dealing with matters relating to cooperation and assistance and concerning the exchange of information, including classified types of information, as well as privileges and immunities. Second, my contribution will survey several specific issues relating to the transmittal of documents by the ICC to the EU and vice versa. Third, the contribution will consider the question of the waiver of immunities by the EU, including the question of hearings.

5 The EU's Competence to Conclude the EU–ICC Agreement

Since the beginning of its engagement with the ICC, the EU has based the competence to deal with ICC-related matters on the Articles in its constitutive treaties that relate to the CFSP. The first legal act of the EU in this respect, the 2001 Common Position, already referred to the then Article 15 of the TEU which provided that "[c]ommon positions shall define the approach of the Union to a particular matter of a geographical or thematic nature" and that "Member States shall ensure that their national policies conform to the common positions".[15] It could certainly be asked whether the EU's activities regarding the ICC would not rather

[14]United Nations Security Council Resolution 1422 (12 July 2002) UN Doc. S/RES/1422; United Nations Security Council Resolution 1487 (12 June 2003) UN Doc. S/RES/1487.

[15]Article 15 of the TEU provided as follows: "The Council shall adopt common positions. Common positions shall define the approach of the Union to a particular matter of a geographical or thematic nature. Member States shall ensure that their national policies conform to the common positions."

fall within the ambit of Justice and Home Affairs, formerly the third pillar, than into the CFSP. In the 2001 Common Position, the EU explicitly acknowledged that the ICC's mandate contributes to "freedom, security, justice and the rule of law". However, since the competences under Title VI (Provisions on Police and Judicial Cooperation in Criminal Matters) focus on the cooperation among the member states and not between the EU and other foreign institutions like the ICC, the only legal basis could be found in the CFSP (Title V). According to Article 24 of the TEU[16] which defines the competence of the EU in this field, the CFSP encompasses any relations in the field of foreign policy, although the adoption of "legislative acts" is excluded. The Article provides that "[t]he Union's competence in matters of common foreign and security policy shall cover all areas of foreign policy and all questions relating to the Union's security […]."

However, in view of the broad competence regarding the CFSP and the necessity to cover also the matters that could reach beyond the EU's competences under Justice and Home Affairs, ICC-related acts were placed under the heading of the CFSP. The treaty-making competence in the field of the CFSP is theoretically unlimited, provided that the respective agreement does not fall within the treaty-making power in other fields of external actions of the EU, such as external trade policy.[17] As long as this is not the case, the EU is entitled, within the ambit of international law, to conclude any agreement with third States or foreign organizations. That such agreements are not concluded against the will of the MS is ensured by the requirement of unanimity for the conclusion of these agreements.

The ICC–EU Agreement only differs from other agreements insofar as it explicitly stipulates that it does not create obligations for the member states. This provision seems to contradict Article 218(7) TFEU according to which agreements concluded by the EU are binding not only on the EU, but also on the member states, thus creating the impression that any agreement concluded by the EU establishes obligations also with respect to the member states. Since agreements do not belong to primary EU law and, accordingly, are unable to amend it, a conflict seems to arise between the Agreement and primary EU law. However, this contradiction does not arise here if we assume that the substance of the EU–ICC Agreement, including the clause regarding the scope of the obligations (Article 4), is binding on the member states. For in that case, the binding effect of the Agreement on the member States is to be distinguished from the obligations incumbent on them.[18]

[16]Consolidated version of the Treaty on European Union, Official Journal 115, 9 May 2008, 13–45. http://eur-lex.europa.eu/LexUriServ/LexUriServ.do?uri=CELEX:12008M/TXT:EN:HTML. Accessed 25 June 2013.

[17]See e.g. Craig and De Búrca 2011, pp. 79–83.

[18]Article 4 (Obligation of cooperation and assistance) of the EU-ICC Agreement reads as follows: "The EU and the Court agree that, with a view to facilitating the effective discharge of their respective responsibilities, they shall cooperate closely, as appropriate, with each other and consult each other on matters of mutual interest, pursuant to the provisions of this Agreement while fully respecting the respective provisions of the EU Treaty and the Statute. In order to facilitate this obligation of cooperation and assistance, the Parties agree on the establishing of appropriate regular contacts between the Court and the EU Focal Point for the Court."

6 The Substance of the EU–ICC Agreement

The Agreement regulates questions of cooperation and assistance, attendance at meetings, the exchange of information, testimony, including the problem of classified information, the cooperation between the EU and the Prosecutor, and privileges and immunities. In its structure it follows *cum grano salis* the UN–ICC Agreement, which is, however, much more detailed.[19] The substance of the agreement raises certain problematic issues that result from the fact that the Agreement affects not merely the two Parties to the Agreement, but also, indirectly, the MS, irrespective of the restriction of the effect of the obligations since no international organization can act entirely autonomously without the involvement of its MS.

7 Major Controversial Issues

7.1 The Exchange of Information

According to Article 7 of the Agreement, the ICC "shall, to the fullest extent possible and practicable" ensure the regular exchange of information and documents. This part of the Agreement is based on Article 5 of the UN–ICC Agreement.[20] The EU committed itself to providing the ICC with such information upon a request in accordance with Article 87(6) of the Rome Statute. This provision entitles the ICC to seek information or documents from any intergovernmental organization. The Agreement obliges the EU to comply with such a request, within the limits of its own responsibilities and competence. However, the ICC itself is bound to provide information relating to pleadings, oral proceedings, judgments and orders of the ICC to the EU, as far as it is in the interest of the EU. Although this provision does not define who is competent to determine the EU's interests,[21] it is hardly controversial. This determination can be only within the powers of the EU as it would be unthinkable that the ambiguity could be resolved in a way as to allow the ICC to define the Union's interests and, thus, also the scope of its obligations unilaterally.

---

[19]Negotiated Relationship Agreement between the International Criminal Court and the United Nations, Doc. ICC-ASP/3/Res.1, entered into force on 22 July 2004. http://www.iccnow.org/documents/ICC-ASP-3-Res1_English.pdf. Accessed 25 June 2013.

[20]Article 5 (Exchange of information) of the EU–ICC Agreement reads as follows: "1. Without prejudice to other provisions of the present Agreement concerning the submission of documents and information concerning particular cases before the Court, the United Nations and the Court shall, to the fullest extent possible and practicable, arrange for the exchange of information and documents of mutual interest. In particular: […]."

[21]See in this context also Article 18 (Settlement of disputes) of the EU–ICC Agreement which reads as follows: "All differences between the EU and the Court arising out of the interpretation or application of this Agreement shall be dealt with through consultation between the Parties."

The central problem in this regard is the delivery of sensitive information. The Agreement distinguishes two different categories of information: First, information that could endanger the safety or security of current or former staff of the EU or otherwise the security of proper conducts of any operation or activity of the EU (Article 8). Second, "classified information", defined in the Annex as "any information [...] or material determined to require protection against unauthorised disclosure and which has been so designated by a security classification [...]".

The first category of documents relates to those that could affect operations and activities of the EU. In view of the increased operational activities of the EU through its civil and military conflict management operations this constitutes a rather important issue. The regulation is modeled on Article 15(3) of the UN–ICC Agreement. In both situations, it is within the power of the ICC to decide on the retention of such information by the other party, albeit in particular on request from the side of the EU, respectively the UN. It is questionable whether this solution is appropriate since the decision on whether the transfer of documents could endanger activities of the EU should be reserved to the latter, or at least involve the latter as the EU would be in the best position to assess the risk posed by such documents. It can only be expected that the EU would be in a position to explain in a sufficiently convincing manner to the ICC the risk entailed by the delivery of such documents. However, the Agreement contains other sufficiently broad clauses that permit the denial of the delivery of documents. So, for instance, Article 7(1) ensures the exchange of documents only to the "fullest extent possible and practicable", and the EU committed itself in Article 7(2) to deliver documents only "with due regard to its responsibilities and competence under the EU Treaty". The reference to "competence" ensures that only documents of the EU and not of the member states can be delivered to the ICC. This conclusion is also supplemented by the reference in Article 7(2) to documents being "in its possession", implying that documents still remaining in the possession of a member state cannot be delivered to the ICC. The reference to "responsibilities" obviously entails the duty to observe the security regulations of the EU itself. Thus, the delivery of classified documents within the possession of the EU is subject to the confidentiality regulations of the EU relating to this category of information, i.e., documents "determined to require protection against unauthorized disclosure and which has been so designated by a security classification".[22]

The basis of the Agreement in EU law as far as classified documents are concerned is Article 12 of Council Decision of 31 March 2011 on the security rules for protecting EU classified information, which addresses the issue of the exchange of classified information with third States and international organizations. In accordance with this provision, the Council concludes relevant agreements (called "security of information agreements") whereas the Secretary-General of the Council concludes administrative arrangements. The decision to release classified information is a matter left to the Council on a case-by-case basis.

[22]See para 1 of the Annex to the EU–ICC Agreement.

The Agreement itself refers in its Article 9 to the Annex where the further rules on this issue are contained. In particular, the Court is required to grant such documents the same protection as is provided by the EU. Documents classified CONFIDENTIEL UE can be distributed only to persons who have been security cleared. Their delivery must be recorded and further security arrangements must be entered into by the Security Office of the Court, the Security Office of the General Secretariat of the Council, as well as the European Commission Security Directorate. These Security Arrangements ensure that "classified Information exchanged with the other Party is protected to a level which is at least equivalent to the relevant minimum standards set out in the providing Party's security rules and regulations". Accordingly, documents classified CONFIDENTIEL UE/ICC CONFIDENTIAL or above are only granted to persons in possession of a valid personnel security clearance. The relevant "Security Arrangements" which were agreed in 2008[23] specify that the release of EU classified information to the ICC is allowed up to the level of RESTREINT UE in hard copy and that "no EU classified information may be transmitted by electromagnetic means to the ICC" (para 34) unless there exists a special arrangement. Accordingly, information classified as TRÈS SECRET UE, SECRET UE or CONFIDENTIEL UE must not be delivered in hard copy.

Thus, there is a cascade of legal acts relating to the security of documents starting from the Agreement, including its Annex. The latter authorizes the security offices of the EU to conclude an arrangement with the parallel institution of the ICC and is still supplemented by a relevant[24] document approved by the Council's Security Committee and the ICC. The reference to the responsibilities of the EU in Article 7(2) of the Agreement amounts to a reference to the security documents of the EU such as Council Decision of 31 March 2011 on the security rules for protecting EU classified information.[25] However, the EU cannot benefit from the clause on the protection of national security information in Article 72 of the Rome Statute (Protection of national security information), since the EU is not a party to the Rome Statute and neither the Agreement nor the Security Arrangements contain a reference to this provision.

Notwithstanding this legal regime which seeks to ensure that the confidentiality provided by the EU for certain documents is respected by the ICC criticism has been expressed. According to the American Non-Governmental Organizations Coalition for the International Criminal Court ("American NGOs CICC"), this exchange of documents "could create the fear that, if the US ratifies the Rome Statute, thus

[23]Council of the EU (15 April 2008) Security Arrangements for the Protection of Classified Information Exchanged between the EU and the ICC, Doc. 8349/1/08. http://register.consilium.europa.eu/pdf/en/08/st08/st08349-re01.en08.pdf. Accessed 25 June 2013.

[24]Ibid.

[25]Council Decision of 31 March 2011 on the security rules for protecting EU classified information, Doc. 2011/292/EU, L 141/17, 27 May 2011. http://eur-lex.europa.eu/LexUriServ/LexUriServ.do?uri=OJ:L:2011:141:0017:0065:EN:PDF. Accessed 25 June 2013.

expanding the Court's jurisdiction over US citizens, the EU could have access to documents related to the proceedings whose contents could be harmful to the US."[26] There is no real safeguard against this since the formulation regarding the documents "which may be of interest to the EU"[27] is very broad. Certainly, this criticism is not totally unfounded, as it is within the power of the ICC to decide which documents are transferred to the EU, provided they are of interest to the EU. Accordingly, documents could be delivered to the EU that relate to proceedings against US citizens, something that is lawful even at present if such a person commits a crime within the jurisdiction of the ICC in the territory of a State Party to the Rome Statute. To assuage such fears, it would have been useful to include a clause concerning the withholding of certain types of information that could prejudice third parties, and to provide a procedure by which other States or persons, possibly prejudiced by an exchange of information, could challenge the exchange of certain documents. The 2008 Security Arrangements contain a procedure for the disrespect of confidentiality, which can be instituted only by the two parties so that third States or individuals cannot interfere. It is quite interesting that, in contrast to the agreement with the EU, the agreement of the ICC with the UN provides a certain guarantee in this respect. According to its Article 20 ("Protection of confidentiality") any information that the UN is requested by the ICC to provide the ICC with that was disclosed to it "in confidence by a State or an intergovernmental, international or non-governmental organization or an individual," requires the consent of the originator. This clause offers at least certain protection to the rights of third parties.

7.2 *The Testimony of EU Staff*

Article 10 of the EU–ICC Agreement deals with the issue of "the testimony of an official or other staff of the EU" and aims to ensure that the testimony of such persons may be heard by the ICC if the latter requests so.[28]

---

[26]American Non-Governmental Organizations Coalition for the International Criminal Court (Simge Kocabayoglu) (4 March 2005) Paper on the Agreement between the ICC and the European Union. http://www.amicc.org/docs/EU-ICC-Agreement.pdf. Accessed 25 June 2013, p. 2.

[27]Article 7, para 3 of the Agreement.

[28]Article 10 (Testimony of staff of the European Union) of the EU–ICC Agreement reads as follows: "1. If the Court requests the testimony of an official or other staff of the EU, the EU undertakes to cooperate fully with the Court and, if necessary and with due regard to its responsibilities and competencies under the EU Treaty and the relevant rules thereunder, to take all necessary measures to enable the Court to hear that person's testimony, in particular by waiving that person's obligation of confidentiality.
2. With reference to Article 8, the Parties recognise that measures of protection might be required should an official or other staff of the EU be requested to provide the Court with testimony.
3. Subject to the Statute and the Rules of Procedure and Evidence, the EU shall be authorized to appoint a representative to assist any official or other staff of the EU who appears as a witness before the Court."

This provision already raises the problem of the definition of the EU staff who should not be put at risk by giving testimony. It must be determined whether all persons engaged in operations of the EU belong to this category, in particular persons seconded by the member states. The Agreement does not contain any definition of "staff" so that this term has to be interpreted by reference to other relevant instruments, first of all the Status of Forces Agreement concluded by the member states.[29] This agreement addresses, in particular, "the status of military and civilian staff seconded to the institutions of the European Union, of the headquarters and forces which may be made available to the European Union in the context of the preparation and execution of the tasks referred to in Article 17(2) of the Treaty on European Union, including exercises, and of the military and civilian staff of the Member States put at the disposal of the European Union to act in this context". It defines as military staff personnel seconded by the member states to the EUMS, or for the purpose to provide temporary augmentation for the preparation and performance of the Petersberg tasks, whereas civilian staff refers to civil personnel seconded by the member States for the preparation and execution of such tasks. Such personnel would be the first to have knowledge of facts that are important to the ICC with regard to its investigations so that, taking into account the object and purpose of the Agreement, namely the support of the effective functioning of the ICC by the EU,[30] the term staff as used in the Agreement must be given a broad understanding as used in the EU SOFA.

However, the EU–ICC Agreement goes beyond the UN–ICC Agreement insofar as it not only obliges the EU to waive the respective person's obligation of confidentiality, but also to "take all necessary measures to enable the Court to hear that person's testimony". The extent such measures may take is unclear. In any case, they are limited by the EU's competencies. However, for instance, measures such as disciplinary measures—which could arguably be deemed "necessary"—could lead to problems especially with regard to persons that are subject to different legal regimes, that of the EU and that of their State, regarding their services such as military personnel. According to Article 17 of the EU SOFA it is the sending State that exercises "all criminal and disciplinary jurisdiction conferred on them by the law of the sending State over military as well as over civilian staff where those civilian staff are subject to the law governing all or any of

[29]Council Agreement between the Member States of the European Union concerning the status of military and civilian staff seconded to the institutions of the European Union, of the headquarters and forces which may be made available to the European Union in the context of the preparation and execution of the tasks referred to in Article 17(2) of the Treaty on European Union, including exercises, and of the military and civilian staff of the Member States put at the disposal of the European Union to act in this context (EU SOFA). Doc. 2003/C 321/02, 31 December 2003.

[30]Preambule para 7 of the EU-ICC Agreement reads as follows: "CONSIDERING that the European Union is committed to supporting the effective functioning of the International Criminal Court and to advance universal support for it by promoting the widest possible participation in the Rome Statute."

the armed forces of the sending State, by reason of their deployment with those forces." Accordingly, it is hardly apparent which measures the EU can take in order to force a staff member to testify before the ICC, unless measures in connection with an applicable contract of service between the individual and the EU would be applied. Moreover, it is also hardly conceivable that the tasks for which such persons were seconded would also include testimony before the ICC.

The situation of staff members or officials of the EU who are subject to the Staff Regulations[31] is different insofar as they are subject to disciplinary measures by the EU under Articles 86 to 89. Accordingly, a clearer picture is only offered if staff is merely understood as persons addressed by the EU's Staff Regulations, namely officials, i.e., "any person who has been appointed, as provided for in these Staff Regulations, to an established post on the staff of one of the institutions of the Union by an instrument issued by the Appointing Authority of that institution".[32] This solution would, however, exclude persons seconded by the Member States, in particular those persons that are engaged in military and civil operations of the Union and would have the best insight in situations that are likely to be discussed in the ICC. Nevertheless, it is again hardly conceivable that the duties of such persons would include also the obligation do give testimony before the ICC so that the only measures the EU could take is to waiver the obligation of confidentiality and, if the EU understands immunities in this sense, also that of immunities.

Accordingly, this article of the Agreement is of limited applicability insofar as it opens the possibility for a testimony before the ICC, but not of a necessary appearance before the Court. The duty of cooperation envisaged by this provision possesses only a permissive dimension, but not a duty of appearance.

7.3 Seconded Staff

According to Article 13 of the Agreement, the Court may employ the expertise of gratis personnel offered by the EU, to assist with the work of any of the organs of the Court. This provision corresponds to Article 44(4) of the Rome Statute according to which the Court may employ gratis personnel offered by States Parties, intergovernmental organizations or non-governmental organizations. During the

[31]European Commission (1 May 2004) Unofficial, consolidated version of the Staff Regulations of Officials of the European Communities and Conditions of employment of other servants of the European Communities. http://ec.europa.eu/civil_service/docs/toc100_en.pdf. Accessed 25 June 2013.

[32]Idem. Article 1a(1) Staff Regulations reads as follows: "1. For the purposes of these Staff Regulations, "official of the Communities" means any person who has been appointed, as provided for in these Staff Regulations, to an established post on the staff of one of the institutions of the Communities by an instrument issued by the Appointing Authority of that institution."

negotiations on the Rome Statute discussions arose with regard to this provision and it is said to have a "long and controversial history".[33] On the one side, the possibility of such gratis personnel was welcomed since it was expected to lead to lower costs for the ICC state parties. On the other side, the fear was expressed that such personnel was not sufficiently independent from particular states and could disturb the geographical balance of the staff. It was argued that the institution could come under particular influence of the States offering such personnel. In any case, the reference to Article 44(4) of the Rome Statute ensures that the limitations provided in the Rome Statute apply also to gratis personnel offered by the EU and that such personnel has the same status with the ICC as any other personnel hired under Article 44(4) of the Rome Statute.

Nevertheless, the doubts expressed by S. Kocabayoglu on behalf of the American NGO CICC regarding a draft Article 11 of the future agreement between the ICC and the EU[34] that was aimed at including the support of the EU in training for Court staff, judges and other ICC personnel could also be applied to Article 13 of the Agreement.

The NGO paper noted that draft Article 11 was considered "as exerting too much European influence on the operations of the Court".[35] It also raised "the fear that the combination of common and civil law principles in the Court's procedure and practice will become unbalanced in favor of the latter".[36] The same fear was expressed during the negotiations of the Rome Statute also with respect to Article 44(4) of the Rome Statute since a great influence by developed-country NGO's personnel on the ICC was expected.[37] It was for this reason that the possibility of using such personnel became extremely circumscribed and subject to the decision of the ICC organs. The application of these limits to the personnel offered by the EU should suffice to remove such fears of the US.[38] The present formulation of

[33]See Lee 1999, p. 17; Lachowska 2009, p. 392 et seq.

[34]American Non-Governmental Organizations Coalition for the International Criminal Court (Simge Kocabayoglu) (4 March 2005) Paper on the Agreement between the ICC and the European Union. http://www.amicc.org/docs/EU-ICC-Agreement.pdf. Accessed 25 June 2013.

[35]Ibid.

[36]Ibid.

[37]It can be noted that an analogous discussion occurred in the context of the WTO discussions relating to the participation of NGOs as *amici* in WTO Panel and Appellate Body proceedings.

[38]However, it should be noted that the reality of geographical, gender-based or other disparities in representation in the ICC have also been subject to empirical analysis. See for some empirical data: ICC Assembly of States Parties (3 December 2010) Report of the Bureau on equitable geographical representation and gender balance in the recruitment of staff of the International Criminal Court. Doc. ICC-ASP/9/30. http://www.icc-cpi.int/iccdocs/asp_docs/ASP9/ICC-ASP-9-30-ENG.pdf. Accessed 25 June 2013; see also Schabas 2011, p. 603.

Article 11 on the cooperation between the EU and the ICC does not give rise to similar expectations: comparable provisions can be found in the Accord de Coopération entre la Cour pénale internationale et l'Organisation international de la Francophonie of 28 September 2012 (Article 8),[39] as well as in the Memorandum of Understanding Between the International Criminal Court and the Commonwealth on Cooperation (Article 8).[40] Hence, it seems to be unlikely that this provision on cooperation would lead to further criticisms for political reasons.

8 The Waiver of Immunities by the EU

Similar to Article 19 of the ICC–UN Agreement, Article 12 of the ICC–EU Agreement provides, *inter alia*, for a waiver of "any" immunities and privileges enjoyed under "the relevant rules of international law" by a person "alleged to be criminally responsible for a crime within" the ICC's jurisdiction. The logic of this provision is very unclear. Neither does it describe the "persons" addressed with sufficient specificity, nor does it identify the character of the immunities and privileges. Moreover, it does not specify which measures ("all necessary measure") should be taken in order to enable the Court to exercise its jurisdiction, but merely highlights "waiving such immunities" as a particular measure.

As to the persons, the only definitional criterion is that the person must be alleged to be responsible for a crime within the jurisdiction of the ICC and enjoy any privileges and immunities under international law. Defined in this sense, this group of persons would comprise an extremely broad range of persons since diplomats of any state could fall under this category so that additional criteria are to be applied.

One of these criteria is the privileges and immunities enjoyed by these persons; since the EU is called to waive these rights, these privileges and immunities can be only those that are possessed by the EU. The EU undoubtedly enjoys immunities and privileges the beneficiaries of which are certain Union officials. The basis of such rights is Protocol No. 36 of 1965 on the privileges and immunities of the European Communities.[41]

---

[39]Accord de coopération entre la cour pénale internationale et l'organisation internationale de la francophonie, Doc. ICC-PRES/13-03-12, entered into force on 28 September 2012. http://www.icc-cpi.int/iccdocs/oj/AgreementwithInternationalFrancophonieOrganisation.pdf. Accessed 25 June 2013.

[40]Memorandum of Understanding between the International Criminal Court and the Commonwealth on Cooperation, Doc. ICC-PRES/10-04-11, entered into force on 13 July 2011. http://www.icc-cpi.int/NR/rdonlyres/F9569B18-0AF3-499E-9352-4D5C91373B31/283598/MOUwithCommonwealthoncooperation13072011.pdf. Accessed 25 June 2013.

[41]Protocol annexed to the Treaties establishing the European Community and the European Atomic Energy Community—Protocol (No. 36) on the privileges and immunities of the European Communities (1965) OJ C 321 E, 29 December 2006, pp. 318–324.

However, although, in this regard, the EU officials are granted immunities in the territory of the member states with regard to official acts (Article 12(a)[42]), it is nevertheless doubtful whether this also applies to international institutions in the territory of a member state, such as the ICC. Quite a lot of considerations militate against the assumption that the immunities addressed by this provision are those enjoyed in relation to the ICC. This latter institution, being a third-party subject of international law not party to this Protocol, cannot—under the law of treaties—be bound by it and is not obliged to grant immunity to EU officials, irrespective of the location of these institutions on the territory of a member state. One state cannot endow its officials with immunity if the other State in which the immunity should provide a bar to the exercise of jurisdiction over the official does not accept such a legal regime. This conclusion does not contradict to a mutual recognition of the legal personality of these two organizations, the EU and the ICC, already through the conclusion of EU–ICC Agreement.

A similar conclusion would be applicable to the military and civil personnel participating in the area operations of the EU. Their status in these countries is regulated by Status of Forces Agreements (SOFAs). These SOFAs, however, such as the SOFA with Afghanistan, only grant immunity with regard to the authorities of the host State. Within the EU, their status is again governed by the EU SOFA.[43] Its Article 8 provides immunity to the personnel in the sense of the SOFA, i.e., including personnel seconded by the member states, without stating against whom such immunity should be applicable.[44] A further difficulty results from the fact that this immunity belongs to both, the EU and the sending State and both are required to waive the immunity "enjoyed by military or civilian staff seconded to the EU institutions where such immunity would impede the course of justice and where such competent authority and relevant EU institution may do so without prejudice to the interests of the European Union". Although this duty seems to be in line with Article 12 of the EU–ICC Agreement, the EU SOFA nevertheless differs from the Agreement insofar as it requires the waiving by the EU and the sending State (Article 8(3)) whereas the EU–ICC Agreement imposes such a duty only

---

[42]Ibid. Article 12 of Protocol No. 36 reads as follows: "In the territory of each Member State and whatever their nationality, officials and other servants of the Communities shall: (a) subject to the provisions of the Treaties relating, on the one hand, to the rules on the liability of officials and other servants towards the Communities and, on the other hand, to the jurisdiction of the Court in disputes between the Communities and their officials and other servants, be immune from legal proceedings in respect of acts performed by them in their official capacity, including their words spoken or written. They shall continue to enjoy this immunity after they have ceased to hold office; […]".

[43]EU SOFA, Doc. 2003/C 321/02, 31 December 2003; see generally Sari 2008.

[44]Article 8 of the EU SOFA reads as follows: "1. Military or civilian staff seconded to the EU institutions shall enjoy immunity from legal process of any kind in respect of words spoken or written, and of acts performed by them in the exercise of their official functions; that immunity shall continue even after their secondment has ceased. […]".

on the EU. Accordingly, if seconded personnel are included in the purview of Article 12 of the Agreement, difficulties cannot be excluded once the need of such a waiver arises.

Finally, a fundamental question arises concerning the need for such a provision. The norm of international law regarding immunities has evolved as a bar to the exercise of national jurisdiction. When the ICJ dealt with the question of whether state officials enjoy immunities, it did so only with regard to national jurisdiction.[45] As to international criminal jurisdiction, the ICJ noted that even the legal instruments creating international criminal tribunals[46] that denied the immunity of persons having an official capacity did "not enable it to conclude that any such an exception exists in customary international law in regard to national courts."[47] This statement indicates that the immunity as rooted in customary international law exists only with regard to national courts, but not in respect of international courts or tribunals. This is confirmed by the ICJ's later finding that "an incumbent or former Minister for Foreign Affairs may be subject to criminal proceedings before certain international criminal courts, where they have jurisdiction."[48]

Accordingly, members of the staff of the EU cannot invoke immunity before the ICC irrespective of the fact that the EU is not bound by the Rome Statute and its Article 27(2) regarding immunity. In the same vein, Article 27(2) of the Rome Statute itself seems superfluous or only of declaratory nature. Certainly, in the *Simić* Case the ICRC claimed immunity before the ICTY. However, this was not accepted by the Prosecutor who denied that the ICRC could prevent any of its former employees from testifying by means of immunity.[49] The Prosecution in *Simić* argued as follows (para 6):

> [First,] the ICRC does not enjoy immunity from the jurisdiction of international courts as a matter of general international law (such immunity does not flow from the ICRC's functional international legal personality, nor does it have any basis in treaty or customary law); and
>
> [Second,] the assertion that an ICRC employee giving evidence in any judicial proceeding would jeopardise the ICRC's ability to carry out its humanitarian mission is not proven.

---

[45]Cf. Arrest Warrant of 11 April 2000 (*Democratic Republic of the Congo v. Belgium*) (Judgment) (14 February 2002) [2002] ICJ Rep. 3.

[46]Referring to the Charter of the International Military Tribunal of Nuremberg (Article 7), the Charter of the International Military Tribunal of Tokyo (Article 6), the Statute of the International Criminal Tribunal for the former Yugoslavia (Article 7(2)), the Statute of the International Criminal Tribunal for Rwanda (Article 6(2)), as well as the Rome Statute of the ICC (Article 27).

[47]Arrest Warrant of 11 April 2000 (*Democratic Republic of the Congo v. Belgium*) (Judgment) (14 February 2002) [2002] ICJ Rep. 3, para 5.

[48]Ibid., para 61.

[49]*Prosecutor v. Simić Case* (IT-95-9), Decision on the Prosecution Motion under Rule 73 for a Ruling Concerning the Testimony of a Witness (27 July 1999). http://www.icty.org/x/cases/simic/tdec/en/90727EV59549.htm. Accessed 25 June 2013, para 2.

However, in the further discussion, the ICRC no longer argued on the basis of immunity but rather on that of neutrality and confidentiality and the Tribunal decided in its favor (para 76).[50] Similarly, Rule 73(4) of the Rules of Procedure and Evidence of the ICC,[51] which provides that information offered by ICRC officials or employees is privileged, no longer refers to any immunity of the ICRC, but merely to the latter's privileged position.[52] When certain Headquarter Agreements of the ICRC such as those with Croatia, Belgium, Kuwait, the Philippines, Switzerland, the Russian Federation, Rwanda and Turkmenistan refer to immunity, this immunity is to be understood only with respect to the local national authorities. So, for instance, the Trial Chamber notes in Footnote 34 that Article 10(3) of the Headquarter Agreement with Croatia provides that the members of the ICRC

> […] shall enjoy immunity from personal arrest or detention and from seizure of their personal baggage, and in respect of words spoken or written and all acts done by them in the discharge of their official duties, immunity from legal process of any kind, even after they have left the service of the delegation. They shall not be called as witnesses.[53]

Accordingly, the EU SOFA addresses the immunity only with regard to competent authorities or judicial bodies of member states, since Article 8(5) of the EU SOFA only refers to member state bodies or authorities in relation to the abuse of immunities.

It must also be recognized that the problem of immunity before international tribunals is only of recent nature due to the relatively short existence of such institutions and therefore a rule of customary international law could hardly have been expected to solidify. Prior to the emergence of such tribunals, no need arose to develop such a rule since international judicial instances dealt with disputes between States. Where individuals were allowed to become parties, such as in the

---

[50]Ibid. The Trial Chamber concluded as follows (para 76): "It follows from the Trial Chamber's finding that the ICRC has, under international law, a confidentiality interest and a claim to non-disclosure of the Information, that no question of the balancing of interests arises. The Trial Chamber is bound by this rule of customary international law which, in its content, does not admit of, or call for, any balancing of interest. The rule, properly understood, is, in its content, unambiguous and unequivocal, and does not call for any qualifications. Its effect is quite simple: as a matter of law it serves to bar the Trial Chamber from admitting the Information."

[51]ICC Rules of Procedure and Evidence, Doc ICC-ASP/1/3 (Part II-A), entered into force 9 September 2002.

[52]Article 73(4) of the ICC Rules of Procedure and Evidence reads as follows: "The Court shall regard as privileged, and consequently not subject to disclosure, including by way of testimony of any present or past official or employee of the International Committee of the Red Cross (ICRC), any information, documents or other evidence which it came into the possession of in the course, or as a consequence, of the performance by ICRC of its functions under the Statutes of the International Red Cross and Red Crescent Movement, unless: (a) After consultations undertaken pursuant to sub-rule 6, ICRC does not object in writing to such disclosure, or otherwise has waived this privilege; or (b) Such information, documents or other evidence is contained in public statements and documents of ICRC."

[53]*Prosecutor v. Simić Case*, n. 50 above, footnote 34.

case of mixed claims commissions, regional human rights courts and tribunals, or in the investment treaty arbitration context, they acted as claimants and not as respondents. The stipulations in the various Statutes of such institutions about the denial of immunity cannot be seen as evidence of the existence of a contrary rule under customary international law, but rather as confirmation of such a rule. As the ICJ acknowledged,

> […] none of the decisions of the Nuremberg and Tokyo international military tribunals, or of the International Criminal Tribunal for the former Yugoslavia, cited by Belgium deal with the question of the immunities of incumbent Ministers for Foreign Affairs before national courts where they are accused of having committed war crimes or crimes against humanity.[54]

The above statement confirms that in customary international law immunity is a bar to proceedings before national and not international judicial instances. Accordingly, if a staff member of the EU is likely to be prosecuted by the ICC, neither can this person invoke immunity nor can the EU waive it. If the person is alleged to have committed a crime under the jurisdiction of the ICC, he or she has the same status as any other person within the jurisdiction of the ICC. Otherwise, staff members of the ICC would be in a better position than State officials, in particular those not enjoying the benefits of a head of State immunity.

Accordingly, if Article 12 of the EU–ICC Agreement should make sense, it must be interpreted as a commitment of the EU to waive the immunity in relation to national instances. Under this perspective, Article 12 stands in contrast to Article 98 of the Rome Statute which seeks to protect immunities.[55] Pursuant to this latter provision, States are not obliged to waive immunity, but the ICC has to exercise certain restriction if confronted with immunities. Irrespective of the different interpretations of this provision, the duty of a State Party to waive immunity can only be derived from the general duty of cooperation with the Court under Article 86 of the Rome Statute.[56]

However, it is not clear whether the intention of the authors of the EU–ICC Agreement was to endow Article 12 with such an effect by committing the EU

[54]Arrest Warrant of 11 April 2000, n. 48 above, para 58.

[55]Article 98 (Cooperation with respect to waiver of immunity and consent to surrender) of the Rome Statute reads as follows: "1. The Court may not proceed with a request for surrender or assistance which would require the requested State to act inconsistently with its obligations under international law with respect to the State or diplomatic immunity of a person or property of a third State, unless the Court can first obtain the cooperation of that third State for the waiver of the immunity.
2. The Court may not proceed with a request for surrender which would require the requested State to act inconsistently with its obligations under international agreements pursuant to which the consent of a sending State is required to surrender a person of that State to the Court, unless the Court can first obtain the cooperation of the sending State for the giving of consent for the surrender."

[56]Article 86 (General obligation to cooperate) of the Rome Statute reads as follows: "States Parties shall, in accordance with the provisions of this Statute, cooperate fully with the Court in its investigation and prosecution of crimes within the jurisdiction of the Court."

to waive the immunity in relation to national authorities of States. The parallel Agreement of the ICC with the United Nations contains a similar provision (Article 19) that raises similar problems and does not offer further clarifications. It remains to be seen how these ambiguities will be resolved in practice.

9 Conclusion

My contribution has sought to discuss a few specific questions of law and policy that have resulted from the EU's engagement with the ICC during the last two decades and in particular the EU–ICC Agreement of 2006. It is clear that through this and other legal acts, as well as the EU institutions' supportive policies towards the ICC, the EU has attempted to promote its international status in pursuance of its goals of fighting impunity and enhancing the rule of law. Some of the ambiguities and questions that arise from the EU's ICC-related legal acts, in particular the EU–ICC Agreement, and that I have discussed above may well be explained by the dominance of considerations of policy rather than legal minutiae in the EU's approach.

However, this approach and its consequences come at some cost: Insofar as the Agreement is one-sided—placing the obligations of confidentiality only on the side of the ICC, not on that of the EU—it creates uncertainty about how confidential information will be treated by the ICC. As such, one unexpected but not too farfetched possible consequence of the one-sidedness the 2006 Agreement could be to impede the intensification of the already "reluctant engagement" of the US[57] with the ICC. Ironically, this result would run counter to the EU's overall strategy of promoting universal adherence to the Rome Statute.

Case law, legislation and documents

Case law

Prosecutor v. Simić Case (IT-95-9), Decision on the Prosecution Motion under Rule 73 for a Ruling Concerning the Testimony of a Witness (27 July 1999). http://www.icty.org/x/cases/simic/tdec/en/90727EV59549.htm. Accessed 25 June 2013

Legislation

Agreement between the International Criminal Court and the European Union on Cooperation and Assistance, Doc ICC-PRES/01-01-06, entered into force on 1 May 2006.

Consolidated version of the Treaty on European Union, Official Journal 115, 9 May 2008, 13–45. http://eur-lex.europa.eu/LexUriServ/LexUriServ.do?uri=CELEX:12008M/TXT:EN:HTML. Accessed 25 June 2013

[57]See e.g. generally Kielsgard 2010.

Consolidated version of the Treaty on European Union, Official Journal C 321 E, 29 December 2006, 5–36. http://eur-lex.europa.eu/LexUriServ/LexUriServ.do?uri=CELEX:12006M/TXT:EN:HTML. Accessed 25 June 2013

Protocol annexed to the Treaties establishing the European Community and the European Atomic Energy Community—Protocol (No 36) on the privileges and immunities of the European Communities (1965) OJ C 321 E, 29 December 2006, 318–324

Rome Statute of the International Criminal Court (adopted 17 July 1998, entered into force on 1 July 2002) 2187 UNTS 90

UN ILC (1994) Draft Statute for an International Criminal Court. GAOR 49th Session Supp 10, 29

United Nations Security Council Resolution 1422 (12 July 2002) UN Doc S/RES/1422

United Nations Security Council Resolution 1487 (12 June 2003) UN Doc S/RES/1487

Documents

American Non-Governmental Organizations Coalition for the International Criminal Court (Simge Kocabayoglu) (4 March 2005) Paper on the Agreement Between the ICC and the European Union. http://www.amicc.org/docs/EU-ICC-Agreement.pdf. Accessed 25 June 2013.

Arrest Warrant of 11 April 2000 (Democratic Republic of the Congo v Belgium) (Judgment) (14 February 2002) [2002] ICJ Rep 3

Council Agreement between the Member States of the European Union concerning the status of military and civilian staff seconded to the institutions of the European Union, of the headquarters and forces which may be made available to the European Union in the context of the preparation and execution of the tasks referred to in Article 17(2) of the Treaty on European Union, including exercises, and of the military and civilian staff of the Member States put at the disposal of the European Union to act in this context (EU SOFA). Doc 2003/C 321/02, 31 December 2003.

Council Decision of 31 March 2011 on the security rules for protecting EU classified information, Doc 2011/292/EU, L 141/17, 27 May 2011. http://eur-lex.europa.eu/LexUriServ/LexUriServ.do?uri=OJ:L:2011:141:0017:0065:EN:PDF. Accessed 25 June 2013

Council of the EU (11 June 2001) Common Position 2001/443/CFSP on the International Criminal Court

Council of the EU (15 April 2008) Security Arrangements for the Protection of Classified Information Exchanged between the EU and the ICC, Doc. 8349/1/08. http://register.consilium.europa.eu/pdf/en/08/st08/st08349-re01.en08.pdf. Accessed 25 June 2013

Council of the EU (15 April 2008) Security Arrangements for the Protection of Classified Information Exchanged between the EU and the ICC, Doc 8349/1/08. http://register.consilium.europa.eu/pdf/en/08/st08/st08349-re01.en08.pdf. Accessed 25 June 2013

Council of the EU (16 June 2003) Common Position 2003/444/CFSP on the International Criminal Court
Council of the EU (20 June 2002) Common Position 2002/474/CFSP amending Common Position 2001/443/CFSP on the International Criminal Court
Council of the EU (21 March 2011) Council Decision 2011/168/CFSP on the International Criminal Court and repealing Common Position 2003/444/CFSP
Council of the EU (28 January 2004) Action Plan to follow-up on the Common Position on the International Criminal Court. Doc 5742/04. http://register.consilium.europa.eu/pdf/en/04/st05/st05742.en04.pdf. Accessed 25 June 2013
European Commission (1 May 2004) Unofficial, consolidated version of the Staff Regulations of Officials of the European Communities and Conditions of employment of other servants of the European Communities. http://ec.europa.eu/civil_service/docs/toc100_en.pdf Accessed 25 June 2013
General Secretariat of the Council (May 2010) The European Union and the International Criminal Court. http://www.consilium.europa.eu/uedocs/cmsUpload/ICC_may%2010_internet.pdf. Accessed 25 June 2013
ICC Assembly of States Parties (3 December 2010) Report of the Bureau on equitable geographical representation and gender balance in the recruitment of staff of the International Criminal Court. Doc ICC-ASP/9/30. http://www.icc-cpi.int/iccdocs/asp_docs/ASP9/ICC-ASP-9-30-ENG.pdf. Accessed 25 June 2013
ICC Rules of Procedure and Evidence, Doc ICC-ASP/1/3 (Part. II-A), entered into force on 9 September 2002
Memorandum of Understanding between the International Criminal Court and the Commonwealth on Cooperation, Doc ICC-PRES/10-04-11, entered into force on 13 July 2011. http://www.icc-cpi.int/NR/rdonlyres/F9569B18-0AF3-499E-9352-4D5C91373B31/283598/MOUwithCommonwealthoncooperation13072011.pdf. Accessed 25 June 2013
Negotiated Relationship Agreement between the International Criminal Court and the United Nations, Doc ICC-ASP/3/Res.1, entered into force on 22 July 2004. http://www.iccnow.org/documents/ICC-ASP-3-Res1_English.pdf. Accessed 25 June 2013.

References

Craig P, de Búrca G (2011) EU law: text, cases, and materials, 5th edn. Oxford University Press, Oxford
Ford S (2011) How leadership in international criminal law is shifting from the U.S. to Europe and Asia: an analysis of spending on and contributions to international criminal courts. Saint Louis Univ Law J 55:953–999
Groenleer M, Rijks D (2009) The European Union and the International Criminal Court: the politics of international criminal justice. In: Jorgensen KE (ed) The European Union and international organizations. Routledge, Abingdon, pp 167–188
Kielsgard MD (2010) Reluctant engagement: U.S. policy and the International Criminal Court. Martinus Nijhoff, Leiden
Kirsch P, Holmes JT (1998) The birth of the International Criminal Court: the 1998 Rome conference. Can Yearb Int Law 36:3–39

Koutrakos P (2013) The EU common security and defence policy. Oxford University Press, Oxford

Lachowska A (2009) The support work of the court's registry. In: Doria J et al (eds) The legal regime of the International Criminal Court: essays in honour of professor Igor Blishchenko. Martinus Nijhoff, Leiden, pp 387–400

Lee RSK (1999) The International Criminal Court: the making of the Rome Statute: issues, negotiations, results. Martinus Nijhoff Publishers, The Hague

Sari A (2008) Status of forces and status of mission agreements under the ESDP: the EU's evolving practice. Eur J Int Law 19:67–100

Schabas WA (2011) An introduction to the International Criminal Court, 4th edn. Cambridge University Press, Cambridge

Schiff BN (2008) Building the International Criminal Court. Cambridge University Press, Cambridge

Strapatsas N (2002) The European Union and its contribution to the development. Revue de Droit Universite de Sherbrooke 33:399–424

Washburn J (1999) The negotiation of the Rome Statute and international lawmaking in the 21st century. Pace Int Law Rev 11:361–377

Annex

Rule of Law and Democracy in Perspective

Laurens Jan Brinkhorst

The issue of the Rule of Law and Democracy is close to the heart of Jaap de Zwaan. He has also written extensively on the subject. After the Treaty of Maastricht of 1992 and, above all, since the Treaty of Lisbon of 2009 a remarkable process of the 'politicization' of the European Union has occurred. This process has had a major impact on the governance of the EU institutions.

After the demise of the European Defence Community in 1954, for the next 40 years the integration process in Europe was fully concentrated on economic, not political integration. We lived in the period of the Cold War when politics and security were primarily a matter for NATO and the issues of welfare and economic growth economics were the domain of the then European Community. As a result, if a conflict arose between the two organizations, NATO prevailed. This was most certainly the case in a country like the Netherlands, where political integration in Europe had never been a priority.

In retrospect, one can say that the period between the early 1950s and 1991 was for the Netherlands, in foreign policy terms, a happy period. Of course the economic stagnation of the 1970s, largely the effect of the two oil crises, also had its political impact on the EC Member States. Nevertheless, the main priorities of the European Community were concentrated on the implementation of the four economic freedoms, resulting in the completion of the internal market. The main institutional innovation of the EC system occurred when it became necessary in the course of the 1980s to harmonize economic rules. Increased qualified majority voting was even accepted by Mrs. Thatcher, its fiercest critic. In national terms the EC had few opponents, mainly as a result of its limited political objectives.

Former Professor of European Law at Groningen, Tilburg and Leiden, former Minister of Economic Affairs and Deputy Prime Minister of the Netherlands.

F.A.N.J. Goudappel and E.M.H. Hirsch Ballin (eds.), *Democracy and Rule of Law in the European Union*, DOI 10.1007/978-94-6265-066-4

The Role of Human Rights

Against this background the main priority for the EC was therefore not so much the Rule of Law and Democracy, but the completion of the internal market. Obviously the accession of Greece, Spain and Portugal had strong political overtones. But their membership of the EEC was seen in the first place as a consequence of the end of the dictatorships of Franco, Salazar and Papadopoulos. The requirements of human rights and the fulfilment of democracy were seen as a prerequisite for EC membership. But the issue of human rights was seen as only marginally affecting the functioning of the EC as a whole.

The viewpoint of the German Constitutional Court became a political and legal guideline: it confirmed in a number of cases that European law prevailed, with the exception of human rights because these were guaranteed by the Constitutional Court. That element also became the basis of what was assumed by the Court of Justice when it stated that the general principles of law, including human rights law, were also principles of the law of the European Community.

In retrospect it is clear that the demise of the Soviet Union and the disappearance of the Berlin Wall had become the turning point in the 'politicization' of the European Union. The membership of Central and Eastern European states, former satellite countries of the Soviet Union, had become a societal choice. It would clearly not have been acceptable to preserve the political separation of Europe in two blocs of countries after the end of the Cold War. On the one hand, a Western Europe which after the War had become democratic, rich and capitalistic. On the other hand, an Eastern part which for half a century had been governed without respect for democracy, with the state dominating the economy and, as a result, low per capita income.

As a consequence, both the deepening of the integration in the West through the objective of Economic and Monetary Union and, at the same time, the whole of Europe having European Union membership can be seen as the beginning of a more political process of unification. If one now looks back over the last 25 years, in political terms, the EU has made remarkable progress. In the first place, in democratic terms, the tandem Commission-Council has been largely replaced by the tripod Commission-Parliament-Council. In about 90 per cent of all the legislation, the consent of the European Parliament is required. The Commission is now subject to firm political control by the European Parliament. Individual Commissioners can now be held politically accountable.

From an internal point of view, there is a strong development of democracy within the institutions of the EU.

Secondly, concerning the rule of law, after the Constitutional Court decisions in Germany and the development of principles of law as being essential to the EU, we have seen two major developments. On the one hand, the requirement is that Member States themselves should guarantee human rights and that sanctions are even possible in case of a persistent violation of human rights. And on the other hand, the Charter of Fundamental Rights as a document with the same effect as the

Lisbon Treaty itself is now formally enshrined as being essential to the functioning of the European Union. It applies to the institutions but does not automatically apply to every action of the Member States. In a sense, it is also a modernization because, compared to the European Convention for the Protection of Human Rights and Fundamental Freedoms of some sixty years ago, its formulation of human rights is more up to date.

Reception in the Member States

At first sight, one would expect that the political support for the Union would have become stronger. In fact, the opposite is the case. There is an increased sense of frustration that competences are being removed from the Member States and taken over by "Brussels". Sometimes, the extent of such competences is not well understood. Another objection is that the institutions are not subject to national parliamentary control in the Member States. There is also a grudging feeling that additional powers and competences have been granted because of the economic crisis. As a result we have the paradoxical situation that even though, in fact, the impact of the European Union in the Member States is increasing, also a growing gap in understanding the European Union has occurred.

In the Netherlands, but also in some other European countries, a profound sense of unease exists. Although subsidiarity and proportionality are guaranteed in the Treaty, the application of these principles is not seen as effectively taking place. It is not unfair to presume that if there would be a referendum today in some Member States, there would be a tendency to retract powers rather than granting new ones.

In my opinion, this paradox is caused by a number of developments. In the first place, the body of politics of most Member States has not grown and become accustomed to this change of reality on the ground, which is also caused by the process of globalization over the last few decades. It is clear that as a result of the growing process of the integration of European economies, also their finances have become more integrated. Nevertheless, at the beginning of the Greek financial crisis, the Dutch Prime Minister, Mr. Rutte, when the issue of support for Greece became urgent, is quoted as having said "I have nothing with the Greeks". Only when he understood that Dutch banks had lent 50 to 60 billion euro to Greek banks did he realize that by cutting off Greece from any support by the European Union, the Dutch economy would also pay a heavy price!

The underlying problem is a lack of understanding that political decision-making has moved away from the nation state. Unease about this phenomenon has been stimulated by the extremist political parties on the right and on the left. This new attitude is not limited to the Netherlands, although the contrast with its traditional positive attitude to more European integration in the past in this country seems to be rather extreme. It is also occurring in other countries like Germany and France, but with less impact on day-to-day political attitudes.

In the second place, this politicization of European decision-making has, for a long time, not been recognized. For a long time there was a profound indifference in the body politic of the Netherlands towards European integration. In the early 1980s, when I was a member of the Second Chamber of Parliament, I advocated the introduction of a parliamentary committee on European affairs. The reaction of the then chairman of the Foreign Affairs Committee was: "you know we have a committee on foreign affairs that also covers Europe. Europe is part of foreign affairs".

Nowadays it has become abundantly clear that European affairs have a major impact on internal affairs. The only way forward is not to remove democratic powers from European institutions, but rather to recognize this new situation and to adjust the national decision-making process accordingly. This implies that at a much earlier phase in the decision-making process, before European decisions are taken in Brussels, national parliaments should be involved. The debate on European legislation should not be limited to the European Parliament.

Similarly, when the internalization of European norms is at stake, also the European Court of Auditors should control the way European legislation and thus also the European budget has an impact in the Netherlands. The same is true for national competition and telecom authorities. This line of thought can also be extended to the European judicial and police institutions, Eurojust, Europol and their national counterparts. Many years ago the French scholar Georges Scelle advocated the "doubling of functionality", meaning that national institutions increasingly have a national and a European function. In my opinion, this insight can help to alleviate the feeling of being overrun by foreign structures, and thus help with creating a sense of the internalization of the European dimensions.

Lack of Confidence in the European Union

The third element is that national political parties and national politics are also increasingly under attack from the general public. There is an enormous lack of confidence in national political solutions and nearly all traditional structures are under attack, whether in the financial sphere, like banking, the police, education or the prison system, and so we find ourselves in a crisis of democracy in a larger sense. That is obviously a matter of concern. This is the general background against which I would like to place these issues.

Knowledge about European affairs, not only in the national parliaments, but also in general, at law faculties or in the business world, is remarkably low. There is an urgent need to change this situation, but it would require political leadership that so far seems to be seriously lacking. Let me add a specific example from my personal political experience of many years ago to demonstrate this.

In 1980 on the occasion of a debate on constitutional reform, I tabled a motion requesting that we should have an interpretation of the Constitution which was in conformity with the EU.

With the exception of the small right-wing Christian reformed parties the motion was adopted with a large majority. Recently the same parties that supported me at the time, the liberal-conservative VVD and the Christian-democratic CDA inspired by the same right-wing Christian reformed parties, the Christen Unie and the SGP, decided to retrospectively "annul" the motion of 1980!

From a legal point of view, this decision is very questionable, because motions adopted during a particular government period only have validity during that period. So repealing a motion from the 1980s is rather bizarre. Secondly, it has no legal effect because the Treaties and also the case law and even the Treaty of Lisbon have established, over many decades, the supremacy of European law over national law, including constitutional law. But in political terms the decision to repeal can only be understood as a profound sign of frustration, a grudge, a negative signal of denying the reality of a changing political situation.

In the early days, there was a kind of indifference, Europe was not seen as very relevant, except for those who were farmers or businessmen as they benefited from European subsidies or were affected by EU competition rules. Nowadays every individual citizen is affected, and the EU has an enormous impact on many dimensions of national society. Nevertheless, the political attitude is characterized by a denial of reality and it reacts as if European decision-making is alien, for the reasons I have just explained.

Subsidiarity

The importance of the subsidiarity principle is clear from the application of the subsidiarity protocol: we have seen some recent examples. One was an interesting one: the Dutch Parliament voted against the liberalization of the railways, they said 'once the decision is annulled, liberalization will not take place, because we have issued a yellow card'.

This statement demonstrates a lack of understanding of the system. In my opinion, a reasonable approach to subsidiarity needs to come from both sides, the national and the European side. There is growing acceptance for this approach, which is clear from the presence of members of the European Parliament in national parliamentary sessions and meetings like the debate on the new European state of the union. Also, there is a more regular appearance of Commissioners before national institutions. Above all, the attitude of the Member States should not be simply a negative one. Both the yellow and the red cards are blocking elements, elements of saying no. On the contrary, we should move from a 'no' attitude to an attitude of thinking along the same lines, adding elements that on the European level are not at the forefront of people's minds; we should aim for a real institutional dialogue.

Because of this, there are two points of view: there is the European one that the European nation states are becoming too small for many issues, and there is the national issue which for the institutions very much depends on national loyalties. And so if these two come together, the yellow card is not the right answer, because it blocks decision-making and debate. And in any case, we should not block the system; we should allow the system to work and to improve it.

Sovereignty

The current prevailing opinion in the Netherlands is to argue that within the European framework too much national authority has been eroded and is now being exercised at the European level. This, I believe, is far too shallow an approach to European decision-making and a parody of the reality which has grown over, by now, half a century.

The current situation of decision-making in the EU context is far from satisfactory, but this is not because too much authority has been removed from the Member States. Rather, the contrary is the case. We are increasingly faced with a situation that purely national decisions are inadequate to resolve a problem. At the same time no European solution can be found either, because diverging national interests are blocking competences at the European level. A very significant issue is the almost total stagnation in Europe in the area of asylum and migration. On a daily basis we are faced with horror stories of people drowning in the Mediterranean, and trucks with dead refugees who had fled their homeland because of the unbearable living conditions they were experiencing. Clearly, a European approach with real competences at the European level is an absolute precondition, otherwise we will be faced with even more dramatic stories.

However, also in areas where European competences do exist, national contributions to decisions at the European level are essential for decision-making. Nearly all European decisions require approval by the Council of Ministers, an institution composed of national representatives at the political level. This has been the rule from the very beginning of the integration process. To pretend otherwise is simply a distortion of the truth.

More fundamentally, I would defend the thesis that the European Union has reinforced national sovereignty, because it has reinforced the possibility of having control over one's own affairs. Even in the formal sense in order to achieve many national objectives, individual Member States depend on cooperation with other Member States, with or without European competences. Alan Milward very forcefully uses the same argumentation in his book *The European Rescue of the Nation State*. If it had not been for the development of democratic and rule of law structures at a higher level, Member States might easily have dwindled from the path and become subject to dictatorships. Or as we have seen with the banks which came under the control of non-democratic structures and other institutions which have never been controlled by the European Union. So I reject the concept that the Netherlands and other Member States have lost sovereignty: it has rather gained sovereignty in a new context.

Some Final Comments

It is also important to note that the future of a country needs to be decided via a 'willful formulation' of ideas, so I should therefore end with some comments concerning some differences between the Netherlands and a number of other European countries.

First of all, the term "Euroscepticism" is a bizarre word because all of us are living in a biotope called Europe; one cannot simply be against our own biotope. With this, I mean that Europe is the framework in which we live, and even if there would be no European Union you would still be living in that biotope and you would be far worse off because we would not have the transnational mechanisms to solve conflicts. Yet, the term "Euroscepticism" continues to be on the rise in the Netherlands. Of course, the crisis and high unemployment risk losing a whole generation from the European idea, therefore one should not want to belittle these issues. Nevertheless, where the Dutch position differs rather fundamentally from most other Member States (with the exception of the Nordic countries) is its purely economic or even commercial attitude to European integration. I referred to this point earlier.

The Netherlands thinks in terms of selling our products better in an internal market: we import, we export, our market is 70% European. What we do not realize at all, or have great difficulty in accepting, is that Europe is also a geopolitical sphere, in which our relative importance in demographical terms is rapidly shrinking. At present one in seven inhabitants of the world is a European and it will soon be one out of 10 or 15. We now have 500 million out of seven billion inhabitants worldwide. The ageing process, demographic changes and the rise of new powers worldwide: all these elements imply that the geopolitical relevance of individual European countries is becoming smaller. We are witnessing a worldwide shift of power, an unprecedented changing power balance.

Countries like Germany, France, Poland, Italy, or Spain, i.e. the larger European countries, consider a strengthening of Europe to be essential in order to increase the relevance of their states also at the European level. Federal Chancellor Merkel remarked at the World Economic Forum in 2012: "Die Zukunft der Euro ist die Zukunft Europas" (the future of the Euro is the future of Europe). And what she meant to say by this is that Germany has 78 million people out of a world population of 7 billion: Germany forms just 1 per cent, and without a European dimension that 1 per cent plays no role at all. So the geopolitical element is very strong in Germany; it is also strong in France as well as in Italy, otherwise Italy would fall away to become part of North Africa. Spain still has vivid memories of living under a dictatorship without democratic institutions, Poland is squeezed between Germany and Russia and if it is not part of Europe, it risks being a vassal, as it was for many years. So that geopolitical dimension with all its underlying differences prevails for the larger Member States and ultimately considers Europe as being also a potential power actor in world terms.

A smaller Member State, like Ireland, depends on the European Union as a counterweight against again being colonized by its larger neighbour Great Britain. A country like Belgium benefits from Europe because otherwise it might fall apart. Therefore many countries have specific reasons for looking at Europe in political as well as economic terms.

The Netherlands does not have that tradition. Twenty-four years after the creation of the Netherlands in 1648, we had a so-called 'rampjaar' (disastrous year) when we were collectively attacked by the French, the Germans and the British. I think somewhere deep in the minds of the Dutch is the impression that we do not like Europe because of our small numbers and a fear that we will be dominated by the continental powers. So with our neutrality in the nineteenth century and the later American dominance, we felt more comfortable as a trading nation.

And because we essentially have an economic attitude, above all we like earning money in a European context, but also outside as has been our centuries-long tradition. That attitude means that we feel uncomfortable in a Europe which exercises power. Recent developments in the world directly around us, such as the illegal occupation of the Crimea, the ongoing war in Eastern Ukraine, the asylum tragedies or the terrorist attacks within Europe and directly adjacent to our borders, constitute ever-increasing challenges They can only be met by a more integrated Europe, mindful of its human values, represented by the Rule of Law and Democracy. This very political dimension of Europe is rarely explained in the Netherlands. It is certainly not the subject of the political debate in our Parliament. The government does not explain its actions in and with Europe in these terms. In short, the country is leaderless in a European vision of the future. The Dutch Prime Minister considers this attitude to be even his identity in Europe. Recently he proudly proclaimed "I don't want any vision of the future".

It is precisely that lack of vision that makes people uncertain. One can argue that we go forward, we go backwards, we do this, we do that, but at least there should be intellectual and political leadership. But if there is no political leadership, the people who are affected by the crisis turn to extremist or populist parties which promise the moon, although they realize that it is not possible.

The manufacturer's authorised representative in the EU is Springer Nature Customer Service Centre GmbH, Europaplatz 3, 69115 Heidelberg, Germany. If you have any concerns regarding our products, please contact ProductSafety@springernature.com

Printed and bound by CPI Group (UK) Ltd, Croydon, CR0 4YY
23/09/2026
02221975-0001